ICE CUBE //
ATTITUDE

Foruli Classics

Published by Foruli Classics 2012
ISBN 978-1-905792-34-4
Copyright © Joel McIver 2002, Nostromo Media Ltd 2012
Cover copyright © Foruli Ltd 2012

First published by Sanctuary Publishing Ltd 2002
This edition published by Foruli Ltd 2012

Cover design by Andy Vella at Velladesign (www.velladesign.com)

Printed by Lightning Source

Foruli Classics is an imprint of Foruli Ltd, London
www.foruliclassics.com

Foruli
Classics

ICE CUBE //
ATTITUDE

JOEL MCIVER

Introduction to this Foruli Classics edition

I wrote *Ice Cube: Attitude* in 2002. It is the first of the many books I have written to really matter.

This reprinted version of what is still the only Ice Cube biography intentionally retains two awe-inspiring errors, inserted by the original copy editor of the first edition. This chap managed to convert the word 'crib' (as in the hip-hop word for a home or refuge) into 'cot', presumably using some form of sub-editing software. He also inserted '[date?]' after an album title and forgot to remove it. You'll notice these glorious errors when you come across them. They were left in this reissue edition because they are funny.

I am very pleased with *Ice Cube: Attitude*, even all these years later. It's still a penetrating, sensitive study of a culture much removed from my own, as a middle-class white boy from the hind end of England. I gave it my all, and I succeeded at least partly in portraying the man behind the public image. Thank you for reading this book, and thank you to Foruli Classics for giving it a new lease of life.

Joel McIver
Buckinghamshire, 2012

Contents

Introduction   9

1   Welcome To South Central   11
2   NWA, America's Bastard Sons   32
3   Armageddon Arrives – Straight Outta Compton 47
4   Going Solo   69
5   Increase The Peace   84
6   LA Under Siege   101
7   The Predator Stands Up   114
8   Violence, Silence And Tragedy   132
9   Caught In The Middle   154
10 Monsters, Movies And Monster Movies   175
11 Heavyweight Values   195
12 The Desert King   210
13 Smoked   236
14 A Piece Of The Pie   248
15 Prophecy   264

Discography 277

Filmography 278

Online Resources 280

Index 282

Introduction

'Our actions are like the terminations of verses, which we rhyme
as we please.'   – *La Rochefoucauld*

'Whom men fear they hate; and whom they hate, they wish
dead.'   – *Quintus Ennius*

Welcome to *Ice Cube: Attitude*.

I hope you enjoy reading it as much I did writing it, although it
wasn't an easy book to put together. Ice Cube is a man of many
contradictions – both sensitive and brutal, tender and violent, rational
and irrational, and alternating positive messages with the bleakest of
misanthropy. How is the author to deal with this and still present a
coherent profile? His career has been a career full of peaks and
troughs, with the only apparent constant his seemingly unshakeable
faith in his own abilities, and the task of following this roller-coaster
ride has been demanding but exhilarating. But now it's done, let me
immodestly assure you that it's one hell of a story.

Furthermore, received wisdom has it that no biography of any
prominent hip-hop artist would be complete without a detailed
analysis of the culture he or she moves in and a full examination of the
sociological and political consequences of his or her work. If that's
what you want, take a look at the postgraduate schedule of any
Western university – the number of doctorate students basing their
theses on hip-hop culture is rising every year, so most of this analysis
has already been carried out elsewhere (and in much greater detail than
could fit into this book).

What I've tried to do here is tell the story of Ice Cube, with nothing held back and nothing underplayed or concealed. This is, I feel, how the man himself would want it – he's always been brutally honest about the things he's said and done in his life, and you, the reader, are intelligent enough to draw your own conclusions about the significance (or lack thereof) of his actions without me constantly invoking the broader picture.

Having said that, this *is* the man who infamously said, 'Life ain't nothin' but bitches and money', invoked the spectre of white people as 'devils' and at one time in his life seemed inseparable from his phalanx of AK-47 assault rifles, so I've addressed the themes of misogyny, race and violence as they come up. But I'm not here to preach. That's Ice Cube's job, and the job of others like him.

The other important point is this. I'm a white guy from Britain, and I don't for a moment pretend to have experienced life from the perspective of a black man from America. I'm sure that when the time comes for Cube to find a writer for his official biography, he'll choose someone who shares his background – someone from the ghetto – and with good reason. But my outsider status in relation to that world gives me both perspective and objectivity, which are valuable assets for any biographer, I feel.

Just keep an open mind, and enjoy the ride.

Joel McIver
May 2002
www.joelmciver.co.uk

1 Welcome To South Central

It was, as the man so famously said, a good day.

Sunday 15 June 1969 was much like any other summer's day in Crenshaw, a district of the South Central region in Los Angeles, California. Although Crenshaw is close to the Watts district, which had been practically levelled during the riots that had taken place there four years earlier, it was still a relatively secure area to live in and had yet to be overtaken by gang-related activities.

On this particular day, however, a local family, the Jacksons, were focusing their attention on the birth of the family's fourth child. Both the father, Hosea, and mother Doris were relieved when the baby was safely delivered and, searching for inspiration for a name, Doris decided to christen her second son after a promising young American football player whose deftness and rugged good looks she admired. Given that the player was the newly debuted O J Simpson, the name she chose for the infant seems – albeit with the help of a blurred consonant – to have been an obvious choice.

O'Shea Jackson was a lucky child. Although Crenshaw was to remain a relatively peaceful suburb for some years, it soon became clear that this would not always be so: crime rose throughout the 1970s, in line with the proliferation of activity on the ever-growing gang scene. Although Hosea (a machinist and groundskeeper, who worked in the latter capacity at University College of Los Angeles) and Doris (a hospital clerk) were diligent, caring parents, the innocence of a child in the area was never likely to last long. As the biggest – and perhaps most infamous – of all America's gangs, the Bloods and the

Crips, extended their influence through the city, the part of Crenshaw where the Jacksons lived was renamed N-Hood (short for 'Neighborhood Crips'), and became known as a district where you needed to watch your back.

O'Shea's luck centred on the strength of his family; specifically, on the discipline and experience of his father and the protective presence of his older brother, Clyde. Of the former, he later simply told *Addicted To Noise* magazine: 'He was there. He kept me on the right track. You don't realize that till you see other people who grew up without fathers, and how their lives turn out.'

Hosea was clearly a man of some vision. Cube remembers: 'He told me at a young age not to worship entertainers, stars, musicians and stuff, but to look up to people that was directly in your life, that was directly helping you – not nobody that you look at on TV...' Most importantly, the boy's parents didn't try to hide the problems of the ghetto from their younger son, especially when he had Clyde around to help him learn. In fact, Hosea positively encouraged O'Shea to go out and satisfy his curiosity: 'My father just gave me the freedom to do what I wanted. He would teach me things at home and [let me] see if it worked. He didn't try to be on me at home and be on me while I'm in the streets... If that's what I wanted to do, he was cool with that.'

A naturally active kid, O'Shea found a way of channelling his energy – by launching himself into sports. For five years, he played football in the children's series, known nationwide as the Pop Warner Leagues. Both stocky and fast, he alternated between the positions of full-back and outside linebacker – and it paid off: 'My older brother and my pops got me into sports real quickly, so that kept me away from a lot of the bullshit,' Cube later explained. He also played basketball at that most harmless of venues, the neighbourhood YMCA, and developed a passion for the game that stayed with him until his adult years. Crenshaw, it seemed, would not make a gangster of O'Shea just yet.

But boys will be boys, and this particularly inquisitive young man wasted no time in learning about the tougher side of life in South Central, which also covers the Hyde Park, Jefferson Park, Leimert Park and Watts districts. 'You know, kids are kids,' he later recalled. 'They want to roll with the crowd, get in fights, jump people – all that little shit – but nothing major.' However, the calming presence of Clyde Jackson kept O'Shea out of the worst trouble: 'A lot of the people who were deep into the gangs…didn't have fathers or older brothers to set them straight. But I had that; I have an older brother *and* a father. My brother had been through all that shit so he was like, "Man, you don't have to do that."'

But why is it that the idea of violence and disobedience entered his mind at all? After all, it's not every urban child that contemplates fights and gang activities. To discover the answer, we have to look at the history of O'Shea's environment – and that means taking a brief look at America's urban history.

The city of Los Angeles was a modest settlement throughout the 19th century. It seemed that it would never expand to unusual limits, until in 1913, when an aqueduct constructed by engineer William Mulholland brought water to Los Angeles from 300km (200 miles) north. This enabled industries to flourish: one such was the movie business, which grew exponentially during the 1920s and 1930s. The city's population doubled in the 1920s alone, and by 1955 the total number of residents had reached two million.

Wartime industries such as aircraft manufacture also boomed, leading developers to buy up whole tracts of land (Lakewood is an example) to house an increasing workforce, many of whom were immigrants of Hispanic and Caribbean origin. Old housing estates in areas such as Watts and Compton in the South Central area became the focus of these immigrant communities. These districts suffered severely from unemployment, violent crime and poverty, and the city's first large-scale disturbances were witnessed in 1943, when visiting sailors clashed with local Hispanic gangs in confrontations which became known as the Zoot Suit Riots. It took several days and nights for the police to curb the violence.

The first African-American police officers and firefighters were recruited in 1955, with the first black city councillors being elected in the mid-1960s. Tensions between black and white communities were high, however, and in 1965 an altercation between a white LAPD officer and an African-American man at a traffic light in the Watts district escalated into a riot in the predominantly black community that lasted for six days. By the time the violence had ceased, 34 people had been killed (31 of them by the police), while an incredible 1,032 citizens had been injured. Almost 4,000 arrests were made, 6,000 buildings were damaged or destroyed, and the damage costs were estimated at £28 million ($40 million).

In the 1980s, Los Angeles' population expanded rapidly, due in part to an increase in immigration from Latin America (especially Mexico) and Asia. In 1990, it was found that 38 per cent of the city's residents were born outside the United States, and ten years later the total population was recorded as about 3.7 million. Social analysts feared that little improvement had taken place in the relationships between communities, and (with the population ever rising) some predicted that racial tensions would inevitably reach boiling point.

Running parallel to this was the rise in prominence of the city's gangs. The first African-American gangs began to coalesce in California during the 1920s, and had established a base in South Central Los Angeles and the southerly suburb of Compton by the end of the 1960s. One particularly aggressive gang was the Crips, whose earliest activities included attacking local neighbourhoods and schools and assaulting and robbing the citizens.

A rival gang soon sprang up around the Piru Street area in Compton, calling themselves 'Piru gangs' or, simply, Bloods. At the time the Bloods were outnumbered three to one by the Crips, but were equally brutal in their activities. Both gangs split into many smaller divisions (or sets) in the 1970s and the two major clans began to develop a bloody rivalry, developing identifying hand signals and adopting colours – blue for the Crips and red for the Bloods. By the beginning of the 1980s, the combined gangs numbered around 15,000 members in the LA area.

Gang activities embraced assaults, robberies, burglaries, car-jacking and drug dealing, with methods of protection and extortion becoming more and more violent as the years passed. By the mid-1980s, a new era of drive-by shootings had begun, from gang members armed with their weapon of choice, usually either the AK-47 or the Mac-10 assault rifle. Police officers also became legitimate targets for the first time, with several sets (the Project Crips, Southside Compton Crips and the Pueblo Bishop Bloods among them) all attacking cops. In 1990, LA saw 135 homicides, 1,416 assaults and batteries, and 775 robberies, committed by either Crips or Bloods.

Although the black gangs are the most notorious entities in California, more gang members in the state are actually Hispanic. Asian gangs formed from the Vietnamese, Cambodian and Laotian communities are also on the rise, leading to an even more dangerous situation. Add to this the growth in number of white supremacist groups such as skinhead and KKK-affiliated gangs, and LA's recipe for violence is a potent one indeed.

So much for LA. But O'Shea and his friends were growing up in the most gang-infested area of all – South Central. The successful rapper Ice-T, who grew up in the area, once explained the situation in South Central with these words: 'You got a gang situation, you got a drug situation, all the Jamaican posses and everybody else killing each other. It's like rats trying to get out of a barrel, they're all drowning and pushing everybody else down. It's real sad, but I made it out…and my objective is to say, yo! I was worse or just as bad as any of y'all fuckers, so listen, this can be done. Ain't really much else I can do.'

Another rapper, Kid Chill, is very specific about life in South Central and the way it is governed by gangs and the police's attitude to them. He points out that 'I didn't know any different as a kid, so it seemed like normal life. There were police helicopters that flew by all night. The police would pull you over in your car, or stop you on the street for no reason and ask you what gang you were in, what's your gang name etc. We were threatened and kicked off of Venice Beach for no reason, stopped a couple of times at gunpoint for suspicion of something or another. We were made to stand against the rail at the mall for a long period of time because we fit the description of some people that did something or other.'

Chill observes that Blood vs Crip distinctions weren't always easy to live with: 'The gang activity wasn't quite like gang activity elsewhere. The reason that it was so bad is because there wasn't a clear line between being in a gang and *not* being in a gang. Some areas were divided by certain streets. There were dozens of gangs. All of the black gangs were divided into Bloods and Crips. All Blood gangs hated all Crip gangs, and some Crip gangs hated each other.'

It wasn't much use relying on your home neighbourhood to keep you safe, either. 'Hoods were defined by certain geographical areas. If you lived in a certain area you were, for the most part, considered to be in that gang unless you were specifically in another gang. If you lived in a Crip neighborhood you would get beat up for wearing red. If you were in a Blood neighborhood you would get beat up for wearing blue. If a Blood asked you what hood you were from, and you happened to live in a Crip neighborhood, you'd get beat up. You could try to say that you weren't involved in gang activity by saying "I don't bang", but dependent on who was asking they may or may not really care.'

So, if gang warfare was so prevalent, why join one at all? Chill explains: 'Regarding South Central, the fact that people would beat you up just because you were from a certain neighborhood influenced you to hang around others from your neighborhood who would protect you. This influenced you to join a gang. I never heard of a case where some gang members forced someone to join as the media implied. It was sort of cool to be in a gang, so people who weren't really even in a gang would sometimes claim to be.'

The suburb of Compton was hardly any safer. At one point the 12th poorest suburb in the USA, its murder rate comes close to that of Detroit and Miami, with the local authorities allocating over two-thirds of their annual budget to public safety. After the rise of gangsta rap in the 1990s, the name of Compton – ironically, still the ancient title of many sleepy villages in Great Britain, where the name originated – became synonymous with murder, brutality and urban decay.

In the early 1990s, a band called Compton's Most Wanted were even briefly well-known, largely due to the violent nature of albums with titles such as *Music To Driveby*. Their rapper, MC Eiht, discussed the inspiration for his lyrics in a January 1993 interview: 'I like to stick to the realism. I don't like to go on subjects that ain't sayin' nothing. I like to leave you with something so you can go "That's real," or "I went through that."' The interviewer asked him if he was familiar with the term 'studio gangsta' – and he certainly was: 'I ain't no studio gangsta. I was there. I hung with the niggas. I seen the niggas getting jacked. I seen the niggas getting killed. I did the jacking, I did the gangbangin'.'

Eiht also expressed his dislike of rappers who spoke of ghetto life without personal experience: 'Other gangsta rappers, all they talk about is "Shoot you up, bang, bang, boom." It ain't even like that. They don't know what they're talking about. They feel just by saying fuck or shit, or putting a strap in their hand, or talking about a 40 ounce that they're in it to win it. It ain't about that. I'm a gangster rapper, but when you listen to CMW, you're always gonna get a story told. It ain't like you gonna be sitting, listening to a nigga go "Yeah, I'm the baddest muthafucka. Fuck, grab my dick. Fuck this".'

But all this was some years away. Despite the intimidating history of his environment, the young O'Shea Jackson showed little sign at this early age of wanting to follow in the footsteps of so many of his peers and join a gang. His academic skills also showed that he was no slouch: he maintained a steady B average across the curriculum and showed particular prowess at drawing, sports and maths. As a person he was keen to show interest and was naturally polite: some years later Doris even went so far as to describe him to *Rolling Stone* magazine as 'a very nice young man'. However, the boy became a teenager, and with the loss of his childhood came a new interest: the opposite sex. Always fascinated with the teenage girls who would come to call on his elder brother, O'Shea wasted no time in boldly walking up to them and attempting to persuade them to talk. Of course, Clyde found these precocious attempts at courtship hilarious and laughed long and hard at how cool the boy thought he was. 'I used to always try to talk to his women,' admitted O'Shea years later. 'Thought I was too cool…'

So cool, in fact, that one day Clyde came up with a nickname for O'Shea – Ice Cube. Initially just a name to lay on his brother when the kid got too confident, the new sobriquet stuck, and soon everyone – with the exception of his parents – was using it. Before too long the newly christened Cube was one of the kids to know in Crenshaw: a boy unafraid to talk to the older girls, who would beat you at any sport you cared to mention and whose natural energy and politeness made him popular. His special friend was a kid called Randy, who lived a block away, and this friendship would affect his growth in an entirely unexpected manner.

After he finished at the local grammar school, the Jacksons had to make a decision about the best middle school for their son. The neighbourhood school, a competent institution called Henry Clay, seemed like the obvious choice, and the young Cube decided that this was where he would go. However, news came that Randy's mother had begun to receive some convincing brochures from a school in the Valley (situated east of Los Angeles) that went by the somewhat superior name of the Hawthorne Christian School. Both Randy and Cube were devastated when Randy's family opted to try their son out at this out-of-district institution, and the two families met in order to try and negotiate a solution.

It was decided that Cube would also attend Hawthorne: after all, he had showed considerable talent at his first school and his parents had every reason to expect that he would excel at this elevated place of learning. Unfortunately, he would later remember it otherwise: 'We had to get up at like six in the morning and get on the bus; it was like 30 minutes away. So we get there – we're in the seventh grade, we think we can go out there with all these white boys and tear shit up – and there's niggas there from every set. They had bussed in niggas from our hood, niggas from the East Side, they bussed niggas from everywhere.' It emerged that there was a political agenda behind Hawthorne's marketing campaign: the idea was that both black and white students would come together from different neighbourhoods, study together, and learn from the experience. A schoolkid who endured a similar experience grew up to be DJ Muggs of Cypress Hill, who remembers: '10 to 15 years ago, the government thought it would be a good idea to bus white kids into black schools and black kids into white schools. It was done for them to be knowing about the other people's cultures.'

It's a plausible – and even admirable – idea on paper, but the school board, and the education authorities above them, had forgotten an important point. Cube recalled that 'This school had neighborhoods bussed in from everywhere. There were Bloods *and* Crips, so the school had a lot of mayhem. The shit was crazy!'

The scheme rapidly went downhill. 'I remember the principal having an assembly saying "You are the worst seventh graders ever." Then they had another one next year: "You are the worst eighth graders." They had to close the school.' Before this could happen, however, Cube learned some valuable lessons on the nature of crime, punishment and loyalty: 'I remember one of my homies my age who had went to [juvenile detention] camp. He had done something for one of the O.G. niggas around, went to camp, and that O.G. nigga didn't even give a fuck. He didn't write that nigga, he didn't do shit.' The hapless inmate's predicament – abandoned by his friends with no credibility or allies – struck a chord in Cube: 'That kind of woke me up because I'm out there trying to prove myself to these niggas, and then these niggas don't give a fuck about you when you get stretched. So I was like fuck this shit! I can hang, but I'm not going to be doing all this crazy shit because there isn't any money in it.'

Cube's parents had heard his descriptions of the environment at Hawthorne and pulled him out of the institution before the situation could worsen, electing to send him to a school in the Woodland Hills district called William Howard Taft High School, or merely 'Taft' to its students. Among his co-students were future House Of Pain frontman Everlast and Epic Mazor of the hip-hop/nu-metal act Crazytown. Like them, it was at Taft that Ice Cube made an important discovery – one that would change the path of his life irrevocably. The object of his fascination? Music.

At the tail end of the 1970s, the popular chart music that ruled the radio airwaves of the United States was an unstable beast. Punk had established a foothold in 1977, and 1978 and was coming closer and closer to overturning the throne of disco, which had developed into a way of life in urban America (especially among black audiences) but was beginning to lose its lustre as the 1980s approached. One of the last hits to come from this glittering, coke-fuelled genre came from Chic, whose 'Good Times' – an unforgettable bassline nailed to a rock-solid beat – ruled the charts in July 1979, just after Ice Cube's family celebrated their prodigal son's tenth birthday.

Three months later, the song exited the chart – and so it was that radio audiences were surprised to hear what they thought was 'Good Times' being broadcast again. The rhythm and the instrumentation seemed identical, but on closer listening it was revealed that this song was something entirely new. The cut – retitled 'Rapper's Delight', and provided courtesy of a little-known New York outfit called the Sugarhill Gang – was an unforgettable sequence of rapped lyrics laid on top of the Chic groove, and an entirely new concept to most music fans. The single became the biggest-selling 12" single of all time.

Ice Cube was rendered speechless when he heard the record. His family had introduced him to funk by way of Rick James, Parliament, Funkadelic and James Brown, but this was an entirely different proposition, as he later remembered: 'My uncle had a tape of "Rapper's Delight", and I was on my way to the dentist. His car didn't have a stereo because someone had stolen it, so he had a radio instead... The fucking shit blew my mind. I listened to it the whole way to the dentist, I thought about it while I was at the dentist, left the dentist playing the song, and I wanted to borrow the tape.'

What was so new, and what was so unexpected about the song, was the fact that it came directly from the street (Ice Cube might not have known it at the time, but the East Coast ghettos of Brooklyn were hosting frantic street parties and rap marathons) and that it was a rap, not a melody, which gave the song its drive. The combination of Jamaican toasting (in which the MC speaks over a song) and scratching (where a DJ spins a record against the stylus to produce a distorted sound) was the foundation of a whole new culture – hip-hop – of which the music was just a part. And, if hip-hop was being born as Ice Cube drove to the dentist that day, 'Rapper's Delight' was its first word. No wonder Cube felt that something was happening.

The roots of rap go back further than many might imagine. Most experts believe that the actual practice of rapping was pioneered in the

1970s by a musician called Lightning Rod, a member of the black nationalist group, the Last Poets, whose poetry and music dealt with the most profound of political issues. Other aficionados point to proto-rappers such as Gil Scott-Heron and Jayne Cortez, who laid their tales of American living over jazz tracks at around the same time. But most observers agree that the Jamaican practice of 'toasting' (producing spoken-word narratives) over records played on bass-heavy sound systems was an enormous influence on the development of the technique.

New York's Brooklyn and Bronx districts housed a large Jamaican community, and the DJs who lived there (DJ Kool Herc was an early leader) were the first to mix their sets from parallel turntables while an MC straddled the microphone. By the time Cube came to hear the Sugarhill Gang's 'Rapper's Delight', the city had established its own hip-hop scene, while Grandmaster Flash's 1982 single 'The Message' would be another classic cut from the early days.

As the hip-hop culture spread, it became apparent that rap was only one facet of the whole movement: breakdancing and graffiti-writing became equally important. As the DJ Afrika Bambaataa later said, 'Hip-hop means the whole culture of the movement. When you talk about rap, rap is part of the hip-hop culture.The MCing and the DJing is part of the hip-hop culture... How you act, walk, look, talk are all part of hip-hop culture, and the music is colorless. Hip-hop music is made from black, brown, yellow, red, white.'

The DJing, however, was the root of it all. By scratching, a turntablist could make his act the focus of attention. Scratching is said to have been invented by either Grandmaster Flash or Grand Wizard Theodore, two DJs who lived in the Bronx, while mid-1980s songs such as Herbie Hancock's 'Rock It' and Malcolm McLaren's 'Buffalo Gals' helped spread the word. Other acts such as Master Don Committee Funky Four Plus One More and Crash Crew pushed the public's awareness of hip-hop still further.

Caribbean-born DJ Kool Herc himself also observed that the history of America's newest music actually had its roots in America: 'The whole chemistry of [hip-hop] came from Jamaica. I was born in

Jamaica and I was listening to American music in Jamaica. My favorite artist was James Brown. That's who inspired me. A lot of the records I played was by James Brown. When I came over here I just put it in the American style and a perspective for them to dance to it.'

By the time the young Ice Cube was listening to hip-hop, it seemed to be a temporary phenomenon that might vanish at any moment. Rapper Busta Rhymes explained its status to the *Addicted To Noise* magazine with these words: 'The respect level is growing, but it still ain't completely established. We're not compromising in the slightest. That's why the creative edge of hip-hop has only gotten better. We're going to continue to drill our hole in the core of the corporate tycoons' loveboats and make those motherfuckers feel our pain and agony until we get it where we wanna get it. But it ain't always a painful, agony thing. It's also a good and happy thing, because not everybody that's depressed and struggling in the ghetto is being successful in hip-hop.'

As CIA performed their first gigs, other artists were coming up from the streets as well. Prominent among them were the aforementioned Ice-T, whose anti-police tirade of '6 In The Morning' had indicated a tougher direction for rap to follow; Run-DMC, whose image made them instant superstars; and LL Cool J, with his ladies-love-cool-James charisma oozing from every pore. Public Enemy's Chuck D had already pointed out that rap was 'the CNN of the streets', and the relatively new TV channel MTV was about to establish a hip-hop show, the hour-long *Yo! MTV Raps*, which first aired in 1988. 'It made the rest of MTV's programming look pale in comparison,' said Chuck. 'All of a sudden MTV opened a Pandora's box, and we're going to open up this black box to the white world.'

However, all this rapidly passing history wasn't at the forefront of Ice Cube's mind – a new school awaited, with the stern hand of Hosea Jackson nearby to keep his son diligent. As Cube later recounted in his song 'Doin' Dumb Shit' ('Fuckin' up at a real fast rate/Till they said I might not graduate/Then I said fuck the dumb shit/Cause Pops'll fuck me up real quick'), Hosea and Doris were only too aware of the problems that a South Central upbringing can bring and were keen for their son to continue his education. Ice himself mused in a later magazine interview, 'It's a trip, because I look at muthafuckas from N-Hood (Crenshaw) now who are killers. I wonder if I didn't have that family structure how I would have turned out.'

Fortunately for Cube, he knuckled down and started to achieve good results. But the rush he had felt on that first hearing of 'Rapper's Delight' didn't fade: as he told *Art Form*, 'I couldn't stop rewinding it… It did nothing but grab me. By the age of 14, I was writing my own raps.'

It was 1983, and Ice remembers his first stab at writing a rap. 'One day I was sitting in class with a friend called Kiddo and we had some time on our hands, so he said let's write a rap.' The class – reportedly a typing course – had clearly lost its charm for Cube in the face of writing his own rhymes, although his early efforts were a little hamfisted: it's said that those first scrawled lines were 'My name is Ice Cube and I'm here to let you know, that I'm not Run DMC or Curtis Blow'.

But Kiddo knew when he was beaten, it seems. 'I told him, you write one, I write one and we'll see which one come out better – and I won,' remembered Cube. But there was little sense of destiny hanging over the wannabe rapper: 'I had been a rap fan, but I had never thought about doing it,' Ice added. 'One day we were talking about rap and he said, "Did you get the new Run DMC?" I think it was "Sucker MCs". He said, "Have you ever tried to write a rap?" I said no… I wrote mine, he wrote his. From then on I never stopped.'

The evident lack of rhyming expertise didn't deter him. Cube's schoolfriend Tony Wheatob (who was known by his contemporaries as Sir Jinx and became a successful producer) was also a fan of the nascent rap genre and, after hearing the results of Cube's competition with Kiddo, suggested that they record a tape together. The tape, made on Jinx's cobbled-together equipment, was less than spectacular. Cube later told *Rolling Stone* that this early recording could best be described as 'pathetic. The beat was going, and I was over in the left corner. The lyrics, they were cool, but they wasn't no exciting type of mind-boggling shit. I was only 15, you know.'

Pathetic or not, the first steps had been taken and the rapping continued, in the less-than-savoury atmosphere of Jinx's garage. 'His mom wouldn't tolerate the music,' said Cube later, 'and he had a dog who lived in the garage. The dog would shit in the garage; we'd be in there smelling dog shit, stepping over dog shit, rapping in the garage.' Slowly but surely, the two rappers were gaining in lyrical subtlety and oral fluency.

By 1986, rap was spreading across the nation and into other Western countries. The West Coast was developing its own scene, and it was with some excitement that Jinx came to the wannabe rap duo's aromatic rehearsal space one day to inform his partner that his cousin, Andre Young, was the producer in an LA rap outfit that seemed to be going places. The act, which went by the typically prideful name of the World Class Wreckin' Cru (WCWC) and featured the soon-to-be-star Michel'le on vocals, had scored a big local hit with a song called 'Surgery'. It also turned out that Andre's mother lived close to the Jackson family.

Intrigued by the success of Young, Cube and Jinx went along to see his band at a gig that they were playing, and were immediately sucked in by the intensity of the show. Jinx's cousin, who as a 21-year-old (also born and raised in South Central) seemed much more experienced than either of the 15-year-olds, was a masterful DJ: he had begun playing as a DJ in a club, Eve After Dark, where he attracted attention by performing a set made up of chart records and Motown soul classics. The club was also equipped with a four-track studio, where he recorded demos with the World Class Wreckin' Cru, which Young had formed in the early 1980s with another DJ, Antoine Carraby (who used the *nom-de-deck* Yella) and a rapper, Lonzo Williams. As a performer Young was magical: holding the attention of the entire audience, he even went by a stage name for a dash of added mystery. This name, derived from the second syllable of his first name, was Dr Dre.

Yella recalled later how the band came into being: 'Hip-hop was like Grandmaster Flash back then. Rap was something from the East Coast. We almost originally started West Coast hip-hop when we were in the World Class Wreckin' Cru. We were broke but we stuck together.' On the creation of their hit, 'Surgery', the DJ explained that 'We'd seen a show with Run-DMC for the first time. It was their first time in California. We sat back and looked at the show and it wasn't nothin'! It was two people rapping and a DJ! We said, "That's it! We can do that!" That's when we started trying to make records.'

By this time Los Angeles was developing its own rap scene, with acts such as Uncle Jam's Army, LA Dream Team, Rodney O & Joe Cooley, Egyptian Lover, Formula V, Captain Rap, Mixmaster Spade, King T and Toddy T all making a local impact. And this impact was felt most profoundly by enthusiastic young musicians such as Cube and Dre. An acquaintanceship grew between the two men, and their friendship accelerated when Dre heard Cube rap for the first time: 'Dre had heard me rap so he was like, "Let me hear what you got."' Apparently the local star was so impressed by the young rapper's talents that he asked him to accompany him on a shopping trip. 'I was like, oh shit! I'm gonna hook up with Dre!' recalled Cube later, and with good reason – WCWC used to enjoy heavy rotation on the local hip-hop radio station, 1580 KDAY, a feat not often matched by West Coast acts of the day.

Dre also invited Cube along to some of the many parties he gave, many of which took place at the Skateland roller rink. At one of these live shows the older man suggested that the teenager prepare a live act with Jinx. 'We had never performed in front of a live audience,' said Cube later, 'so I said, "What kind of shit do you want?" He said, "People like shit that is funny, and people like shit with a little bit of cursing in it."'

People did, it seemed, like 'a little bit of cursing', as Cube soon discovered when he and Jinx made their debut at Dre's club. Their set was made up of semi-obscene versions of established chart hits. He remembered: '"Roxanne Roxanne" [a 1984 hit by UTFO] was out back then, so I said why don't we do a parody of that? We did a song called "Diane Diane". We changed it around and put cursing in it... We did, like, dirty versions of Weird Al Yankovic-type shit. Beastie Boys had a record out called "Paul Revere", and we kinda mimicked the lyrics, but we was talking 'bout how we rode into town, fucked a couple of women, shot up the place... We took "My Adidas" by Run-DMC and did a song called "My Rubber".'

This live success led to a demand for some product, so Cube and Jinx made up mix recordings of their raps on top of the hits of the day. As Cube recalled, 'We was doing these dirty raps strictly for the club audiences... When that started catching on, we started making mix tapes. We would rap on what was going on in the neighborhood and they were selling.' Clearly there was a market for a vulgar – but truth-based – form of rap. An indicator for the future, perhaps?

Dre and Cube were firm friends by this stage: 'I used to ditch school and run around the corner. He'd pick me up,' said Cube. 'I'd roll with him the whole day, hanging.' But this didn't stop Cube from forming his own band outside the influence of Dre: he was still a 16-year-old schoolkid despite the rap kudos, and put together an outfit called the Stereo Crew at Taft. At the time, rapper Kid Chill was a student at a neighbouring school, and remembers the activities of the Stereo Crew well. 'They had a catchy tune called "Gettin' Sweated" that was pretty popular. Back then, "popular" meant that everyone at your school knew you, and quite a few people that didn't go to your school had heard about you. The fact that they had a tape that people from other schools was buying was popularity back then. They probably sold over 50 copies.'

Kid Chill was a well-known school 'battle rapper', and recalls how 'battles' went: 'Rapping wasn't about getting a record deal when I started, it was about drawing a huge crowd and getting them to cheer louder for you than for the other guy. It was the same as breakdancing at the time. You'd go to the malls, to the festivals, to school and find an opponent and prove that you were better than them. Although it was about beating someone else, it wasn't a violent type of confrontation.' And, although the Stereo Crew didn't show up to take on the rapping talents of Chill (who now sometimes goes by the name InSite), he recalls that Cube was known as a 'smart kid'.

Along with 'Gettin' Sweated', the Stereo Crew were known for their song 'She's A Skag', but the act couldn't last and a more capable outfit was formed by Cube with Sir Jinx and another rapper, Kid Disaster (who later changed his name to K-Dee and launched a successful solo career). Calling themselves CIA – derived, apparently, from 'Cru In Action' – the three young rappers made their first steps on to vinyl on a Dre-produced single containing the songs 'My Posse', 'Jus 4 the Cash $' and 'Ill-Legal'.

At around this time Ice Cube went to a show by the rapper Ice-T for the first time. Later to become a hugely influential figure in several arenas, the former Tracy Marrow was a true product of the ghetto and was producing hard-edged rap tunes, albeit with far less violent lyrics than his later work would contain. To Ice Cube – who had come from a similar background but had enjoyed the benefit of a strong, supportive family unit – Ice-T must have come as a revelation, a true ghetto prophet who (along with Dre) was an enormous inspiration to him.

But a still more important and influential meeting lay ahead of Cube. Although Dre had certainly been a mentor to him, it was the Compton-born rapper Eric Wright – better known as Eazy-E – who shaped Cube's career path more profoundly.

Hip-hop experts nowadays number the key players in the genre as Grandmaster Flash, Kool Herc, Afrika Bambaataa, Ice-T, Public Enemy's Chuck D and Dr Dre as pioneers. The more astute among them would include Eazy-E in this select group, as it's certain that without him the development of West Coast rap would have been slower and far less publicised. The roots of Eazy's enormous influence can be traced to his personal background.

Quite simply, Eazy-E was a true, dyed-in-the-wool original gangster. Born in 1964, he spent his middle teenage years making a buck from mowing lawns, delivering newspapers and the usual domestic tasks that adolescents traditionally perform to earn pocket money. It wasn't long, however, before he realised that dealing drugs was a faster and more efficient way of making a profit, and turned to it with alacrity after dropping out of high school in 1979.

After a couple of years, Eazy had made enough money to make him think about future career options. Life in the ghetto had given him a keen awareness of the short-term prospects of the dope dealer (he later told *Spin* magazine: 'I've seen a lot of shit. I seen a hoe get chopped up. Eyes took out. Legs cut up') and wanted to get out of the drug business altogether. In an April 1989 interview with *BAM* magazine, he seemed almost to regard his decision to withdraw from dealing as a moral issue, saying, 'I seen that it wasn't really worth it. It wasn't worth my life. My cousins got killed. It really wasn't worth it so I got out of it, I figured I could do something right for a change instead of something wrong.'

In a later interview with journalist Brian Cross, Eazy talked about his roots. 'I used to sell drugs. And if I wasn't doing what I'm doing now I'd probably be in jail or dead.' He also vented some spleen about World Class Wreckin' Cru manager (and rival business player) Lonzo Williams: 'Lonzo had more than me at the beginning, he had a house and a car, and thought he was the shit. If he wasn't so fucked up, he'd probably be right along now. Lonzo's a fuckin' loser.'

Clearly unimpressed with the 'glam' look that the WCWC attempted to emulate at Williams' instigation, Eazy added, 'That fuckin' lipstick and lace and boxers and shit didn't last too long. Trying to sound like Cameo, it was hittin' back then, but you can't do it nowadays. Lonzo Williams [his manager and co-artist in the World Class Wreckin' Cru] even had Michel'le, you know something was wrong. You can't have somebody blowing up and getting on the radio, then give them 100 dollars. Damn, when Michel'le came out and her record was doing good, this muthafucker tried to rerelease [her earlier single] "Turn Out The Lights".'

Eazy knew he could do better – and soon the idea of founding a record label was discussed, as he knew several local musicians and producers, including Dr Dre. The two men had first worked together in 1986 after Eazy received a phone call from the producer (who had been arrested for a series of outstanding traffic violations), asking him to loan him £640 ($900) as bail money: reportedly, Dre had already approached Lonzo for the loan, but had been turned down because he already owed Williams a considerable sum. Eazy agreed to provide the bail as long as Dre promised to come and produce acts for the label, which Eazy planned to call Ruthless Records.

Although Dre had agreed to work with Eazy-E out of sheer necessity, he soon found his new role as producer at the ex-dealer's newly christened label a highly enjoyable one. E gave Dre near-total autonomy, allowing him to stretch the skills which he had honed over so many nights at the Eve's After Dark club. Finding a band to produce took some time, but eventually Dre unearthed a new band, HBO, from New York, whose demo impressed Eazy enough to offer them a deal. The rap outfit from the East – whose name supposedly stood for 'Homeboys Only' – looked like a competent bunch, but none of them were songwriters and it became apparent that a song would need to be written for them, which Dre would produce. Neither E nor Dre had much talent as a songwriter at this stage – the former was a businessman learning to rap, while the latter was at his best at the mixing desk or on the decks – and for a moment it seemed that a deal with HBO might not come to pass.

Enter Ice Cube. Dre hit on the idea of asking the young CIA rapper to pen a song for the New York band, and Cube was more than willing to give it a try. Sequestering themselves in the studio for a couple of days, Ice and Dre put together a song called (prophetically, as it turned out) 'Boyz N Tha Hood', a visceral tale of gangland violence and homicide flowing over a typically hardcore Dre beat. Confident that the record would make HBO a name to conjure with, Eazy summoned them to the studio and handed over copies of the lyrics to the rappers, ready to record.

But all was not well. The Big Apple musicians read Ice Cube's uncompromising lyrics in obvious incredulity and immediately dismissed the song as 'West Coast shit' and 'too West Coast-sounding' for them, before flatly refusing to record it. Dre and Eazy were surprised, as was Cube when the news was passed on to him, but HBO could not be persuaded to change their opinions and left for New York shortly afterwards. This left Eazy with a problem. Recording time in the studio had been booked, and the still-unstable Ruthless label would not be able to handle an immediate loss without serious implications for its future.

It was Dre – always a lateral thinker – who came up with a solution, just as he had when he picked Ice Cube to write lyrics at short notice. This time, he simply suggested that Eazy record 'Boyz N Tha Hood' himself. Although this sounded like a good idea on paper – why not ask a genuine boy from the hood to rap the song of the same name? – it was less so in practice, simply because Eazy had never rapped before. Even his nickname was a fairly recent innovation for the Compton street-kid-turned-record-company-chief. In the end, however, Dre and Cube managed to persuade him to take the plunge and the trio entered the studio as scheduled. Cube later recalled with some amusement that 'It took *forever* to do that record. Nigga was in the studio for days, trying to do some lyrics!'

New to the game as Eazy was, however, the results were awe-inspiring. E had hit upon a drawling, almost ranting style with his high-pitched tenor voice, which gave Cube's cruel tale of a murderous daily routine in the ghetto a strangely convincing atmosphere, and the trio knew that they had something special on their hands.

It was now Eazy's job to finance the Frankenstein's monster that he and his cohorts had brought to life. A deal was struck with the small Macola label, which agreed to manufacture 10,000 12" singles of 'Boyz N Tha Hood' in its tiny DIY pressing plant for the sum of £4,900 ($7,000). Initially, Eazy, Dre and Cube sold copies of the single from the boot of a car on the streets of South Central, but it's reported that Macola later offered to distribute the record officially, although the details of the record's early history are now scarce.

The single sold fairly rapidly, and a neighbourhood buzz began to grow around Eazy's cut and his new label, attracting the attention of the other rap crews in the district. The success of 'Boyz' tied in with the growing atmosphere of discontent in Dr Dre's own band, the World Class Wreckin' Cru: his co-producer in the band, Yella, had (like Dre) begun to feel some irritation at the business practices of Williams. Eazy-E later told Brian Cross what exactly happened between him and the Cru: 'Me and Dre was buddies from way back. We used to DJ and shit... Yella and Dre and [Williams] were in the Wreckin' Cru, but they were doin' all this work, and he used to give 'em like peanuts. Dre had a fucked-up car, he gave 'em like 25 dollars [£17] a week.' Eazy also revealed that Williams had taken on the management of CIA. 'He used to give Cube and Jinx 25 dollars [£17] a week *between* them. From watching him fuck everybody over I learned that what you do is you take care of [people], and they'll be cool to you.'

Given the bad vibes in the WCWC camp, it didn't take much persuading to get Dre to agree to another collaboration with Eazy and Cube, this time with Yella watching with interest from the wings (as he later put it, 'Me and Dre were getting tired of the Wreckin' Cru 'cause the money situation wasn't right, and we were always broke'). The success of his first single had prompted Eazy to request more lyrics from Ice Cube, who had come up with two songs, '8-Ball' – an insane homage to the brain-shredding effects of Olde English 800 malt beer – and 'Dopeman', a much more insightful description of the lifestyle and inevitable fate of the neighbourhood crack dealer. Rehearsals were put in place, Ruthless arranged for studio time to be booked, and Cube's lyrics were committed to memory by Eazy, who would share rapping duties on the two tracks with Cube himself. 'We were all committed to [our own] groups,' explained Ice Cube later, 'so we figured we'd make an all-star group and just do dirty records on the side.'

As sessions progressed, the idea of a fully fledged rap supergroup took shape in the trio's minds. Two other rappers – friends of Cube and Dre who went by the names of the Arabian Prince and The DOC – were also in line to be recruited, as was Yella, but before the line-up could be completed there was one small matter to be decided. A name for the band.

Ice Cube remembers the exact moment when he first heard the name of the band that would go on to shake the music world to its foundations. He was waiting outside his house for Dre and Eazy to appear and take him to the rehearsal studio. Speaking to *Vibe* magazine in 1998, he recalled: 'One day Dre and Eazy picked me up in the van and they was like – you know what we gonna call the group? I was like, what? And they said: Niggaz With Attitude.'

A slow smile spread across Cube's features. With a shrug, he concluded: 'Sounded like a plan...'

2 NWA, America's Bastard Sons

'We're the number one in your town. All the niggas love us.'

These words, spoken by a black man, might not sound unusual – many members of the American black community, especially if they are young and urban, refer to each other and themselves as 'nigga'. Coming from a white person, however, they make for a different story, with the spectres of Deep South lynchings, racial segregation, colonialism, imperialism and plain old race hate immediately raising their ugly heads. In this case it was the infamous radio DJ Howard Stern who used the n-word in a live interview with Eazy-E and LAPD chief Darryl Gates in 1992. In this instance the controversial jock was attempting to speak to E using 'black' language – presumably as a light-hearted dig at Eazy's fearsome gangsta background – and the studio was filled with genuine (if slightly tense) laughter, while the rapper himself chose to respond in his usual laid-back manner with a tolerant chuckle.

But, even though the circumstances were relaxed, the word 'nigga' had been used by a white man to a black man, which made the interview a slightly confusing experience for most listeners of all races. Should we laugh? Should we frown? Should we ignore it? Little help was given by the band themselves in a 1991 *Spin* interview, in which Dre claimed: 'We don't say nigga as a racial thing. Anybody can be a muthafuckin' nigga... Depends on how you say it. Say it wrong, we fuck you up.' Furthermore, the overall confusion wasn't helped by a rumour that had started to spread – that 'NWA' actually stood for 'No Whites Allowed' – with those believing it averring that even this most hardcore of groups wouldn't dare to use the word 'nigga' commercially.

There's an underlying stratum of meaning here, though, which focuses on the differences between 'nigger' (with its malignant, racist overtones) and 'nigga' (which has long been a positive term of mutual affection between black people). Many writers have explored the semantic connotations of both words to a degree to which many listeners, mostly from the white audience, remain ignorant. When Dre and his posse chose their name, they made a more intelligent decision than they knew – one which would shock white listeners who assumed the word 'nigger' was being used, but which actively focused on 'nigga'. The word's controversy is its strength, as the producer Quincy Jones once pointed out: 'Richard Pryor went to Africa and said, "I will never say that word [nigga] again"… But back to the significant tone coming from Africa, it can be done affectionately. It can become straight from the heart where it is literally taken and meant and felt as what the word was invented for. [There's] too much subjectivity out there to be that careless with the word. I've had a lot of arguments with rappers about this. They think it's "just a thang". Just lay down like a lot of other things they say. I think that they'll grow out of that though.'

The 'nigga'/'nigger' dilemma was just one thought-provoking issue raised by the Dr Dre and Eazy-E's decision, back in 1987, to name their new band Niggaz With Attitude. In the late 1980s, the response was no different. The entire mission of the band at that stage seemed to revolve around shocking people into a Technicolor awareness of NWA's existence – or, as Eazy said, 'We wanted to do some shit that would just shock everybody, that we could relate to, and obviously everybody else could relate to.' As for the crudely sexual lyrics, which Ice Cube had discovered would routinely delight live audiences, Eazy observed: 'We just wanted to do something new and different and talk about what we wanted to talk about – like dick sucking, we wanted to talk about that. Like people say, well you can't talk about dick sucking, or this or that in order to get [a record] deal. I be like, *fuck* the deal, I'll just wait. I'd rather take nothing and do what I want to do, than take a lot and do what they want to do. That's why we never signed with any major label. We just did it.'

This moral stance notwithstanding, the newly formed NWA were going through the period of limbo which all artists endure at this stage: the time when they have to commit themselves full-time to their project and simultaneously survive without a regular income. Eazy had his record label dealings to keep him going, while Dre was a known producer – but for Cube the options were limited. Ultimately he resorted to parking cars in a car lot, an experience which he later referred to as the worst job he'd ever done. 'At the age of 17 I got my first real job, for minimum wage – not counting whatever I could steal from people's ashtrays and glove compartments. I parked cars in downtown Los Angeles. I was just out of high school in that summer of '87, Mom wanted me out of the house and I needed a new engine for my '68 Volkswagen Bug. My car-parking gig coincided with the recording of NWA's first single. After I got off work each night, I'd spend another six or eight hours in the studio. I barely had any time to sleep.'

It was a busy time, all right – Eazy-E was being carefully shepherded into artisthood, while the newly formed band was learning to work together and make the project come to life despite all the other commitments. Parking cars all day wasn't the best way to lyrical inspiration, and being forced to dress like a lackey wasn't conducive to Cube's status as a force to be reckoned with in his neighbourhood: 'Getting up at 4:30am wasn't all bad – by getting out of the hood early I could avoid the embarrassment of my polyester tie, polyester pants and starched white shirt; it wasn't fashion, it was an *embarrassment*. And believe me, my friends couldn't wait to see me walk out of the house for the second shift dressed like that. They'd stand in my way, clowning me, holding up their keys, yelling "Hey, come park mine!"'

And he evidently learned from the experience, concluding that 'These days, when I hand over my car in a parking garage, I always leave an extra-large tip. And I don't leave anything too important behind, because they'll go through all my stuff anyway. My address book and the master tapes of my brand new albums – they'll find legs. I should know.'

One advantage of Ice Cube's graduation from high school (he was now 18 years old) was that he could devote his time to NWA for the moment. Despite the various logistical problems, the sessions were providing tangible results and the two singles, '8-Ball' and 'Dopeman', were clearly a step up in production and lyrical terms from the straight-ahead thrust of 'Boyz In Tha Hood'. The former, an account of a booze-fuelled trip evening from the viewpoint of Eazy-E, was the more humorous of the two (and therefore the more disposable, said many observers), although the casual violence which E dispenses, as well as the volley of insults he hurls at the women he encounters, are far from forgettable.

The body count that mounts during E's intoxicated rant isn't selective: his targets are pretty much anybody who gets in his way. Ice Cube's lyrics effectively evoke the all-guns-blazing approach of any drunken, aggressive thug, singling out for particular malice an immigrant driver who comes close to hitting Eazy's car when the rapper slams on his brakes at a stop light ('Stopped at a light and had a fit/Cause a Mexican almost wrecked my shit'), a nervous liquor-store owner who is worried about E's drunken state ('Nigga on tip cause I was drunk/See a sissy ass punk had to go in my trunk') and, of course, the cops and their drink-driving laws which would hinder his enjoyment of his treasured 8-Ball beer ('Drink it like a madman, yes I do/Fuck the police and a 502').

The women don't come off any better, with E cursing out girls who dislike his drunkenness ('Three bitches already said, "Eric your breath smells!"') and girls who won't dance ('Stepped on your foot, cold dissed your hoe/Asked her to dance and she said, hell no!'). 'Bitch', 'hoe' – the terms of endearment for which NWA would receive endless criticism, were all evidently in place, even this early in the band's career. Eazy winds up his diatribe with the customary props to his posse, with the words 'Dre makes the beats so goddamn funky' and 'Ice Cube writes the rhymes, that I say/Hail to the niggas from CIA'.

Not a pleasant trip, then, although the song is not without a certain self-deprecating humour – at one point Dre includes a sample of a partygoer asking, 'Yo man, you see Eazy hurlin' in the parking lot?' But '8-Ball' is a mere inside joke compared to the threatening sentiments of 'Dopeman', which paints a brutal picture of the persona of the average hood drug dealer. Narrated by Ice Cube, the song is a simple description of what the successful pusher can do to you if he so desires, untouchable as he is by nature of his job and the constant need of his presence by his clients. Cube sets the scene with a simple, grim image: 'It was once said by a man who couldn't quit/Dope man, please can I have another hit?/The dope man said, I don't give a shit/If your girl kneels down and sucks my dick'. Once he's got your attention, Cube points out that the dealer is a man to admire in some ways – with 'Gold around his neck 14 k... Bitches on his dick 24-7... Clockin' much dollars on the 1st and 15th', the dope man has it all, in hood terms: money and sex on tap. If this seems unlikely, remember that 'From a kid to a G [gangsta] it's all about money'.

The rest of the song is a description of the dealer's cruelty to his women, whom he knocks around as he chooses, and a crack addict who accompanies him called Strawberry, as in 'Strawberry just look around you'll see her/But don't fuck around she'll give you gonorrhea'. Charming stuff. But, just when you think the song is going to end with a round of applause supporting the dopeman and his activities, Eazy E steps in with a surprising threat: 'Hey mister dopeman, you think you're slick – you sold crack to my sister, and now she's sick/But if she happens to die because of your drug, I'm putting in your quto [head] a 38 slug'. It seems the dealer's future isn't so secure after all – as Eazy himself had realised.

Like it or not, the two songs were in the can, and NWA began to focus their thoughts on how to promote their product. Issues to be resolved included the setting-up of some live dates, the sourcing of a manager, and the consolidation of the band itself, which still revolved around Dre, Cube and Eazy-E. Rappers Mik Lezan (whose stage name was the Arabian Prince) and The DOC had been duly recruited, but a gap was felt alongside Dre, whose production skills were well honed but who needed a right-hand man to manage the beats and samples behind the four rappers. World Class Wreckin' Cru's DJ Yella (Antoine Carraby) was the man who stepped up to the plate, a logical choice for the role as he had worked for so long alongside Dre.

Of all the members of NWA who would come and go across the years, Yella remains the person about whom least is known. 'I was born and raised in Compton,' he pointed out some years later. 'I'm an original member of NWA, and I was here until the end.' He was always remarkably honest about his role, stating, 'I'm a producer. I don't play any music instruments except for drums.' As for his name, he explained that 'When I was just DJing, there was a song by the Tom Tom Club called "Mr. Yellow". [Another] DJ heard it and said "That's what your name should be!" – and from that day on, that was my name.'

Once the line-up had stabilised, with the six members meshing with each other's particular strengths, it was time to do business. The responsibility for advancing the band commercially fell squarely on Eazy-E's shoulders: although Dre was no novice and the others all had some experience, it was Eazy who had the most business acumen and the other members looked to him for advice on the band's commercial strategy, such as it was. As it happened, business issues were well advanced by this stage. In March 1987, Eazy had become acquainted with a record industry veteran by the name of Jerry Heller, a man with several years of management experience to his name. Meeting Heller during a trip to the Macola pressing plant in Hollywood to pick up another batch of 'Boyz In Tha Hood' singles, which were still selling well, Eazy was struck by Heller's obvious expertise (among other coups, Heller had been the man responsible for bringing the music of Pink Floyd and Elton John to the American public in the 1970s), while Jerry was curious about the commercial potential of this diminutive but intense kid from the ghetto. Heller asked for an Eazy-E demo and was impressed enough by what he heard to invite E to sign a management deal.

On first sight Heller and Eazy made an unlikely partnership. The former was a white Jewish man in his 50s, for starters – but he had a vision for NWA, and immediately set about finding a deal for them using his many contacts in the industry. This proved to be no simple task: the Eazy demo, plus the 'Boyz In Tha Hood' single, was a pretty powerful introduction to the South Central rap style, and most of Heller's contacts turned him down immediately. In the summer of 1987, however, he struck lucky when he approached the Priority label, whose headquarters are situated on LA's Sunset Boulevard. The label managers at the time were the sometime K-Tel executives Bryan Turner and Mark Cermai, both men who wanted to advance the front line of black music – and the NWA recordings convinced them to offer Heller's latest act a distribution deal, whereby Ruthless product would be added to the Priority roster.

The members of NWA were delighted, if slightly suspicious of Heller in the early days. The appearance of a white manager in the midst of South Central was an unexpected development, after all. However, Heller displayed immediate motivation by suggesting and then finding a spot on a 14-date tour for them for the autumn of 1987. To date, NWA's live dates had been confined to the venues at which Dr Dre would host his DJ sessions, plus private parties and clubs – and a scramble ensued to rehearse a set that would match the standards of the other tour acts, which included the young Salt-N-Pepa (whose first international hit, 'Push It', would be released within months) and Heavy D (who had enjoyed some minor success with his 'Mr Big Stuff' single in late 1986, but who wouldn't make much further chart impact until 1991's 'Now That We Found Love').

The tour was a success, according to reports from eyewitnesses and reviews at the time. Yella recalled that, while NWA groupies did appear, it was hardly a debauched experience ('We had two pool parties...there wasn't no orgies going on'). More importantly, the band learned about life on the road, along with the pitfalls to avoid and the art of stagecraft. This last area was their strength – having honed their crowd-stimulating skills to a fine edge from the South Central shows that each man had performed, NWA were able to tap into an audience's energy simply by telling violently sexual stories and swearing abundantly. The tour also took place at the height of the golden age of party hip-hop: the gangster-isms had yet to permeate the music and fast beats were the key ingredient, rather than the slower, more laid-back vibes that would become the linchpin of the music in the following decade.

By the end of the tour in November 1987, NWA had evolved into a relatively seasoned touring band. One slight setback was the departure of The DOC, whose ambitions drove him towards a solo project – but the slimmed-down band simply divided up his raps between them and moved on. There was no acrimony between the band members, it seems: The DOC would reappear as a Ruthless signing in 1988 and go on to enjoy a moderately successful solo career.

But more serious twists in the career of NWA awaited. Shortly after the tour ended, Ice Cube surprised his colleagues by informing them that he would be leaving the band for a while to study at college. At the time he had no idea if this would would be a temporary or permanent departure, and for a while it seemed as though NWA would carry on without him. However, the decision was made jointly – Cube would attend college for a year before the issue of whether he would stay or go was finally resolved (after all, he was the band's main lyricist, and his loss would have serious implications). In the interim, the band agreed to work on promotional activities under the guidance of Jerry Heller.

What were the reasons for Ice Cube's sudden departure? Apparently a combination of parental pressure and simple common sense, as Cube later recalled: 'The rap game wasn't looking too solid at that time, so I decided to go ahead and go to school.' He had a point – although hip-hop had been in existence for almost a decade, it had been a relatively short time since the music had penetrated the mainstream and not even the most experienced pundits could have predicted its eventual worldwide dominance, or even if it would remain a force of any significance for the next couple of years.

The most obvious motivation for Ice Cube to attend college, however, was his family, who were a strong influence on him to a degree not often found in a depressed urban area. Although Hosea and Doris had allowed their youngest child to live a relatively free life, their guidance remained firm, and neither parent wanted to see him throw away the chance of a normal life if his musical project failed to make an impact. He also pointed out later that 'it's just somethin' I did to have somethin' to fall back on, and I'm lucky I ain't never *had* to fall back'.

When it came to choosing a college degree, Cube followed the advice of a Taft high-school teacher and opted to study architectural drafting, a precursor to enrolling for a full degree in Architecture. The institute he chose was the Phoenix Institute of Technology in Arizona, a large, multicultural organisation situated about 560km (350 miles) away from Los Angeles. When the recording of 'Dopeman' and '8-Ball' was finally completed after the tour came to a close, Cube packed his bags and bid his family (and his band) goodbye.

Once settled in Phoenix, Cube embarked on his course, which would take him through until September 1988 and provide him with a Diploma in Architectural Drafting and Design. The Institute of Technology is a well-known school for engineering, arts and science degrees, with several well-known alumni: however, Ice Cube – always a fairly private individual – has never revealed much about what he did there, whom he met or what he gained from the experience. However, it is what went on in LA while he was seated at a drawing board in Phoenix that would play by far the greater role in his future career.

Back in LA, Eazy-E was rapidly becoming a star, and NWA were benefiting from this. The 'Boyz In Tha Hood' single – a deceptive slow-burner – had made an enormous impact on the Californian rap scene, focusing attention on South Central (and Compton in particular) and leading Jerry Heller to propose that Eazy record a full album. The rapper was keen to exploit his existing success and plans were laid for more recording sessions.

While on vacation, Ice was contacted by Eazy, informed of the impending album and asked to provide lyrics for a handful of songs. Cube duly obliged, handing rhymes to Eazy as and when his studies permitted. The other members duly cobbled together the album, which was titled *Eazy-Duz-It* and issued by Ruthless in early 1988.

The impact of *Eazy-Duz-It* was immediate. Characterised by E's high-pitched, almost whining vocal, plus the tough beats developed by Dre and Yella, it was a powerful record for the time (remember, hip-hop was almost synonymous with party music, rather than gangsta beats, at this stage) and heads began to turn. The track-listing ('Prelude', 'Still Talkin'', 'Nobody Move', '2 Hard Mutha's', 'Boyz In Tha Hood (Remix)', 'Eazy-Duz-It', 'We Want Eazy', 'Eazy-Er Said Than Dunn', 'Radio', 'No More ?'s', 'I'mma Break It Down' and 'Eazy: Chapter 8 Verse 10') may read like a series of bad puns on the rapper's name, but several of the songs – particularly the title track, 'Radio' and 'No More ?'s' – have gone down as early classics of hip-hop.

In essence, *Eazy-Duz-It* was a clarion call from the ghetto – a precursor of the much more violent albums to come, and among the first major stirrings of hip-hop life from South Central. Its influence was unexpectedly wide, with a notable devotee of the 'Boyz' being a 20-year-old Film Studies graduate called John Singleton, who had been born and raised in South Central and who would go on to play a major role in Ice Cube's career in the early 1990s. Back in the last years of the 1980s, however, it merely seemed like a hot, fast record with plenty of graphic imagery and a smooth production (although the 'Boyz' remix was a primitive affair)...but, of course, hindsight changes everything.

DJ Yella, who looked after the majority of the percussion on the album, remembered a slight clash in the songwriting process: 'The four of us put in a lot of free hours before we made the actual album. Cube was writing a lot of Eazy's stuff that Eazy didn't like because it wasn't him, he wasn't a rapper.' On why Eazy was so popular, Yella explained: 'We liked Eazy because originally, he had the money, but also because the sound of his voice sold. He sounded and looked like a little kid. That's why we pushed him out front; he was the image. When you thought of NWA, you thought of Eazy-E first. It was just a look.'

As Eazy's profile grew, the idea of an NWA album was mooted and batted around the various parties involved, although initial suggestions were almost immediately countered by the seemingly insurmountable problem of Ice Cube's absence. However, by the time the spring and early summer of 1988 rolled around, the band knew that Cube would be returning to the fold in the autumn (he had decided that a one-year course would suffice for the moment, especially as the unexpected success of Eazy-E seemed to indicate that NWA might have a potential market to exploit). This gave the band a boost, but it seemed that full album sessions were still some way away.

Another single, the unequivocal 'A Bitch Is A Bitch', had been recorded and was ready for release. In this song Ice Cube had attempted to defend his labelling of women 'bitches' by defining the term: 'Now, the title bitch don't apply to all women/But all women have a little bitch in 'em...' It turns out that bitches are arrogant women ('Are you the kind that think you're too damn fly?') who only want men with money ('You're through without a BMW'). Memorably, an enraged woman butts in, shouting, 'Who the fuck you think you're callin' a bitch, you little motherfucker? I dunno who the fuck you think you're talkin' to'.

Needless to say, the song had simultaneously attracted droves of negative criticism from critics, mostly on the LA music scene (NWA had yet to break beyond state boundaries), and enthralled club crowds, both male and female. This contradictory effect remained true of much later work by NWA and Ice Cube and, in fact, isn't much different from every other big-selling, but politically incorrect, song ever recorded. Except, of course, that in most such songs the singer didn't go on to warn, 'Now, what I can do with a hoe like you/Bend your ass over then I'm through'...

But the four songs that NWA had recorded ('Boyz In Tha Hood', '8-Ball', 'Dopeman' and 'A Bitch Is A Bitch') were too popular simply to leave in the studio and, while the band deliberated, the Macola label stepped forward to suggest an album made of these four songs and a few others by associated rap acts. The album would be titled (and credited to) NWA And The Posse and would, in effect, be NWA's first album. Some years later, Eazy-E said: 'That wasn't really a NWA album, that was just a bunch of artists that they had...it was like a compilation. And I guess they just used NWA to sell it, you know.' More seriously, E alleged that the label head, Donald Miller, had compiled it as a money-making scheme: 'He [Miller] just threw that together himself, just to make some money. Macola had a lot of big people over there at one time but he just ended up fucking everybody. He had 2 Live Crew, Hammer, Timex Social Club, us, and a couple of other different groups...he was always slippin' shit out the back door.'

The album was duly compiled and released in 1988, shortly after *Eazy-Duz-It*. The track-listing was 'Boyz In Tha Hood', '8-Ball', 'Dunk The Funk', 'A Bitch Is A Bitch', 'Drink It Up', 'Panic Zone', 'LA Is The Place', 'Dopeman', 'Tuffest Man Alive', 'Fat Girl' and '3 The Hard Way'. Like Eazy-E's album before it, the record was an immediate hit among hip-hoppers who preferred their beats fun and fresh rather than slow and threatening – but many listeners today would find it somewhat lightweight in comparison with the intimidating power of the gangsta-rap movement and the slick beats that followed it. All that still lay in the future, however, and on its release NWA And The Posse was hailed by many DJs as a worthy effort. The cover was a generic shot of the band, plus the other rappers who appeared on the record (Dr Rock, the Fila Fresh Crew, Ron-De-Vu – a sometime rapping partner of Eazy-E in his early days – and Fresh K among them) in a typically urban graffiti-wall setting. It bore a black sticker listing the 'guests' on the album, as well as one of the first 'These songs contain explicit lyrics' stickers – probably attached as an incentive (rather than a deterrent) to the buyer. The cover also mentioned the 'smash hit' that was 'A Bitch Is A Bitch' – perhaps an overestimation of the song's actual impact.

On the whole, the album was a decent club record, but not one that would turn many heads for its technical brilliance or even its profanity – as Ice-T would so famously tell a white audience on Oprah Winfrey's chat show, 'My music wasn't a problem until it was in your home... No one had a problem with my lyrics until Jane, Billy and Jonathan started bringing it home and listening to it.' At this stage, NWA were lodged firmly in the black clubs of the West Coast: in America it's radio airplay that pushes an act into the public's awareness, and at this stage few programmers would consider any song that referred to 'niggas' and 'bitches' for rotation.

A mixed success, then, although NWA themselves were more than happy to have some product with their name on it on sale. The future seemed bright and plans were made for further recordings. However, just as the album was beginning to sell, it became clear that all was not well in the ranks. Dre and Eazy had become aware of a young rapper named Lorenzo Patterson – like Cube, still at high school at the time – who was ambitious enough to suggest to them that he would like to record a solo album in affiliation with Eazy's new record label. Auditions showed that he had the necessary skills to do the job, and he soon became part of the Ruthless circle.

Almost at the same time, the Arabian Prince (like The DOC before him) started to evince signs that he wasn't happy with his role as an NWA member, for reasons that have never been fully disclosed. After some discussions, the Prince announced his departure after only a matter of months in the band. Although he issued a handful of solo albums in the ensuing years (his first album, *Brother Arab*, released by the Orpheus label, entered the bottom of the R&B charts in 1989, while another record was issued by NWA's label, Macola), he would never make much of an impact as a solo performer. Nowadays he has reverted to his name of Mik Lezan and works in an animation studio.

A gap had been created in the band, and without further ado Lorenzo Patterson, who (like Dre) used a portion of his first name to become MC Ren, was drafted into NWA, a move that completed the 'classic' NWA line-up. Now a solid unit, Cube and Eazy gave Ren the space he needed to exercise his rapping skills, an opportunity that he immediately seized. Like Cube before him, Ren had been a convert to the rap cause from the first day he heard the classic beats of New York hip-hop. He later said: 'Without Run DMC I wouldn't even be rhyming, really. 'Cause when I saw Run DMC, that just set it off. I had an interest to do it, but when I saw them on this show called *Graffiti Rock* back in the day, that just made me want to just start rhyming, rhyming for real. Run DMC is like my all-time favourite.' Hip-hop had also saved him from a career in the armed forces. 'A small concert me and Eazy went to…was really my first one. And 'cause I was about to go into the Army, when I saw that I said, "I gotta do this!"'

The final stage in the assembling of the band was a satisfying one. At last NWA was complete, with no weak spots. Dre was one of the most talented producers on the West Coast; Yella was a master drum-machine programmer and DJ; Ice Cube was the lyricist with the skills to pay all the bills; Ren was the hot kid straight from college, all attitude and a nimble tongue to match; and Eazy-E, of course, was the charisma behind the band, with the money, the aggression and the confidence to make the project fly. NWA had finally become a force to be reckoned with.

It had been a slow and steady process, but the way Eazy described it to Brian Cross some years later made it seem easy – as hindsight always does: 'Figure you got Dre as the producer, and me. We came up with the name, and then we added Ice Cube and Yella. I put [Ren] in the group and it just happened. Before that everybody was doing their own thing.' It almost seemed as if the players had deliberately chosen to leave their own projects to join NWA, according to Eazy: 'Ice Cube was in another group, Ren was doing his little thing, Yella and Dre was in Wreckin' Cru at the time. They left all that.' Ren, in particular, had his eyes on an individual career, it appears ('I had Ren, he wanted to do his little solo thing'), but together the five men were unstoppable ('We never did anything we didn't want to do. We did what everybody else was scared to do'), as demonstrated by the name they chose to spread their message: 'You couldn't really tell us what to do and what not to do. We came up with a name to shock ya.'

Ah, yes, shock tactics – always an ace up NWA's collective sleeves. When Ice Cube graduated in the summer of 1988 and returned to Los Angeles as a qualified architectural draughtsman, he found a tougher, more focused band awaiting him, and realised that the venom of the lyrics he had written for the old line-up would have to be doubled to match the potential of the new NWA. The band hit the rehearsal studio once more: Ice knew that a career in architecture could be his if necessary (a diploma from the Phoenix Institute is a respectable one), but he wanted to give NWA his best shot before admitting defeat and taking the right-hand path to financial security. Songwriting commenced in earnest, with Eazy now a fully fledged rapper (his early uncertainty had left him, and his ranting, sometimes apocalyptic-sounding raps were a chilling feature of the band's beefed-up sound), Ren and Cube working at full power, and Dre and Yella taking advantage of the march of computer technology to upgrade their studio equipment.

By late 1988, an album had been almost completed, and the group (together with Heller) debated its title before agreeing to issue it in time for the end of the Californian summer. The record, which took the group's aggression to levels that neither they nor anyone observing the West Coast rap scene had deemed possible, was ultimately released under a simple title. A title which, like the name of the band itself, was a no-frills admission of where they were from, what they were about, and what they intended to say.

The album was called *Straight Outta Compton*. And nothing – *nothing* – like it had ever been heard before.

3 Armageddon Arrives – Straight Outta Compton

Few albums have ever gone triple platinum in America in less than three months. Fewer still have done so without the benefit of radio airplay. And *Straight Outta Compton* remains the only record to have done so but which also specifically instructs the nation's trusted police officers to go fuck themselves.

If the world of white rock music was shattered and reshaped by *Never Mind The Bollocks: Here's The Sex Pistols* in 1977, the nearest equivalent in the arena of black hip-hop would be *Straight Outta Compton*, released 11 years later, notwithstanding the awesome fire power of contemporary albums by Public Enemy and Ice-T and later records by Dre, Cube and Eminem. To this day, people new to rap are listening to the album for the first time and experiencing the rush that starts with Eazy-E's drawled proclamation of 'You are now about to witness the strength of street knowledge' and the four bars of Yella's raw-but-funky beat that lead into that first, insanely aggressive rap courtesy of Ice Cube.

The album would ultimately sell over three million copies, boosted by sales of versions on different formats (the CD issue was especially popular in the 1990s) and later reissues. Not bad for a record which (as Dr Dre later told *Rolling Stone* magazine) had been 'thrown together in six weeks so we could have something to sell out of the trunk'.

Make no mistake: *Straight Outta Compton* is a bleak ride. It takes the listener on a journey into a nightmare world populated by Uzi-toting gangsters, witness-beating cops wielding nightsticks, abused girls screaming from the pavement, drunks staggering and cursing in the cold night air, the evil dopeman grinning out from his Mercedes and, bizarrely, finishing up at a club where the only concern is getting the right beats going for a night of dancing. Even the cover art is intimidating – a stark worm's-eye view of the band frowning down at the camera, with Eazy pointing a rifle into the foreground, ready to deliver the death sentence.

On the other hand, it's a garish, lurid world which is oddly hard to resist: the colours seem bright, almost hyperreal; the interplay of the rappers makes it seem like a patterned, regulated place to be; and the inventiveness of Dre gives it all a multifaceted aura which makes the Compton depicted on this record seem like a weird, Tim Burton-esque playground of thugs and murderers, painted in the primary colours of blood, wrath and intense envy. The blood drips both from the cops and the victims; the wrath spills from the clenched voices of Cube, Eazy and Ren, who survey their domain with a sneering violence that knows no boundaries; and the poisonous green envy oozes from the characters depicted in the tracks – envy of the rich, of the privileged and of the powerful. Vengeance will be theirs, we are informed, whether against the oppressors (the police), the exploiters (the dopeman) or simply – and horribly – against each other, in a sick, cathartic killing frenzy in protest against their cruel world. There's no pity here.

The agenda is immediately set by the album's title track. Cube introduces himself as 'a crazy motherfucker' with a 'sawed-off' – and you believe him. Spraying bullets like there's no tomorrow, the rapper goes on to promise dire retribution to anyone ('You too, boy, if ya fuck with me') who gets in his way, specifically 'niggas' – it isn't a race of white oppressors he's railing against here; it's anyone, black or white, who messes with him. This was one of the aspects of NWA's world-view that so shocked the popular press: that their 'own people' could be as casually targeted as those supposedly handing out oppression. If you're still in doubt about his veracity, Cube points to his AK-47 as the weapon of choice (to which Dre adds a burst of gunfire) and compares his killing tendencies to those of mass murderer Charles Manson.

The strength of this song is its simplicity – that and the economy with which it introduces this brutal environment. The chorus, insofar as there is one, is the rappers' payoff line – 'Straight outta Compton' – plus a female shriek of 'No!' and a repeated, low-pitched sample of the line 'City of Compton'. The second verse is the province of MC Ren, who is introduced by the leering Eazy with the command 'Tell 'em where ya from!' One of the grimmest aspects of the track is the layering of anger – each verse is more enraged than the last. Ren takes the harsh standards that Cube has established and rewrites them ('Shoot a motherfucker in a minute') and targets women for the first time with the eloquent words, 'I'm a call you a bitch or a dirty-ass hoe/You'll probably get mad like a bitch is supposed to'. He also identifies himself as the Villain, a nickname he would retain for many years.

But it's Eazy, as always, who brings the most vitriol to the table, embarking on a frenzy of lyrical acrobatics and beginning to sound more than a little deranged ('I don't give a fuck – that's the problem') after the first few lines. However, he's also using his brain here, rather than screaming through a sequence of bloody threats as Cube and Ren have done before him. Painting a picture of himself as a cunning, demonic lurker, he observes: 'I'm smart, lay low, creep a while... Never seen, like a shadow in the dark.' But, just as the listener is beginning to smile, picturing Eazy as a trickster eluding the dumb-ass cop, E reminds you that it's not a game with the words, 'So what about the bitch who got shot? Fuck her! You think I give a damn about a bitch? I ain't a sucker.' Suddenly, it's not funny any more – just as Eazy likes it.

A video was shot for 'Straight Outta Compton', featuring the band in a black uniform, black boots and perma-frowns facing an onslaught of police aggression, but it was rarely seen, as MTV refused to play it, claiming that it was a glorification of violence. In many ways they were right: the song is as much a celebration of anger as it is a simple description of it. The other reason for its impact was its stark contrast to the peaceful, let's-all-live-together vibe of previous rap hits by Public Enemy and KRS-One, who had enunciated in their songs the need for the ghetto boys to stop shooting each other and settle down. NWA's songs countered this eminently sensible policy by insisting that, not only would you get shot for getting in their way, you would get shot simply for being in the wrong place at the wrong time. No apologies, no excuses.

While many press reviews were disapproving (*Newsweek* summed up the record as '*The Godfather* in gutter language', for example), the fans were ecstatic. Perhaps this shouldn't be a surprise: Ice-T later found that, although he was rapping about events in South Central, a location culturally and physically distant from most of the world, he had a huge fanbase in Europe and Asia: 'I just think they picked up on the vibe – I mean to them, all of us are foreigners, and they just liked the rough and rowdy vibe we were kickin'.'

If 'Straight Outta Compton' had been the album's fearsome opening salvo, the next track, 'Fuck Tha Police' (with the f-word replaced by —— on the sleeve), would be the most controversial recording NWA ever made. The LAPD had always been known for the severity of its methods (the city's history is littered with litigation for unnecessary violence during arrests, for instance), and NWA chose to return this – but multiplied several times – in song form. Initially shocking simply because of the 'cop-killer' concept – a line that even hardened criminals will refuse to cross – the song details the many instances of police methods that are perceived to be unjust.

In a masterstroke of production, Dre sets the whole song up as a courtroom trial, using crowd-noise samples and spoken-word sections to create the atmosphere. A voice yells, 'Right about now, NWA court is in full effect, Judge Dre presiding, in the case of NWA versus the police department.' The hum of the audience rises, and it's clear that tensions are running high. The 'prosecutors' are introduced as MC Ren, Ice Cube and 'Eazy Motherfuckin' E' before Cube is ordered to the stand. 'Do you swear to tell the truth, the whole truth and nothing but the truth, so help your black ass?' Dre asks him, before he grimly responds, 'You're goddamn right' – a prophet with something to say. A powerful beat comes in after a bar of scratching and Ice's famous opening lines are heard, laced with venom: 'Fuck tha police, coming straight from the underground/Young nigga got it bad 'cause I'm brown.' In the first section he invites his arresting officer to go 'toe-to-toe' in the prison cell, adding that, simply because he is young and black, cops are constantly searching his car looking for narcotics.

Within seconds Ice has introduced: the idea of police homicide ('And when I'm finished, bring the yellow tape/To tape off the scene of the slaughter'); the mother of all ghetto accusations, ie that the police might be gay ('I don't know if they fags or what/Search a nigga down and grabbin' his nuts'); and, most tellingly, the notion that even a black police officer is not to be trusted ('they'll slam ya down to the street top/Black police showin' out for the white cop'). It's a pretty comprehensive agenda, and a bewildering listen for anyone new to this type of music. And it's obvious why this song kicked up such a storm in America, whose middle classes (like those in Europe and the West generally) tend to admire local cops as family people doing their duty for the community.

The chorus is a repeated sample of Eazy's 'Fuck tha police' line, before NWA stage a scene of police harassment. An impassive voice remarks, 'Example: Scene One', and a brief interchange is played out of Eazy being pulled over in his car and made to sit on the pavement at gunpoint. 'Why don't you tell the jury what you think about this fucked-up incident?' leads MC Ren to the microphone, and he wastes no time in informing us that the cops fear him ('They're scared of a nigga, so they mace me to blind me') and that, as soon as the cop puts his gun away to begin hand-to-hand combat, he will whip out his own gun ('gat') and kill him ('I'm sneaky as fuck').

After Ren's verse, the scene re-enacted in the studio is a raid on Eazy's cot. The police burst in, ignoring the gang members' protests, leading to a frenzy of shouts and threats. Dre's cold, emotionless voice commands, 'Please give your testimony about this bullshit', which is Eazy's cue to commence an extended rant about his ill treatment at the hands of the law. He describes himself as a wanted man ('They put up my picture with silence/'Cause my identity by itself causes violence') and the cops as 'suckers waiting to get shot'.

Finally, the judge reads the verdict – that the jury finds the LAPD collectively guilty of being a 'white-bread, redneck, chickenshit motherfucker'. There's laughter from the public galleries and the sentenced man (voiced by Ice Cube) is dragged away, shouting, 'That's a lie! That's a goddamn lie! I want justice! I want justice! Fuck you, you black motherfucker!' before fading into the distance. A final round of the chorus, and the song is abruptly stopped.

To put it bluntly, the cops weren't pleased when the album took off and graffiti of 'Fuck Tha Police' started appearing on urban walls across the nation. In some areas, entire police forces subsequently refused to provide security for NWA concerts. But a more powerful enemy than the police had been awoken by the song – the FBI. To the surprise (and satisfaction) of NWA, a letter was received at Ruthless Records' HQ from FBI Assistant Director Milt Ahlerich, condemning the record as encouraging 'violence against and disrespect for the law-enforcement officer'. Ahlerich allegedly stated that 'Advocating violence and assault is wrong and we in the law enforcement community take exception to such action.' The full text of the letter has never been revealed, but it was clear that the government organisation's feathers had been ruffled. Ahlerich would not have known how much interest there would be in his protest, but it certainly didn't do his career any harm. He left the FBI in 1990 to become Senior Director of Security at the NFL (National Football League), responsible among other duties for security at the annual Superbowl.

Eazy-E brushed off the feds' concerns in a later interview, saying, 'The FBI? Who cares? They in Washington DC. They way across the country.' Maybe he was right to do so, since it's probable the FBI voices its concerns whenever an anti-establishment statement is made with sufficient strength, irrespective of the medium it comes from. Or perhaps he was wrong, for the FBI is not an adversary to be dismissed lightly.

In either case, it is interesting that an organisation as powerful as the FBI would take offence at the actions of a backroom posse of LA rappers with only a local record label as its platform. Maybe Ahlerich's office was monitoring 'the black situation' in order to assess the likelihood of insurrection or rioting at the time – several decades of racial tension had made South Central a hot spot (as later events proved). What's slightly unusual is that the Department chose to voice its concern publicly rather than make private moves to close down Ruthless's activities. Who knows how the future of hip-hop would have been affected if the FBI had managed to gag NWA?

Another song, 'Gangsta, Gangsta', marks the first time that the g-word was used on a successful mainstream album. But what does it mean? 'I'm a gangsta,' sneers Eazy-E on 'Fuck Tha Police', 'but still I got flavour'. It would appear that in NWA terms a 'g' is a fighter, a pimp, a dealer and a lover rolled into one; a man who breaks the law and betrays his enemies without a second thought, but who still retains some moral values, twisted as they may be. 'It's not about a salary,' goes the chorus on this chaotic song, 'it's all about reality'.

Yes – reality. As the barrage of critical opprobrium that was levelled at NWA in the wake of *Straight Outa Compton* intensified, the most-used argument raised by themselves and others in their defence was that they were simply telling the truth – painting an accurate portrait of the hellish lifestyle of the hood without exaggerating or embellishing the details.

In one late 1990s interview, Ice Cube looked back on NWA from some years' distance, explaining that 'We told it like it was in our neighborhoods. Most of the people who sit around asking themselves why we was so angry have never set foot in Compton. They don't know any prostitutes or drug dealers personally. They don't know poverty.' He also observed in the *New York Times* magazine, during a conversation with sometime Black Panther Abiodun Oyewole, that 'I have to speak the language of the street... See, the teacher, the preacher, the politician won't talk real to the kids. So that's why they won't listen to them. You got to talk in their language and guide them to the place, and that's exactly what we're doing.'

He was right, in a sense, since many of the most vocal critics, primarily middle-class journalists, had never ventured into the ghetto – why would they? For Cube and his posse, it was a different story: 'None of us really had a lot of money when we was growing up. There was a lot of gang activity where I came from [in Crenshaw], and in the Compton neighborhood where Dre and the rest of the guys came from. There would be a shooting every day. You just hoped it was someone you didn't know. Since they were from Compton, I had to get in where I fit in, and I always came correct. Every day we'd see fighting, drug activity and problems going down involving us, our friends and the police. So that's what we discussed on our records.'

The other members of NWA were equally outspoken about the it's-just-reality standpoint. The acceptable face of rap at the time of the release of *Straight Outta Compton* was a recent hit by Jazzy Jeff and the Fresh Prince (aka the soon-to-be-megastar Will Smith) entitled 'Parents Just Don't Understand'. In the wake of this single, MC Ren told the *Los Angeles Times* that 'What Jazzy Jeff and rappers like them talk about is phony, man. They're not talking about what's really happening out there. They're talking about what the white world and the white kids can identify with. If you're a black kid from the streets and somebody is rapping about parents not understanding, you'd laugh at that. You might not *have* parents, or you'd have parents that were into crack and prostitution.'

Dre explained: 'I wanted to make people go, "I can't believe he saying that shit". Everybody trying to do this black power and shit, so I was like, let's give 'em an alternative: "nigger nigger nigger, fuck this, fuck that, bitch bitch bitch bitch, suck my dick", all types of shit, you know what I'm saying?' Yella was more concise in his explanation, observing in *Props* magazine that 'NWA was real. We weren't talking about fairy tales. We talked about life in Compton. That's all we knew. But there's 1,000 Comptons all over the nation.' As for Eazy-E, the clown prince of hardcore, his take on NWA's music was the simplest of all: 'I'm a reporter, man, I'm writing pulp fiction.'

If only the issue *were* so simple. In fact, for many years observers of gangsta rap were split more or less into two camps: those who believed that NWA had an absolute right to freedom of speech, and that their honest evocation of gangsta life was a much-needed wake-up call for both black and white America; and those who wanted them to use their platform to try to improve the situation – perhaps by depriving the violent gangsta environment of the oxygen of publicity and simply keeping their mouths shut, or perhaps by calling for peace. The latter course had been pursued in 1988 and 1989 by a group of performers calling themselves Stop The Violence, led by KRS-One and including rap luminaries such as Public Enemy's Chuck D and Flavor Flav, Doug E Fresh, MC Lyte, Just Ice, Ms Melodie, Kool Moe Dee, D Nice, Heavy D, Daddy-O-Wise, Fruit Kwan and MC Delight. Still others didn't care either way – the violence was happening universes away, in a strange place called Compton, a long way from their own lives.

Another point made by the performers was that whatever they said, and however profanely they said it, they were exercising a basic right: that of earning money to keep their families alive. No one could deny that all the men came from genuinely underprivileged backgrounds with little or no disposable income, so why deny them the right to rectify the situation? Eazy told *Spin* magazine that 'Whatever goes on, we gonna talk about it. Like underground reporters. Brings home the bacon', to which Dre added, 'That's the bottom muthafuckin' line.'

So, are we to conclude that NWA were honest working men earning a crust for their children by telling truthful stories about life in the hood? Again, if only things were so simple... No matter how many times Eazy proclaimed his messenger's role, no matter how many times Dre and Cube held up their hands and claimed to be simply telling it like it is, there is the issue of the luridly violent overtones of the album – and if any listeners had grown inured to the ceaseless slayings and beatings of *Straight Outta Compton*, they always had Eazy to spell it out in plain terms for them. He also told *Spin* that shooting a person was no big deal: 'Of course. It's nothin'. It's like shootin' a bird with a BB gun. I don't feel bad. No conscience... I don't give a fuck about nothing.'

'Not giving a fuck' is clearly at the root of the problem. If you don't care, you don't worry, and if you don't worry, you don't try to change anything. Ice-T said something similar when asked if he ever feared for his life, having made many unpopular statements in his career: 'First off, once you die, you're dead. No more cable bill, nothing. So what is there to be afraid of? I don't have bodyguards. I couldn't live like that. Like when Malcolm X got rid of his bodyguards, *you* might not understand it, but I understand it. Because there's a point when you realize how diabolical the enemy is, and you realize that when they want you dead, there's nothing you can do about it. I could have 100 bodyguards here

– I mean, the bullet's gonna come right between my eyes. So how can you be in fear?' He added that there comes a point when not caring gives a person strength: 'As soon as you're not afraid to die, you become extremely dangerous. The ultimate epitome of expression is the brink of insanity, when you take that "I don't give a fuck" attitude and you start creating shit nobody else would do.'

Furthermore, it's not just the people who don't care what happens to them or anybody else in NWA's world. In the Compton depicted by these five young men (all in their late teens or early twenties) the system itself doesn't care if you live or die. The world goes on with or without you. All that matters is the outcome of the struggle between gangsta, cop, dopeman, 'bitch' and innocent bystander. Might makes right – and he who has no might has no right to life or wealth. Like a game with no point or objective, the wheels turn, the figures move along their random courses and only the system endures. The late Tupac Shakur expressed it succinctly (and prophetically) in an April 1996 interview, saying: 'It's the game of life. Do I win or do I lose? I know one day they're gonna shut the game down, but I gotta have as much fun and go around the board as many times as I can before it's my turn to leave.'

The many listeners who liked NWA's music, but not the sentiments they expressed, couldn't understand why the band refused to make the same funky, hard-assed music but with more palatable lyrical themes. 'Why not use their power to help curb the violence?' they asked. Cube himself told *BAM* magazine in April 1989 that 'There's been violence since the beginning of time. There ain't no such word as peace. There ain't never gonna be peace' – a gloomy (or realistic, depending on your viewpoint) attitude which many others shared, unlike Ice-T, who by the 1990s had developed into a sophisticated social commentator: 'all you can do is *try*, you know. I mean, if I go out there and sing an anti-drug song it sounds like a cliché to say that if one person gets the message that's all that matters, but it's really true. You don't want to become so cynical that you just say "fuck it" and just let it go. You know you've got a voice, you've got a chance and you've been blessed to be up here on stage having people cheering for you. What the fuck you gonna do – be an asshole?'

The issue would remain as important in the following decade. When the rapper Snoop Dogg emerged as a major artist, after a couple of years at the top of the game he quickly learned not to celebrate violence too overtly. For one of his later albums, *The Doggfather*, he toned down the guns'n'hoes rhetoric that had typified his earlier work, explaining this with admirable clarity: 'It was a decision I made because I had just won a murder case for one [Snoop had recently been found not guilty of the murder of a dealer, Philip Woldemariam]. I didn't wanna be glorifying or glamorising gangsta life, like I just killed somebody and got away with it and fuck everybody. I didn't wanna be glamorising it cause I felt remorseful to the situation. I felt like takin' a different approach, an educational approach – bein' like a big brother and tryin' to give the people some messages and something to grow on and something to live for.'

But all this positive thinking lay ahead, a result of years of unthinking brutality in hip-hop sparked off by the success of *Straight Outta Compton*. Violence was only part of the controversy aroused by the album, and one aspect of the NWA world-view, however. The other accusation that has always been laid at the door of NWA is their misogyny – and they would find this much harder to justify. In their world, women are bitches and hoes or, at best, playthings to be used and discarded.

It was often argued with some justification that these outpourings of vitriol were simply the juvenile bile of teenagers, who had neither the experience nor the maturity to reflect on the accuracy of their statements. In his later years, for example, Ice Cube would reveal himself to be a sensitive and respectful provider for many women. But he would always remain a tissue of contradictions: he once said, for example, 'I'm an ass man myself... You don't have to have no breasts at all – I'm with that. The more ass, the merrier. But you got to be careful. You can get hypnotised by that ass and you can't see straight. I'm just telling guys like me to be careful. But fuck it, big asses rule.' Is he praising the sensuality of women, or is he telling his homies to back off in case they get ensnared? 'Who knows?' was the standard reaction of many listeners who enjoyed the sound of NWA but realised that their stance towards women was unreconstructed to say the least.

Perhaps one way through this conundrum is to attempt to define what Ice Cube and rappers like him actually mean by the word 'bitch', the label of choice they apply to so many women. Cube was later asked how he had come to regard women this way, and responded thoughtfully. 'I remember, after NWA, I had a song called "You Can't Fade Me" and it was about a dilemma I was having. A girl that I and everyone else on the block had slept with got pregnant. She said it was mine, and I didn't believe her...or at least wasn't sure. Anyway, I thought about kicking her in the belly or pushing her down some stairs, but then at the end of the song I come to the reality that if I hurt her, I'll go to jail. You may think about killing your boss, but you don't, because you'll have to pay. Even if you don't go to jail, you'll have that on your conscience forever. That's a small part of the song, but that's the part that everyone remembers. There's a lot of guys with babies on the way who could relate to what I was sayin'. I always try to make songs that other people can get with besides myself.'

So much for violence against women, imaginary or otherwise. Ice-T had a different angle: 'One time I was in an interview with Ice Cube, and they were asking us about the way we dealt with women. We said, "Man, basically, we rap about problems." You know, Ice-T, Ice Cube, we don't really rap about the great things in life, we rap about problems: drugs, guns, things like that. And *bitches are problems,* you know? For every woman out there who may not identify with these records, there are women that are out there who fall into the categories that we sing about, and I hate to say it, they're more interesting. A girl who is very nice and is friendly – it ain't nothin' to write a song about. I scan this bitch who's knockin' at your door and sliding rubbers under your door, trying to let you know she's out there...that's an interesting story!'

So a bitch is a conniving or aggressive woman? Maybe, but Ice-T wasn't prepared to commit himself, on this occasion at least: 'But it's only entertainment, and I can honestly say none of my records are meant to really hurt anybody. My records are meant to be listened to by the girls who can listen to it and say, "Fuck you Ice", and let it roll off. It's not really meant to be listened to by somebody who's going to be totally bent out of shape and identify.' Once again, the it's-just-reality argument is invoked: 'We're from the ghetto, and girls in ghettos, you can call them any kind of thing, they just turn around and they say, fuck you.'

Ice Cube was clearer about which women qualify as 'bitches' and which don't: 'Women conduct themselves like ladies. Bitches don't. Now those women who say that I've written songs against women haven't listened to my whole body of work. I talked about the girls I knew growing up – not my own mama, 'cause she's a lady and I love her – but the other women from the hood, ones who acted shady, lied, cheated, tricked and tried to get over on a brotha. Now does that sound like proper behaviour for a lady?'

Furthermore, it's no simple matter to identify such a woman. The listener has to give it some careful thought. Cube added, 'If my opposition listens to [my] songs carefully, and if they're intelligent, they'll be able to see who I'm referring to when I say the word "bitch". On my block, preserving my manhood and standing up for myself was most important. Early on in my life, I met scandalous women. I've seen the world now, and I've met a lovely woman [his wife, Kim], so I know good women are out there. But saving face meant being strong. I talk about how I'm not gonna let a woman play me, and by not letting a girl take advantage of me, I was considered strong in my friends' eyes. I was writing songs for my friends, not my enemies.'

At the time of writing about 14 years have passed since the release of *Straight Outta Compton*, and it's over a decade since the aggression of gangsta rap was smoothed down into the still-popular vibes of G-Funk. This time period has allowed a whole host of academic thinkers to mull over the causes and consequences of this most aggressive of musics and to commit these thoughts to paper. One of these writers was the American activist Gloria Watkins, who usually goes by the name bell hooks (lower case intended), a homage to her great-grandmother, who also bore the name. She was born in Kentucky in 1952 and became Distinguished Professor of English at City College in

New York in the 1990s. hooks made several deadly accurate observations about gangsta rap and its environment, all of which illustrate the story of the NWA/Ice Cube axis a little more.

One of the most interesting juxtapositions of Cube's career took place when hooks interviewed him for *Spin* magazine. On the face of it, the confrontation might well have been pretty heated: hooks later wrote 'Folks (mostly white and male) had thought if the hardcore feminist talked with the hardened black man, sparks would fly; there would be a knock-down drag out spectacle. When Brother Cube and I talked to each other with respect about the political, spiritual, and emotional self-determination of black people, it did not make good copy. Clearly folks at the magazine did not get the darky show they were looking for.' The edited interview was published in *Spin* in April 1993, and the complete version was later published as *Ice Cube Culture: A Shared Passion For Speaking Truth* in one of hooks' collections.

hooks initiated the conversation with the words 'People have been really, really excited about me talking to you because they think that we exist in worlds apart', but the interview was an enlightened exploration of race and gender issues, with Cube observing that to be black in modern-day America 'you gotta damn near fight your body to love yourself', but that his intended audience was a black one all the same: 'I do records for black kids, and white kids are basically eavesdropping. White kids need to hear what we got to say about them, and their forefathers, and uncles, and everybody that's done us wrong.' He also said that one day he would move towards making 'straight political records' but didn't want to make this move abruptly or without careful evolution.

By now a man in his late twenties, Cube had developed into a more rational, global thinker than the ghetto prophet of before, saying that 'Black women have always been the backbone of the community, and it's up to the black man to support the backbone.' He also spoke against male-on-female violence, although hooks couldn't dissuade him from the view that some women are 'bitches' and some are not, simply because of the way they 'carry' themselves.

Many readers were intrigued to hear hooks' further thoughts on gangsta rap itself; in fact she published several learned articles on the subject. She once perceptively pointed out that 'Mainstream white culture is not concerned about black male sexism and misogyny, particularly when it is unleashed against black women and children. It is concerned when young white consumers utilize black popular culture to disrupt bourgeois values.' This is exactly the point that Ice-T had made on Oprah Winfrey's TV show – that white indignation had not been seen until the white community had become involved.

More profoundly, hooks argued that 'It is much easier to attack gangsta rap than to confront the culture that produces that need.' She added that misogyny would always be part and parcel of a society which is a 'white supremacist capitalist patriarchy', although this was by no means to excuse or condone the anti-female sentiments of the gangsta rappers: 'Without a doubt black males, young and old, must be held politically accountable for their sexism. Yet this critique must always be contextualized or we risk making it appear that the behaviors [that] this thinking supports and condones – rape, male violence against women, etc – is a black male thing.'

There is no doubt that *Straight Outta Compton* remains a difficult pill to swallow for anyone who values human respect and tolerance. But even amid all this violence and misogny, one song on the album seems to praise strength and self-esteem – 'Express Yourself'. Based squarely on a bass-and-guitar-riff sample lifted from the 1970 song of the same name by Charles Wright (for some years incorrectly supposed to be related to his namesake Eazy-E) and the Watts 103rd St Rhythm Band, the song is musically funkier and lyrically more uplifting than any other song on *Straight Outta Compton*. In fact, the NWA version is basically a straight repetition of the older song, but with more bass, the added raps and a fatter beat. Cube's lyrics had also started to flow more smoothly: 'Blame it on Ice Cube/'Cause he said it gets funky/When you have a subject and a predicate'. The song is a sign that even NWA could be positive about their ghetto status, despite all the hood fatalism and apathy – but whether the true face of NWA represents the ghetto killer or the optimistic saviour, only the listener can decide.

As for Cube himself, *Straight Outta Compton* is a fairly accurate evocation of where his thinking and political world-view were at as a 19-year-old. Anger at the hood conditions – plus a disgust for the women he perceived were trying to exploit him and the authorities who want to erase him – are the two main emotions that informed his lyrics at that point. In 2001, he said: 'Have I done records I regret? Of course, I have... With records, y'all get to hear what I said at 18, 21, 22, 23, 25, 27. Now I'm 32. Think about what you thought when you were younger and what you think now. So it's all growth, man.' He knew perfectly well that some listeners would assume that the Cube on record and the Cube of real life were one and the same: 'Still, there's a lot of people who think what you say in your songs represents who you are. Well, my records are just a hint of who I am. That's why they don't have *The Cube Show* like *The Truman Show*.'

What this particular interviewer didn't ask Cube was whether he felt any sense of responsibility for what he had unleashed on the world – but this is probably just as well, because the answer would have taken some time to debate. Put simply, *Straight Outta Compton* changed the nature of hip-hop profoundly, opening rappers' and listeners' eyes to a host of political issues and kickstarting the entire West Coast rap movement, which had previously been in the shadow of the pioneering New York/East Coast scene. The music they made was soon to be called 'gangsta rap', a feared term that for years was accompanied by the nasty whiff of controversy, before events overtook it and it was superseded. 'Fuck Tha Police' was perhaps the song that the movement adopted as its anthem, and to this day few songs can claim to be as gleefully violent as this seminal four minutes of bile.

On the issue of responsibility, Cube was asked if NWA had started gangsta rap. 'Yeah,' he replied. 'There were a lot of signs that it was coming, and I can't take away from what people like Ice T and Schooly D and Boogie Down Productions did, but I think we perfected it. We crystallized it.' Yella discussed the same issue a few years later, pointing out that 'Ice-T was rapping, but some people didn't know where he was from. Some people thought he was from New York. He had a different style from us. We were almost the first ones to cuss on a rap record, because that's how we talk – so I think we started "street music" first.'

Ice-T was indeed almost simultaneously rapping along gangsta lines, although Yella added: 'We were just different from him. NWA started a legend and that legend has now opened the doors for all these gangsta rappers, or whatever you want to call them. We didn't think of it as gangsta rap. To us, it was just street music. We rapped about what we knew. We couldn't rap about New York because we didn't know nothing about it.'

The rap author and record label chief Bill Adler was even more specific about who started it all: 'I give NWA all the props in the world, but the auteurs were Dre and Cube. NWA was unquestionably the first group to command respect for West Coast rap. It was urgent and artful and sent rap in new directions. Their records were like the great concept albums of the 60s, designed in absolute genius fashion.' Adler also compared their work with the film industry: 'Cube and Dre created a cinematic texture to rap that had never been there before, like the most vivid blaxploitation films. Maybe it's no accident that it happened within shouting distance of Hollywood.'

Perhaps it should be left to Ice-T to explain how it started. He told *Props* magazine: 'Here's the exact chronological order of what really went down. The first record that came out along those lines was Schooly D's "PSK". Then the syncopation of that rap was used by me when I made "Six In The Morning"... At the same time my single came out, Boogie Down Productions hit with *Criminal Minded*, which was a gangster-based album. It wasn't about messages or "You Must Learn", it was about gangsterism. That was the New York shit.'

But where were NWA in the picture? Had they beaten him to it? He went on: 'If you go back to 1982 with "Cold Wind Madness", I was talking about being "the pimp, the player, the woman-layer", but "Six In The Morning" would be the first "gangsta rap", so to speak. After that, Cube wrote "Boyz In Tha Hood" which was like a bite of "Six In The Morning" [with the syncopation]. It's like "Six in the morning, police at my door..." and "The boyz in the hood are always hard..." If you play "Boyz In Tha Hood" at the same time as "Six In The Morning", you'll hear they even break at the same point. I had my *Rhyme Pays* and *Power* albums before the NWA album came out.'

But, like Cube, Ice-T believes that NWA took the newborn genre to an entirely different zone: 'NWA did it louder, more crazy, and better for what it was. They took gangsta rap to a whole other level. So I'll split credits with NWA, but it was kinda happening on the East Coast too with Schooly and KRS-One. But it was us four groups who really got it going. I also wanna include Too $hort because he was doing shit, so I connect him in with that flavor at the time.'

Although *Straight Outta Compton* was basically an underground record that broke big because it made concrete the various gangsta references that had existed in other artists' songs, the movement it spawned would not remain an underground concept for long. As soon as America's youth (both black and white) began talking enthusiastically about 'Fuck Tha Police', the corporate world sensed that money was to be made from gangsta rap – and a whole host of cussin', frownin', Uzi-totin' artists suddenly gained a platform. As Public Enemy's Chuck D later told *Addicted To Noise* magazine: 'Gangsta rap didn't take over. Gangsta rap was highly financed and endorsed more than [Public Enemy's earlier] Afrocentric rap.' Typically, Chuck was quick to identify the political motive behind this phenomenon: 'I never got mad at my peers. I just got angry at the puppeteers. And then I see this overproliferation of the word "nigga" or "I'm gonna kill the nigga rat-a-tat-tat, never hesitate to put a nigga on his back". Whole bunch of white kids cheering with it. Black kids yelling. And then when I ask a question about it, they say, "Well, it was black kids talking about it." Yeah, but it's a white company endorsing it! "Oh well, it's not censorship."'

His point was that the white powers behind this black music defended their promotion of gangsta rap by hiding behind the rappers' we're-just-reporting-reality defence and selling the violence to the white audience. 'Yeah, you say it's not censorship because you don't come from our community. But you're endorsing it, financing it. And who else would let an 18-year-old person be a voice of the community without any accountability or responsibility attached to it?'

Quincy Jones once commented on the phenomenon of gangsta rap with the words: 'Playing the game, and unfortunately, playing the *gangster* game, is very profitable. It's a strange, strange animal... You are making entertainment out of something that is just probably the most negative aspect of what we are all about.' His point was that the exception was being portrayed as the norm: 'It's been marketed very well. Between the films and the newspaper articles...you would believe that the whole spectrum of black America is "Boyz In Tha Hood", [but it's actually] a huge rainbow... There are so many colors in that rainbow, but this fear is created because you are taking two or three percent of the population and making it the norm, and making everybody think that everybody is like that – so it gives everybody a great justification if they have even a seed of racism inside to just keep it up and so forth.'

The maze of conflicting opinions grew rapidly and organically, with few obviously 'right' points of view. The fact that extremists such as Luther Campbell of the rap outfit 2 Live Crew (whose sex-based lyrics made even NWA's seem tame) were enduring high-profile court battles at the time didn't help clarify the situation, largely because many listeners who felt duty-bound to defend the gangsta rappers' right to freedom to speech were also genuinely appalled by the misanthropy of their work. To this day, more than a decade after the *Straight Outta Compton* furore died down, most observers are still not certain whether gangsta rap was a good or a bad thing.

As for NWA? They loved it all, relishing the near-global impact that their record had made. When *Spin* asked Yella what his goals were, he replied, 'A house in Memphis, money in the bank, and pussy... Anything beside that's irrelevant!' Dre, a more profound thinker, who knew exactly why the album had sold so well, added, 'Everybody else doing this peace shit. Nobody wants to listen to that.' He had a point: just as many otherwise 'normal' people love to watch horror films, and just as people will slow down in their cars to look at a traffic accident on the road, people enjoyed *Straight Outta Compton*'s lurid stories of murder and brutality. Add in a dash of black humour (Ice Cube later said, 'If you really listen to NWA, there's comedy all through it: that's the story of black people – making light of tragic situations') and the recipe is an attractive one indeed. That's the simple truth: the record's success is not hard to understand. Whether or not that says good things about society is a decision people must make for themselves.

Perhaps the album's success was due to its unreconstructed nature: Cube also claimed that 'Most of the rap records at the time avoided cuss words and stuff like that because they wanted to get on the radio. But we were just trying to appeal to our own crowd...the homeboys down the street.' More importantly, *Straight Outta Compton* needed to be heard outside the ghetto: 'We needed to talk about stuff that other people are scared to talk about. We're speaking in the language of the neighborhood. The homeboys know exactly what we're saying.' And NWA's motives always remained pure, he argued: 'People sometimes act as if we are making up the stuff we talk about on the records...that we are trying to be controversial and shocking. It *is* controversial and shocking, but it's also real.'

For better or worse, *Straight Outta Compton* was also an influential album. Cube later said, 'Even though that was a hardcore underground record...that record was still pop. Everybody had that record, and everybody knew about that record. [It] has had [a bigger] impact on rap music than any other album to this day... We opened the door where you can say exactly what you really want to say without having to sugar-coat, without having to hold back.' Yes indeed: the floodgates opened in the wake of *Straight Outta Compton* and, whereas heavy metal had been the prime establishment-scaring musical genre in the past, hip-hop soon rose to take its place. As for the record's influence, by bringing Ice Cube, Dre and Eazy-E to the mainstream, *Straight Outta Compton* changed the face of music. All three became industry movers unlike any black artist since Quincy Jones and Stevie Wonder, and (with Prince to a certain extent) would shape the way black music evolved until the early 1990s. Dre especially played a role in introducing new talent to the field – among them the young rappers Snoop Dogg and Warren G, whose debut albums ruled the airwaves for a couple of years.

Snoop in particular was hailed as 'the son of NWA', and never ceased to demonstrate his respect for the music of his mentor's old band, along with an accurate take on how Dre himself evolved ('He wasn't really with all that gang-bangin' and shit...he likes to make music, be the family man and do what he gotta do. He got burned out on that shit 'cause he did all that shit when he was with NWA') and the longer-term influence of gangsta rap itself. Asked by writer Eric Berman whether Snoop would let his young son listen to gangsta rap, he replied: 'I do. Whether I show it to him or not, it's going to be out there in front of his eyes every day. The streets don't have no love for him. They're not going to teach him. I'm going to love him and show him the right way of going about it. I didn't have no father in the home to stop me from gang-bangin', but he does.'

In many ways, the development of the major players (each of whom, as we will see, would follow shockingly different paths) mirrors the evolution of their music. A journalist for NME.com perceptively asked Dre: 'If you had the 20-year-old Dre sitting opposite you right now, do you think you'd like the guy?' in a late 1990s interview. The rapper was clearly taken aback by the question, never having thought along these lines before. 'That's a different question! I never got asked that one... Would I like him? You know what? I would have to say yes and no. I think I would like the person but I would hate his ways. The immaturity, the fucking, um, because I was wild... I would definitely like the person if I was with them solo. I would love them. But if I was with that person at a club I would hate them. Obnoxious, wild, careless – I was really obnoxious. You got to realise that when I was 20 years old, I had a house, a Mercedes, a Corvette and a million dollars in the bank before I could buy alcohol legally. And taking a guy that grew up the way I did, out of Compton and put him in this fucking mansion, you couldn't tell me shit at that time. It was pretty bad, actually, now I think about it. But I got through it. I grew up.'

Back in 1989, however, such enlightened self-analysis was several years away, and once *Straight Outta Compton* had ignited a wave of national controversy (and praise – *Yo! MTV Raps* devoted a whole hour to the band at around this time) it was time for NWA to take it on the road. A tour was set up by Heller and his associates, and the five-piece began spreading the word. Support came from The DOC, whom Eazy had signed to Ruthless in March. Crowds flocked to see them and controversy was generated almost immediately after NWA ignored a ban in Detroit on the song 'Fuck Tha Police', chanting a few lines from the song at the Joe Louis Arena on 6 August. According to MC Ren, 'Muthafuckas chased us off the stage!' before the band were briefly detained by their nemesis, the local police. Details of NWA's treatment at the hands of the local law enforcement are not known, although it's safe to presume that no love was lost between the two parties. More seriously, an Alabama woman claimed in August that she had been raped by Ren on the band's tour bus after a concert, and later filed a paternity suit against him. Once more, the outcome is not known.

And so the NWA machine rolled on, causing more establishment headaches than ever. The fans loved them, the cops despaired of them – but the press were finding plenty to say about them. At about this time, an unknown writer first coined the phrase 'America's Most Dangerous Group' – a sobriquet that was among the more accurate labels placed on them. Perhaps just as appropriate was the term 'America's Most Wanted'. More evocative still would be '*Amerikkka's Most Wanted*', as events would subsequently prove.

4 Going Solo

As the *Straight Outta Compton* tour rolled on into the summer of 1989, Ice Cube struck up a friendship with Priority Records' publicity officer, a competent, media-savvy industry player called Pat Charbonnet. Possibly a little too talented for the moderate demands placed on her by the Priority label (which had had little mainstream success before the advent of NWA, other than some chart presence from an R&B act called the Raisins), she was full of ideas for NWA and how to exploit the band's new-found status. One day Cube and Charbonnet were discussing the band's management structure and, out of curiosity, Pat asked him about his royalties arrangement with NWA manager Jerry Heller. Pondering the question, the rapper realised that he was unsure how the system operated and started to ask himself one or two questions. By the time the band were due to play in Phoenix, Arizona – where, ironically enough, Cube had only recently spent a year as an impoverished student – he was worried enough about the situation to call the band together and demand to be told the truth about any agreements that Heller and Eazy-E might have made regarding cash flow.

Eazy duly asked Heller to fly down to Phoenix with new contracts for each band member. Allegedly, Heller also brought cheques to the value of £53,000 ($75,000) for each man who signed up for the new arrangement. Cube told *Rolling Stone* magazine in 1990: 'Heller gave me this contract, and I said I wanted a lawyer to see it. He almost fell out his chair. I guess he figure, how this young muthafucka turn down all this money? Everybody else signed. I told them I wanted to make sure my shit was right first.' This decision clearly took some courage, especially as Cube had little money, remained the only member who hadn't signed and was faced with the other players' mockery. 'I remember them niggas joking. They say "Yo! $75,000! If that shit ain't right, ain't *nothing* right."'

Cube passed his contract to an accountant, who (in collaboration with a contract lawyer) came back to him advising him that it would be a bad idea to sign it. Investigations proceeded and after some weeks Cube was advised of the following figures (all of which are alleged). The NWA tour had grossed £460,000 ($650,000), of which Heller had retained £92,000 ($130,000) and paid Cube £16,000 ($23,000). More seriously, Cube had written approximately half of *Straight Outta Compton* and *Eazy-Duz-It*, which had sold about three million units between them – but for this he had received only £23,000 ($32,000). Most urgently of all, Cube's contract had reportedly included an agreement with Ruthless but no official confirmation that he had ever become a full member of NWA. On the advice of his lawyers, Cube filed a private lawsuit against Heller, which was later settled out of court for an undisclosed sum.

However, the relationship between Cube and NWA had clearly soured, and in 1990 he made the decision to leave the band. It was a brave decision – after all, he had made some money for his efforts, but it wasn't by any means guaranteed that a successful solo career would await him. As he later said, 'I was broke before I jumped in that shit, so it wasn't hard to walk away. I preferred it that way.' It seems that he had wanted to attempt some solo recordings in any case: according to Yella, Cube had approached the other members of NWA with an idea for a solo album, possibly to be recorded in collaboration with Public Enemy, called *Amerikkka's Most Wanted*: 'We told him "Not now, we're going to work on Eazy's album." He wanted to do his first.' The DJ also recalled that Cube was taking advice from unknown sources at the time (although he may have been referring to Charbonnet and Cube's legal advisers): 'Plus, somebody was in his ear at the time telling him this and that. That was his major problem.'

The other members of NWA didn't make it easy for Cube to leave, making him the butt of their jokes. 'I was like, fuck it! I'm going to go solo,' he said later. 'Everybody was like, go ahead, nigga – *be* like Arabian Prince. I was a joke. Them muthafuckas had jokes for me.' It's also been alleged that Heller later stirred up extra trouble by claiming that Cube left because he was jealous of Eazy-E's talents. But his resolve was firm (after all, he knew that his raps were the heart of NWA's approach) and he began to make contacts on the East Coast, where he had decided to move to record a solo album. His choice of producer was Public Enemy, and specifically their Bomb Squad studio team: 'At the time the two producers that was worth fucking with was Dr Dre and the Bomb Squad,' he said. 'If I couldn't get Dre, I was going to the Bomb Squad.' He was also in contact with his old friend Sir Jinx from CIA and had agreed to collaborate with him on the new project. Cube's new manager was to be none other than Pat Charbonnet, who left Priority to devote her considerable business acumen to the job of artist management.

The press, of course, were following these developments with an eager eye: some praised Cube's decision and others crowed over what they saw as his imminent slide into obscurity, while still others interpreted his departure as the beginning of the end of gangsta rap itself, the genre which NWA had started and which would surely never outlast them. But, as Ice-T said, it's not the media, but personal integrity, which counts: 'To get up on that stage and spill your guts and bust your ass, and take a chance at getting booed, that's the risk, man. Whether or not you win or lose, you were up there. The dude sitting in the audience writing about ya? Fuck him.' Or, as Chuck D put it: 'This is a society that is always treading on black people, who are being thrown negativity and are adopting the negativity. Being positive is like going up a mountain. Being negative is like sliding down a hill. A lot of times, people want to take the easy way out, because it's basically what they've understood throughout their lives.'

And so the classic NWA line-up came to an end. Ironically, it was money – which they had praised, glorified and relished in their lyrics – which split them up. Looking back on this traumatic time from some years' distance, Cube reflected: 'I came into the rap game at a time when it was all about skills and talent. That's what everybody was trying to work on, getting better at what they do. Nowadays, everybody knows how much money it is, and sometimes you can get caught up in that, you know, "If I release this album, I can get this much money". And the money starts to become more important than the album, and then you start to see the quality slip, even in artists that were bangin'.'

As it happened, NWA themselves had plenty of talent left among their ranks, and in some form or other their grim spectre would remain with the former O'Shea Jackson for some years yet. But for now it was time for the group rapper to reinvent himself as a solo artist, and to do so Ice Cube required a fresh start in a new city. Without further ado, he migrated to New York.

In 1990, the Big Apple was still very much the spiritual home of hip-hop, with the Brooklyn and Harlem districts regarded with semi-religious awe by the faithful fans who flocked there to visit the 1970s-style block parties that still cropped up from time to time. In choosing to reside there for the recording of his debut solo album, Cube affected the course of hip-hop's history more than he could have predicted: as Cypress Hill rapper B-Real later explained: 'For a while, the East looked down at [West Coast hip-hop acts], like we weren't real rappers. And we came up and started saying, hey, look, we're here. And then they began respecting us. Ice Cube started that when he did his record on the East Coast with the Bomb Squad. That automatically opened the door for us. And then East and West was down... [We] could do shows over there and they could do shows over here. And it was all good.' An ironic twist, for who would have thought that Ice Cube, whose raps had defied the 'peace-loving' convention laid down before NWA came to power, would unite the new and old schools?

Cube's choice of the Bomb Squad as producers was logical as well as inspired. He had previously helped out on Public Enemy's ground-breaking *Fear Of A Black Planet* album, producing one of the album's highlights, 'Burn Hollywood Burn', which also featured a cameo rap by Big Daddy Kane. In doing so he had forged a firm friendship with Public Enemy rappers Chuck D (Charles Ridenour) and Flavor Flav (William Drayton). Chuck told *Shut 'Em Down* that Cube was 'like a little brother' and that working with him on his debut album was 'one of the prouder moments' of his career. He added that Cube was no innocent babe in arms when he sought the production expertise of the Bomb Squad: 'You know, Cube wasn't no rookie, because he actually came from the NWA camp, and was working with Dre. He wasn't no rookie, but he just wanted to do it on his own. All he needed was a little bit of confidence, like, "Oh shit, you're ready to go."'

A less obvious choice of co-conspirators was Da Lench Mob, who assisted Cube in a couple of recording sessions for *Amerikkka's Most Wanted* at New York's Greene Street Studios. A talented rap trio consisting of West Coasters Shorty, J-Dee and T Bone were similar to Cube politically and musically, and therefore it isn't clear exactly why their presence was required. However, Cube was probably giving them a leg-up (he would later produce their debut album), as well as benefiting from the comradely feeling of being back in a team.

Da Lench Mob weren't short of a sound bite, either, and were happy to sound off about racial issues, like their mentor before them. When asked in a 1992 interview if they saw any solutions to the problems of black America, rapper Shorty responded: 'Yeah, I see a lot of solutions. First of all, we got to wake up. And everybody has to quit putting the whole muthafucking load on the entertainment's shoulders, 'cause we only learn, and then we try to reach out through entertaining. If we was big fucking professors or activists, we would know how to speak to the masses, but we're entertainers. Everybody say, "Why ain't rappers doing this?" or "Why ain't y'all doing that?" What the fuck are the people who are talking doing?'

Perhaps Shorty went further than Cube would have done, in giving an affirmative answer to the question of breaking America into two countries – one for whites and one for blacks. 'Yeah, that would be the best thing that ever happened to us. The majority of the foolish negroes would be like, "Fuck that. I'm going where the white man's going. He's breaking me off a check." They would be scared to do for themselves. That's lack of knowledge of self.' (Such a question was first suggested by the Nation Of Islam, which had lobbied the UN for reparations on the basis that the US government is in violation of UN Article 27, covering the right of individuals to speak their own language, follow their own religion and practise their own culture.) His response to the question 'Do you think there can ever be peace between blacks and whites?', however, was not without reason, in a grimly apocalyptic kind of way: 'Only if they bear witness to what is ours and what they owe us and know that what was done wrong many years back can never be done again. But there ain't gonna be no peace until we have separation or war.'

But the combined efforts of Da Lench Mob, the Bomb Squad and Ice Cube himself made the finished result a spectacular record. Released in the USA on 16 May 1990, *Amerikkka's Most Wanted* was, like *Straight Outta Compton* before it, an exhilarating ride. The cover, featuring the beanie-clad Cube still sporting the *jheri* curls of old, pointed directly to the Technicolor nature of its contents – the track-listing was 'Better Off Dead', 'The Nigga You Love To Hate', 'Amerikkka's Most Wanted', 'What They Hittin' Foe?', 'You Can't Fade Me', 'JD's Gaffilin'', 'Once Upon A Time In The Projects', 'Turn Off The Radio', 'Endangered Species (Tales From The Darkside)', 'A Gangsta's Fairytale', 'I'm Only Out For One Thing', 'Get Off My Dick And Tell Yo Bitch To Come Here', 'Rollin' Wit The Lench Mob', 'Who's The Mack?', 'It's A Man's World' and 'The Bomb'. 'Endangered Species (Tales From The Darkside)', 'I'm Only Out For One Thing' and 'It's A Man's World' were listed as featuring Chuck D, Flavor Flav and Yo-Yo respectively.

On first listen, it's a funk-driven, powerfully percussive album, with plenty of old-school beats (ie raw, chopped-up sounds with little polish but not lacking in subtlety). There's a new sense of self-awareness in evidence, however, with Cube barking out one of his most misogynistic songs ('Get Off My Dick And Tell Yo Bitch To Come Here') but counterbalancing it with the Yo-Yo duet, 'It's A Man's World', in which his female co-rapper Yo-Yo (born Yolanda Whitaker in 1971 in South Central, LA) admonishes him for his primitive attitude towards women. Props are given to the street lifestyle on 'Rollin' Wit The Lench Mob', and 'A Gangsta's Fairytale' invokes the darkest of Compton-style ghetto imagery, but this is nowhere near the '*Straight*

Outta Compton Volume 2' that some fans had feared (and others hoped for): there's far too much sophistication, lyrical and musical, for that analogy to hold much water.

On the other hand, Cube has serious bile to impart, underlining his anti-police brutality stance in 'Endangered Species (Tales From The Darkside)' with the words 'Every cop killing goes ignored/They just send another nigga to the morgue/They send ten of them to get the job correct/To serve, protect, and break a nigga's neck'. Moreover, although the title track is partially the tale of a housebreaker sent to jail, there's a moral point to be made: 'I think back when I was robbin' my own kind/The police didn't pay it no mind/But when I start robbin' the white folks.../Every motherfucker with a colour is most wanted'.

The album went gold in America inside a week, and platinum in three months. Clearly the hip-hop fans of the nation had been watching Cube's progression with interest, and had not been deterred by the album's most controversial song, the aforementioned 'You Can't Fade Me', in which the rapper relates a tale of deception: like everyone else on his block, he's slept with 'the neighborhood hussy', but she now tells him that she's pregnant with his baby. He doesn't believe her, but fears being sued for child support nonetheless, and has a momentary fantasy about solving the problem: 'Then I thought deep about giving up the money/What I need to do is kick the bitch in the tummy'. A brutal solution, and one that shocked many observers, although in the very next line Cube dismisses the idea with the words: 'No, 'cause then I'd *really* get faded/That's murder one 'cause it was premeditated'.

Album high points for many included the chorus of 'The Nigga You Love to Hate', an inelegant group scream of 'Fuck you, Ice Cube!', although this wasn't the response of many impressed critics, including Brian Cross, who wrote in his book *It's Not About A Salary: Rap, Race And Resistance* that '*Amerikkka's Most Wanted* sought to give a face to [the] criminal underclass and this face was to be furrow-browed, jheri-curled, beanie-clad face of Cube himself. Cube to this day is the foremost hip hop meta-critic, providing listeners not only with stories, but potential criticism of his practice from different perspectives.' Meanwhile, *Spin* called the album 'a masterpiece', helping it enter the Top 20 *Billboard* chart, while *Source* awarded it a coveted five-microphone rating out of a possible five – a rare honour indeed. This acceptance on both coasts made Ice Cube briefly the American rapper with the widest sphere of influence, and the 'Amerikkka's Most Wanted' single, while merely a moderate radio success, kept Cube's profile still higher.

Across the United States, the intelligent message of rappers such as Public Enemy was beginning to sink in a little, in one evident way at least – young black men who made money were starting to invest it carefully, in businesses and in property. Ice-T, a man who would later have his fingers seriously burned at the hands of a major record company, underlined this with these words: 'If you want to have free speech, you also have to have your own network to put it out. I learned that lesson…that you're never really safe as long as you're connected to any big corporation's money.' Two men who heeded his words were Ice Cube and Eazy-E, both of whom established companies at or around this time. Eazy's Ruthless label had been in existence for two years by the time Cube first laid plans for his own organisation with Pat Charbonnet, which he labelled Street Knowledge Productions after those first, prophetic words on *Straight Outta Compton*. The fact that Charbonnet was managing his business affairs was thought by some to be a counter to the accusations of misogny that had temporarily increased in the wake of 'You Can't Fade Me', although, of course, it's much more likely that he appointed her simply because she was a competent and trusted associate.

In the meantime, NWA weren't resting on their laurels: the West Coast hip-hop scene had exploded around them and the south was also beginning to show signs of life in the rap arena. The presence of Ice Cube was only one issue provoking them into activity, and in August 1990 they released the *100 Miles And Runnin'* EP, which gained them some ground by selling over half a million copies. The title track – a fast, uncompromising song – was released as a single and accompanied by a video depicting Eazy, Dre, Ren and Yella making a hustled getaway from a platoon of cops. Dre had excelled himself in the production, introducing guitars and bass to the mix and adding in police sirens, running footsteps and a variety of ambient sounds to add immediacy. One song, 'Just Don't Bite It', an unsympathetic paean to fellatio, kept the controversy high, fuelled by the casually violent lyrics co-authored by The DOC. In September, a 110-shop retail chain in Kentucky called WaxWorks refused to stock the EP on grounds of obscenity.

Although no real enmity existed between NWA and Ice Cube at this stage (the two parties usually chose not to speak about each other in interviews), this uneasy truce was dramatically broken when Eazy's group appeared on a TV show called *Pump It Up* in November 1990. The show's presenter was a woman called Dee Barnes, a member of the rap group Body And Soul. During the recording of the programme, Barnes interviewed NWA, who finally had some negative – even insulting – things to say about the departed rapper. On another occasion Ice Cube was also interviewed for the show, and had some similar comments to make. During editing, Barnes was informed that the two interviews would be intercut, to show the two sides bad-mouthing each other. She told the producers that this might be a bad idea, but her concerns were dismissed and the show was duly broadcast with the interplay between the two parties intact. The crucial moment came when Yella pulled an ice cube from his glass and deliberately crushed it beneath his heel. Simultaneous footage of Ice Cube grinning and bragging that he had NWA '100 miles and running' seemed to imply that NWA were on the losing side of the battle.

As Barnes had feared, NWA didn't take this lightly. According to *Vibe*, on 27 January 1991 she met Dre and Eazy at a launch party for a record by a female rap group called Bytches With Problems (the aping of the name 'Niggaz With Attitude' by this group of women is a whole story in its own right). According to reports, Dre picked her up by her shirt and began slamming her face against a wall near a staircase before attempting to throw her down the stairs. He then punched her repeatedly on the back of the head before leaving her on the floor.

This shocking episode was followed up a few days later when Barnes filed criminal charges to the value of £16 million ($22.7 million) against Dre and the members of NWA. Six months later (by which time NWA were embroiled in much deeper controversy), Dre was fined £1,800 ($2,513) plus £700 ($1,000) to be donated to the California Victims Restitution Fund, and ordered to perform 240 hours of community service and make a public-service announcement. A further civil case was settled out of court.

What was almost as concerning as the fact that the assault happened at all was the blatant lack of remorse the band displayed later that year in *Spin* magazine. Eazy-E, who had clearly enjoyed several cocktails, recounted with obvious glee how Dre had beaten Barnes. The interviewer asked Dre what had happened, who responded, 'Nothing, man... I was drunk', at which Eazy interrupted, 'You lying! You beat the shit out of her!... I seen everything. He grabbed the bitch by the little hair that she had. Threw the bitch to the bathroom door. Pow! She hit her head. He just start stompin' on the bitch... Threw the bitch down a flight of stairs! Bitch didn't even know her name!' Draw your own conclusions.

As 1990 waned, Ice Cube was a busy man, not overly concerned with the *Pump It Up* debacle nor wasting much time paying attention to Dre's caveman brutality. Demand for material had increased since the unexpected success of *Amerikkka's Most Wanted*, and he had recruited Sir Jinx and another associate, Chilly Chill, for an EP, which he titled *Kill At Will* and released on 18 December 1990. Like its predecessor, it sold rapidly, attaining gold status in a short time. But its true impact was felt in the breadth of emotion it explored, which directly influenced many other songwriters in the field to broaden their own approaches.

Specifically, it contained the song 'Dead Homiez', and was nothing less than a funeral elegy to a murdered ghetto homeboy, with little of the splatter-movie glamour that had so attracted America's youth to *Straight Outta Compton* and (to a lesser extent) *Amerikkka's Most Wanted*. In contrast, the club-friendly 'Jackin' For Beats' appeared to have little message other than a simple let's-get-down vibe – two songs of such opposite depth have rarely appeared on an album together, let alone on a five-track EP. Another highlight is undoubtedly the paranoid, twisted remix of 'Endangered Species', on which Cube and Chuck D spar alternately, leading some commentators to liken the song to a vengeful version of Stevie Wonder and Paul McCartney's 'Ebony And Ivory'.

The success of the EP demonstrated one clear fact: that Ice Cube was learning to gauge his audience. The violence that had typified all the gangsta-rap releases to date was almost absent, but the public still flocked to buy it. It seemed that the country's hip-hop fans were ready for a break from all the murderous sentiments of yore, and Cube had known that this was coming. *Art Form* magazine described 'Dead Homiez' (which was released as a single) as a 'harrowing and sorrowful tale of a funeral for a friend'. Cube added in a contemporary interview that the song deals with the influence of our environment: 'It says [that] a kid is just a product of his social background. Put him around lawyers, he's gonna want to be a lawyer. Put him around gangbangers, he's gonna want to be a gangbanger.'

As Ice Cube's profile rose, and his face and words appeared in more and more press, production commissions began to come his way. There was a notable early studio role for Yo-Yo, who had appeared so memorably on *Amerikkka's Most Wanted*: she had scored a solo deal with EastWest and wanted to record her debut album with Cube at the controls, although ultimately Sir Jinx shared production duties. The result was *Make Way For The Motherlode*, released in 1991 – a respectable success among more educated rap fans who could appreciate Yo-Yo's political message, which was based on a positive message to women. She later co-founded the IBWC (Intelligent Black Women's Coalition) to act as a platform for her agenda, and remained a successful career rapper and actor throughout the 1990s.

Another act whom Ice Cube mentored at this early stage in his career was his cousin, Teren Delvon Jones, who rapped under the stage name of Del after beginning his hip-hop career as an 18-year-old MC in Da Lench Mob. Cube produced his first album, *I Wish My Brother George Was Here*, which was released in 1991 by Elektra. A Parliament-/Funkadelic-inspired record with several deftly rapped sections by the young MC, *IWMBGWH* was a success in limited quantities – but some listeners felt that Ice Cube's influence was just too audible. In fact, Del seemed to share that opinion, opting to work without Ice Cube on his next album (which failed to shift many copies and Del faded into backroom obscurity soon after).

And so Ice Cube had made a number of transitions: from rap apprentice to master and mentor; from misogynist to an (almost) enlightened standpoint regarding women; and from team-mate to a confident solo artist. In line with these changes came a new-found maturity (many of the interviews he gave at this time displayed an evident thoughtfulness in his approach), and alongside this came a profound spiritual development, tied in with a new political awareness. Like so many young black men before him, he encountered the Nation of Islam (NOI).

'Up to that point, I was just rolling through life trying to get money,' he explained at the time. '[Then I started] reading a lot of books. I was just learning about the world, paying attention to world history, political views.' Two of the political voices he admired most were those of the NOI's spiritual leader, Minister Louis Farrakhan, and Elijah Muhammad. Although it isn't clear how much religious belief Cube has (or even if he has any at all), it's certain that when it comes to his stance regarding the black struggle in America and the world at large, the writings and activities of the NOI have profoundly shaped his development.

For those unfamiliar with the Nation of Islam, a brief history is in order. It's a branch of Islam concentrated in urban America dedicated to restoring African Americans to what they believe is their ancestral religion, as their ancestors (sometimes defined as the Tribe of Shabazz from the Lost Nation of Asia) were supposed to be Muslims. As part of the process (its main aim, in fact), the NOI desires to restore faith and self-esteem to black people, who have been crushed and oppressed by whites (described as 'devils'). The NOI describes its centres of learning as Universities of Islam, which prescribe a strict moral code focused on the Principles of Divine Unity and the Universal Brotherhood of Islam.

The NOI was founded in the 1930s by a visionary called Wallace D. Fard, who established the principles of the organisation on his return to America from a visit to Mecca, Islam's holiest city. Devising a theological system (part of which involves a rebellious deity and evil scientist, Yakub, creating white people as a race of devils to harass and oppress blacks), and recruiting a disciple, Elijah Poole (who would later be renamed Elijah Muhammad), Fard (who took the name Wallace Fard Muhammad) began to attract followers. On his death, Elijah Muhammad led the NOI until 1975, when he was supplanted by Louis Farrakhan.

Farrakhan himself is a seminal figure and has made the NOI what it is today. Born Louis Eugene Walcott in Roxbury, Massachusetts, in 1933, he was a child-prodigy violinist, calypso singer and dancer until he attended his first Nation of Islam meeting, where he witnessed a pivotal speech by the NOI minister and black activist, Malcolm X. He renounced his show-business activities altogether, joined the Nation himself, and from 1956 rose gradually through its ranks until he became its leader in the 1980s.

Farrakhan has a charisma for his followers which is almost biblical. Even Ice-T was impressed with him, recalling: 'I talked to Minister Farrakhan, and he's a cool guy, but we disagree on a whole bunch of shit. I was sitting in front of Minister Farrakhan, and I'm like, "Look, I'm a eat some sausages, and I ain't gonna tell you that you won't catch me with no white woman", right? And he said to me, "Ice-T, I'm going to tell you something. I've never had anybody come and talk to me the way you do. You're either a very crazy man or you're very powerful, and I'll bet my life on the second." And then he also said, "Don't even worry about anything happening to you, 'cause anyone who kills you, their children will slaughter them in their sleep."' It's perhaps evidence of the man's power that (at the time of writing) the UK Home Office has just won an appeal against a previous High Court ruling that stated Farrakhan should be allowed to visit.

The NOI sums up the aims of the organisation as follows: 'We are taught never to carry arms, to make war or to be the aggressor, for this is against the nature of the righteous... We are taught cleanliness inwardly and outwardly, with the practice of good manners and respect to one and all. We are taught that the family is the backbone of society and that our children must be reared to reflect the highest morals and training to perfect our society. We are trained to eat and to prepare the best of foods for the longevity of life, without the use of alcohol, smoking and substance abuse which endangers the ethics of healthy living. We are taught to respect and protect our women who are the mothers of civilization. Our women are taught a dress code of modesty that will lead to the practice of high morality. We are trained to be an exemplary community expressing the highest spiritual goals for the reform of ourselves and others based on wisdom, knowledge and beauty.'

In practice this means a regime of almost military discipline, which the NOI advocate as the true path to spiritual awareness and self-fulfilment. Anyone who has seen the NOI's members leafleting America's city centres will attest that they – usually young black men – are smartly dressed and extremely polite. The numbers of members nationwide are uncertain, with estimates ranging from as low as 19,000 to as many as 3,000,000.

However many members there are, the NOI showed its power on 16 October 1995, when Minister Farrakhan called for a Million Man March to converge on Washington, DC for a mass meeting. Many thousands of men were present – even more than had attended the march on Washington called by Martin Luther King, Jr some three decades before – and the NOI's national profile was raised significantly. Inevitably, detractors began to raise their voices, among them black members of Christian churches as well as the predictably moronic white supremacist groups, but the movement appears to be unstoppable, bolstered by its *Muhammad Speaks* publication, which addresses a variety of black issues, whether focused on the NOI or elsewhere.

Several prominent black people had joined the NOI before (one of the earliest men to support it was boxer Cassius Clay, who changed his name to Muhammad Ali after his conversion). Several were affiliated with the hip-hop movement, perhaps because so much rap has concerned itself since the rise of Ice-T, Public Enemy and NWA with social injustice against blacks. Ice Cube's conversion to Islam came as little surprise to those who knew him, as his raps had long been based on the black vs white conflict, or to the NOI itself, which was used to having prominent hip-hop alumni among its ranks. Its association with rap went so far that, in the early 1990s, an officially approved Nation of Islam MC existed, charged with representing the NOI accurately with his raps.

Cube could immediately see what the NOI meant and what it could do – after all, it had grown at an apparently unstoppable rate since its inception. Mary Ellison, Professor of African-American Studies at Keele University in the UK, explains how the NOI rose above its more arcane roots to a wider public acceptance: 'Elijah Mohammad, really on the back of Malcolm X, was able to propound a theory that wasn't based so much on the idea of white people being devils – it was far more on self-reliance and self-help.' And the results of this adapted approach were spectacular: 'The rate of recidivism went right down. Malcolm X wrote all the early issues of *Muhammad Speaks* before it became nationwide – and it became a real articulation of black community spirit and independence from white control.'

Cube also partially supported the concept, laid down by the Nation of Islam, of a separate black country. Ellison explains that the NOI wanted 'A southern state – Mississippi maybe – plus an urban centre like Chicago. The issue was never seriously addressed at the time, but now the movement now for reparations is getting seriously discussed.' Cube, however, argued later that he was better placed as an advocate of NOI ideas if he was *not* a member of the organisation. If he declared himself a member, he feared that his listeners would cease to see him as an individual with something interesting to say, that any sudden conversion would result in a loss of the credibility he had built up, and he would be written off as merely another mouthpiece for the NOI. It seems that his support for the organisation came from without, and that he had never actually sought membership.

Cube has always kept an open mind about religion in general: during a Web chat with fans in the late 1990s, he was asked, 'How do you reconcile your beliefs in the Nation of Islam with your work in Hollywood, where there's so much sin?', but answered merely, 'Religion questions, to me, are boring bullshit. I ain't gonna answer that.' However, had it not been for the NOI, a crucial step in his career might never have been taken. At a rally hosted by Farrakhan in 1990, he met the young film director John Singleton, who told him that he was about to make a film and was hoping that Cube would play the lead role. The movie was to be titled *Boyz N The Hood*.

5 Increase The Peace

'You wanted to know what "black" was like,' says Flipper Purify, played by Wesley Snipes in the 1991 film *Jungle Fever*, directed by Spike Lee, America's most prominent black moviemaker. He's addressing this remark to the Italian-American woman with whom a brief affair is coming to an end – and in many ways his comment is parallel with the situation that black film-makers found themselves in as the 1990s began. The black community had had its own film culture for years (not least since Lee's own movies, the seminal *Do The Right Thing* and *She's Gotta Have It*, started making filmic waves in the mid- to late 1980s), but they hadn't made a lasting impact on white cinema-goers – that is, until two gripping, violent films appeared in 1991 which opened a few people's eyes to the blockbusting potential of that slightly vague label, 'black film'.

The first movie was *New Jack City*, released in the US on 8 March. It was directed by Mario Van Peebles and starred the aforementioned Snipes opposite none other than Ice-T, appearing in his first role. A slickly edited piece of moviemaking aimed directly at the audience of Sylvester Stallone and Arnold Schwarzenegger (both of whom were at the peak of their acting fortunes at the time), *New Jack City* is the story of a cop who goes underground to ensnare a drug overlord, with predictably bloody consequences. In a masterstroke of casting, Van Peebles' team decided to reverse the role that many pundits might have chosen for Ice-T and Snipes, handing the former the role of police officer and the latter the chance to portray a criminal. Ice-T recounted in his book, *The Ice Opinion*, that the decision to play a cop –

sympathetically, no less – was no easy step to take, and that the producers themselves were taking an enormous risk by even making the film. He later pointed out that there was no way of knowing if an audience would pay to see black actors in serious films: 'Now every other [TV] situation comedy in America is black, so they know that white people will laugh at us, but like, damn, will they *cry* with them? Will they get serious?'

The white audience was, it seems, ready to get serious – the film was a success. But there was another film in development at the same time, and on 12 July the first queues formed from screenings of *Boyz N The Hood*, a less-publicised movie than *New Jack City* and one that lacked the advantage of a big name associated with it, ie that of Wesley Snipes. The film's director – John Singleton – was also a rookie and, to cap it all, the lead role was being taken by an unknown, the young Cuba Gooding, Jr. Laurence Fishburne, who played Gooding's father under the name of Furious Styles, was a known actor (he had debuted in Francis Ford Coppola's epic Vietnam film *Apocalypse Now*) but was hardly the name he has become today. The name of Ice Cube only rang a few bells among hip-hop-literate movie fans.

The film had been a long time in the making. Singleton, born in South Central Los Angeles and educated at the University of Southern California (USC), where he majored in Film Writing, had been tinkering with the *Boyz* plot since 1988, when (as a callow 20-year-old student) he had first approached Cube, just one year his junior. 'I wasn't thinking about acting,' recalled Ice later, 'but I ran into John Singleton [when] he was just a junior at USC and he was telling me that he had this script, and hopefully in a couple of years he'd be doing it and he had people looking at it, and you know, I didn't pay him much attention.' In his second year at USC, Singleton won a series of awards, however, and struck a deal with the Creative Artists Agency. When he next met Cube, he was on steadier ground. 'Ended up running into him early in 1990,' remembered the rapper, 'and he had graduated, and he said "Yo man, Columbia's looking at my script, and I'm gonna send it to you." He sent it to me, it was *Boyz N The Hood*.'

The reasons for Singleton's long-time eagerness for Ice Cube to play a role in his project are clear. First, Cube was the correct age and had the right background to play the role convincingly; and second, he had written the song of the same name for Eazy-E back in 1987. But the transition from rapping to acting wasn't an easy one for Cube: 'I went and read for [the part], I was wack. He asked me if I read the whole script, I told him no. Went back, read the whole script, came back and got the part,' said Ice some years later.

Once the actor was installed, the project could take shape. Ice's role was that of Doughboy, a troublemaking teenager with a blindly violent, destructive nature whose only interest in life is to sit on the porch of his mother's ghetto house, sipping on a bottle of bourbon, leering at the neighbourhood women, or cruising the streets of South Central in his car. Doughboy is a strong, malevolent character designed to personify the stagnant, violent environment of the ghetto, which seeks to prevent the main protagonist, his neighbour Tre Styles (Gooding), from fulfilling his potential and escaping the streets to a higher education. He's also a grim foil to his half-brother, Ricky Baker (Morris Chestnut), a likable youth who (along with Tre) wants to enter college, with a sports scholarship his chosen method of entry. Against the polite, intelligent personalities of Tre and Ricky, Doughboy is like some kind of malicious gargoyle – frowning, cursing and quick to rage.

Cube took to the part with apparent ease. When required to lay a string of obscenities on his homeboys ('Yeah, I heard you been gettin' that dopehead pussy. See, me, I probably get more pussy than you get air with yo' wannabe mack daddy ass'), he does so with a grim stare, grinding out the words through clenched teeth. Conversely, when Doughboy is casually insulting the girls (one of them asks him, 'Why is it every time you talk about a female you gotta say bitch, hoe, or hootchie?' he replies with an evil grin, ''Cause that's what you are'), he does so with an insouciant, almost charming smirk. Yet Cube never gives away the fact that his character is doomed: the final scenes of the film handle the sudden, shocking execution of his brother Ricky in a drive-by just as he is about to learn of his successful entry into college, and the viewer assumes that Singleton has made his point. But there's another scene to go before the final message – 'Increase The Peace' –

fills the final frame: the scene in which Doughboy turns to leave Tre, crosses the street and vanishes, with a solemn subtitle informing us that two weeks later, he was dead. The message of the film is multilayered, but one of its strands is the simple fact that, despite the ghetto-prophet strength of Furious Styles and the honest intelligence of Tre and Ricky, the hood often claims its own in the most brutal way of all. Moreover, Singleton's simple, human approach – which makes this among the least affected or implausible of films – reminds us that the violence is real, and the violence is now.

With or without its message, *Boyz N The Hood* is a memorable film for its dialogue and its casting. Fishburne, especially, shows a smouldering, unpredictable power. When his house is burgled at night, he shoots at an intruder and calls the cops (who arrive late), and tells one of the officers – a black man – 'Something wrong? Yeah. It's just too bad you don't know what it is...*brother*.' When instructing the young Tre about the nature of responsibility, he informs him that 'Any fool with a dick can make a baby, but only a real man can raise his children.' And in his most memorable scene, he takes Tre and Ricky to a South Central street corner populated by drunks and gangbangers and calls them all to him, declaring, 'Why is it that there is a gun shop on almost every corner in this community?... I'll tell you why. For the same reason that there is a liquor store on almost every corner in the black community. Why? They want us to kill ourselves.'

The locations are also colourful – but not like the street scenes in *Straight Outta Compton* were colourful, when street homicides are glorified and where the dopeman is a devil rather than simply a paranoid young man. At one point the three boys and their friends bump into a rival gang and, despite the reasoning of a female companion, who asks, 'Can't we have one night where nobody gets shot?' violence erupts after Doughboy draws a gun. There's no funk-laced cool beats to accompany the scene and no laconic laughter from the rappers telling the story – just a lot of panic, a lot of screaming, and an almost palpable sense of fear when Doughboy and the others are forced to run for their lives after the other side produces assault rifles.

Boyz N The Hood was a critical success. Reviewers almost universally praised it, and Singleton was rewarded with Best Screenplay and Best Director Oscar nominations and a New York Film Critics Circle Award for Best First-Time Director. It also made a resounding commercial impact: it exceeded its budget of £4m ($6m) in its opening weekend and went on to earn £40m ($57.5m) at the box office and a further £19m ($26.7m) in home-video rentals.

Ice Cube remembers *Boyz N The Hood* as the moment when, as he put it in an interview with *Music Monitor* magazine, he entered mainstream awareness: '*Boyz N The Hood* kind of threw me over that fence to where OK, everybody at least knows my face, that they've seen me somewhere. I mean, the people who don't really know anything about me, they [still ask] "What movie did I see you in?"... And from there, doing one movie, that experience gave me the bug, and from then on I've just been trying to get involved with any project that I feel I can contribute to.'

John Singleton also had some profound things to say about his first film. 'When I first got into the film business, I always thought that I had to make some kind of cultural identity to show my uniqueness as a filmmaker. Woody Allen has a certain part of Manhattan, Spike Lee had Brooklyn, Martin Scorsese had Little Italy. I felt South Central Los Angeles was going to be my thing, where I can make these little stories about where I had grown up and where I'm from. It would be unique because I did them from a personal standpoint.'

This film and his later work had a message about human relationships as well as social injustice, he revealed. 'It seems like dysfunctional relationships have become the norm and not the exception... It seems like men and women are at war with each other. There's less communication and more fighting. You can't use sex to solve problems. This kind of infantilism is perpetuated by being raised within a racial, institutionalised society that basically has created these dysfunctional rite of passages for black men.' And the culture of gangsta rap doesn't offer any help: 'They believe – it's perpetuated in music and culture – [that] to be a man, you have to be a killer. What are they talking about? Killing each other. Or, they set the notion that you will do prison time. And that's a mark of honor. Everything else is perpetuated toward that end. That path is just there in front of a lot of people.'

But Singleton, a man of wisdom beyond his years, never expected movie-goers to understand his work immediately. 'I always believe that a film doesn't truly have a life until years afterward. People tell me things they have seen in my films years afterward. They look at them on different mediums and they learn something.' This is a perspicacious observation and, given the events that would shake North America in the months after *Boyz N The Hood*'s release, also prophetic.

The number of so-called 'ghetto dramas' that were made in the years following the success of *Boyz* was wholly unexpected. Many of these were excellent, but some were tedious exercises in plagiarism or simple glorification of violence, even cheapening the sensitive approach that both actors and directors had employed to give *Boyz* its human edge. But a precedent had been set: movie fans and critics accepted that top-level drama could be created in an all-black scenario, and all eyes were on the black community to prove them right.

In retrospect, it seems that *New Jack City*, which was so much more polished but so much less 'significant' in the critics' eyes than *Boyz N The Hood*, has become something of an underrated classic. Although it's primarily a cop film (as opposed to the worthier status of *Boyz* as a rite-of-passage picture), it helped create an audience for the later film – and Ice-T's brave decision to step into the Hollywood limelight must have been an encouraging move for Ice Cube, too.

As the number of ghetto movies proliferated, Ice-T said: 'The ball started rolling. It's not a revolution of black films, just a new commodity that had been brought to Hollywood – and there's money to be made... It's really because of Spike Lee and Robert Townsend, because they started making movies with their own money and they showed that they could make a movie for $100,000 [£70,000] and make $6 million [£4 million].' Always able to detect the money changing hands beneath the table, he added: 'It's not like Hollywood all of a sudden became black conscious: they became conscious that people would pay to see a black film. And it's selling. And now that *New Jack City* does like 60 million dollars in the US, it is the number three video over there, there's gonna be a lot more, [but] as soon as there's no more big money to be made, there will be no more black films, it's no revolution. For it to be a revolution it would have to be a whole bunch of black people with their own money running in there all of a sudden and making movies – but at the moment we're all still getting money from the white film companies.'

A few days after *Boyz N The Hood* started attracting attention for its encouraging performance at the box office, music as well as film pundits began talking about gangsta rap in shocked terms again. The reason for this was the unveiling by NWA of their third album (date?), the none-more-controversial *Efil4Zaggin* (which, read backwards, is 'Niggaz4Life'). Although *Straight Outta Compton* had been raw and misogynistic enough, this record took those sentiments to an entirely different level. Listeners wondered if Eazy-E had finally gone too far – to the point where the group had begun to parody themselves, with little serious message remaining in their work. Nonetheless, two weeks after its release, *Efil4Zaggin* hit the top spot on the US albums chart, to the simultaneous despair of the parents of white America and the delight of their teenage children.

The album was as fascinating as it was grim, however, to those who were watching with interest the development of gangsta rap. For example, it marked the rapping debut of Dr Dre, who had emerged from behind the mixing desk with a deliberate, baritone style that was the perfect foil to Eazy's high-pitched, fast-moving rants. It also contained the first real signs of the NWA–Ice Cube rivalry that would escalate into a full-blown slanging match in the next few months: the track 'Message To BA' is a series of phone calls received by Priority Records from fans disgusted with Cube for leaving the band, with MC Ren delivering the warning, 'when we see your ass we're gonna cut your hair off and fuck you with a broomstick. Think about it, punk motherfucker'. The BA in question is – somewhat bizarrely – Benedict Arnold, a Revolutionary War general who infamously betrayed his own country to the British, and whose name, to many Americans, is synonymous with the concept of 'traitor'.

Of the album's other songs, 'Findum, Fuckum And Flee' and 'She

Swallowed It' are the most deliberately controversial, while 'Real Niggaz Don't Die' and 'Niggaz 4 Life' don't really contain anything that wasn't heard on *Straight Outta Compton*. But there's no sense of the ghetto prophecy that Ice Cube had made his forte; the record is just too cartoonish to be taken seriously.

This view was not shared by the British authorities, however, who invoked the Obscene Publications Act on *Efil4Zaggin*'s release: after issuing a warrant, a police raid saw 23,000 copies of the album removed from Polygram Records' property. A trial ensued, with Geoffrey Robertson QC (who had defended in the *Oz* trial two decades before) acting as counsel for the defence. Testimony was provided by an Aston University academic, Guy Cumberbatch, acclaimed rap author David Toop, and Wendy K of Talkin' Loud Records. The judge eventually cleared the album for release in November, although a number of British MPs subsequently indulged in some sabre-rattling calls for the law to be toughened up in this area.

The controversy lasted some months, although *Efil4Zaggin* was never destined to become a huge seller outside America. The Irish musician Sinéad O'Connor, who had previously supported the work of NWA, told the *NME* that their 'attitudes have become increasingly dangerous' and that 'the way they deal with women is pathetic'. Others didn't understand what all the fuss was about, however, regarding the album with amusement, although the violence it depicted would seem to be genuine. Eazy-E told *Spin* magazine that if the interviewer should 'piss me off enough to make me wanna fuck you up', then he would do it, 'and show no shame'.

MC Ren looked back on the album some years later with evident nostalgia: 'It's my favorite classic 'cause we did it with our back against the wall. 'Cause that's when Cube had left, and everybody thought we couldn't make another record, so it's gotta be that one 'cause that one came out classic.' He had a point: since the success of *Amerikkka's Most Wanted*, Ice Cube had come to be regarded essentially as the creative nucleus of NWA, who might not be able to create any meaningful statement without him. Whether or not *Efil4Zaggin* is the sound of NWA defeating that prophecy is still open to debate. Perhaps its most enduring legacy is its demonstration that Dr Dre had become a force to be reckoned with in his own right – as subsequent events would demonstrate. Like Cube before him, Dre had started to evince signs of dissatisfaction with the group's financial set-up, and talks with Eazy, Jerry Heller and the rest of the group about NWA's future were under way.

As for Ice Cube, he wasted little time either resting on his laurels after the success of *Boyz N The Hood* or poring over the strange story of *Efil4Zaggin*. One consequence of his foray into the world of film was that more people knew his name. But they knew him as an actor – and so, without further ado, he entered the studio, this time with his old colleague Sir Jinx and a production posse called the Boogie Men in tow, to record a follow-up album to *Amerikkka's Most Wanted*. The success of *AMW*, and the apparent ease with which his role in *Boyz* had complemented his choice of music, made it all the more imperative that he remain ahead of his game in his chosen field.

Autumn 1991 was a busy period for Cube. No sooner had he finished interviews after *Boyz* opened in the summer (its international cinema presence extended until after the US run was complete), than he was recording sessions for his new album, which was due to be released in November. Somewhere along the line he found time to spend with his girlfriend Kim, whom he had met some months before, and who must have appreciated the time she had with her ever-active partner.

Death Certificate was Cube's second full-length solo record and, once again, he recorded it with Da Lench Mob, into which he invited Jinx, the three original Lench members (T-Bone, J-Dee and Shorty), plus Kam, Yo-Yo, Chilly Chill and several others in a kind of collective. The album was to be split into the Death Side and the Life Side, early reports suggested, with a bevy of spoken-word inserts between the tracks and a heavy debt paid to texts taken from writings by Nation of Islam ministers. The press – who had bought into the Ice Cube/Doughboy persona with enthusiasm as the *Boyz N The Hood* virus spread – were eager in their anticipation of Cube's newest work, and as review copies arrived were quick to spin the album. Editors held open review space in magazines nationwide, waiting for the reviewers' responses to come flooding in.

There was a palpable sense of shock as reviews began to run in November, however. Far from the initial flurry of praise that had been expected from most hip-hop experts, the first impressions were of shock, disgust, and even anger. Ice Cube had produced his most controversial work yet in *Death Certificate*. Although this album was the third phase in the gangsta-rap story of 1991, neither critics nor fans seemed any less shockable than before – and the battle between liberal free-speech supporters and anti-sexism and anti-violence campaigners raged higher.

Death Certificate was released on 29 October 1991, just before Halloween, after advance orders of over a million copies had generated a sense of expectation among press and public – a bonus in commercial terms, as the still-B-league Priority label had only allocated £13,000 ($18,000) to its promotion. It entered the *Billboard* charts at No.2 and would later go platinum – a remarkable achievement for a record which spoke of inner-city life without any of the evil glamour that had characterised both *Amerikkka's Most Wanted* and *Kill At Will*'s more upbeat cuts – and clearly appealed to the steadily maturing rap audience, with its combination of intelligent propaganda and Nation of Islam-based rhetoric. The sleevenotes contained the introductory lines 'Niggas are in a state of emergency. The Death Side: a mirror image of where we are today. The Life Side: a vision of where we need to go. So sign your Death Certificate', and pointed clearly towards Cube's concept of two polarised sides reflecting different sentiments. Ice Cube explained to Dimitri Ehrlich, a journalist at *Interview*, that 'The "death" side is the condition we're in now: the records are real negative, and that side starts out with a funeral. Now, the "life" side starts off with a birth, meaning that we get knowledge of self...while the "death" side shows you where we at, the "life" side shows you where we going.'

Both sides contain unenlightened threats and evocations of violence – 'The Wrong Nigga To Fuck Wit'' on Death and 'I Wanna Kill Sam' on Life – the latter a rant against the American government and a link with the album sleeve, which depicts Cube standing next to a corpse in a morgue, which is draped in the Stars and Stripes with an 'Uncle Sam' tag attached to its foot. An immediate delineating point is two excerpts of speeches from the Nation of Islam's Dr Khalid Muhammad: 'Death' (in which the minister announces, 'Let me live my life: if we can no longer live our life, then let us give our life for the liberation and salvation of the black nation... Look the goddamn white man in his cold blue eyes... Open your black eyes for the rebirth, resurrection and rise'), which closes the Death side; and 'The Birth' (whose key sentiments are 'History...will record the black father and mother of morality, medicine, music, and mathematics. The father and mother of all natures of religion, philosophy, art, science and civilization... Before we can make a way for the peace maker, we must kill and get rid of the peace breaker'), which opens Life.

It's a concept that doesn't reveal itself immediately, however – and most listeners' attention wasn't focused long enough on the intricacies of Cube's vision anyway, thanks to two songs on the Life side, which caused the most scandalised critical response of his career to date.

The two songs in question were 'Black Korea' and 'No Vaseline', both of which were short, direct and to the point. The first is a 45-second description of Cube's treatment at the hands of Korean shopkeepers in LA, who (he says) view all black customers as potential robbers and treat them with undeserved suspicion. Although the simple reporting of this problem is not particularly controversial, Cube's promise of revenge certainly is: 'Oriental one-penny motherfuckers/Pay respect to the black fist/Or we'll burn your store right down to a crisp'.

Just as shocking was 'No Vaseline', a funk-laden cut produced by Sir Jinx, which was the answer to NWA's Benedict Arnold accusations on *Efil4Zaggin*. Cube begins by levelling accusations at Dre, Eazy and Ren of moving 'straight outta Compton' to districts 'without another nigga in sight' and of having lost their aggression, appearing in videos by Michel'le while he, Cube, kept his edge. He then points out that they're 'getting fucked...by a white boy, with no Vaseline' (one would presume he means manager Jerry Heller) and that 'Eazy's dick is smelling like MC Ren's shit' – it appears that the enlightened ghetto prophet has temporarily regressed into the frat-boy thug of 1988 with this line. (Not that Eazy laughed it off: he told the press 'How would you know what my dick smells like?... Not unless my nuts was on your chin, and my dick is in your mouth. That's all I got to say.') It gets worse: Cube adds that Ren is being 'gang-banged by your manager', that 'you let a Jew break up my crew', that Eazy had moved to the affluent LA suburb of Riverside (Eazy: 'I don't know anybody in Riverside, let alone live there').

Cube also repeats three times the line 'I'll never have dinner with the President' – a snide reference to the unlikely fact that in March 1991 Eazy-E had attended a lunch party at a Republican function, with none other than George Bush present. How this came about is one of the more surreal episodes in the history of hip-hop. Eazy received an invitation from the then Senate Majority Leader Bob Dole, which read: 'It is my privilege to invite you to accept membership in The Republican Senator's Inner Circle... I believe your accomplishments prove you're worthy of this important organization.' The rapper reasoned that Dole's office had unearthed his name while examining a list of people and organisations who made regular donations to charity in Los Angeles, and that when the name Eric Wright had come up, no one was any the wiser, and the invitation – which offered the recipient the opportunity to attend the function at the mere price of £1,750 ($2,490) – was sent out without further investigation.

Needless to say, the press had a field day, either laughing along with Eazy – whose evident glee at attending the event was infectious – or condemning him for collaborating with his supposed enemies, the Republicans ('Blacks are too fuckin' broke to be Republican', reproved Cube in 'Look Who's Burnin'', a song on *Death Certificate*). In an interview, *Spin* magazine asked Eazy if his attendance had been a publicity stunt, to which the rapper replied: 'You know it! Everybody was dumb to that fact. Like Spike Lee, little bastard. He thought I was selling out or something. I paid $2,500 [£1,750] for a million dollars' [£700,000] worth of publicity! I'm not a Republican *or* a Democrat. I don't give a fuck. I don't even vote.' He also told the *LA Times*: 'How much press did I get? I would have paid $100,000 [£70,000] for that press... Most likely he [Dole] wrote because not long ago I gave a large donation to the City Of Hope. But does he know who I am?... I'm the one who started NWA, the group that got a letter from the FBI taking exception to our song "Fuck Tha Police". The group from Compton where nobody ever gets invited to join Inner Circles.'

Eazy was most succinct on the matter when speaking to Brian Cross, who asked him if he was a Republican: 'Hell no, I don't give a shit really. How could I do a song like 'Fuck Tha Police" and be a Republican? I guess you can really, but I don't even vote. I just went 'cause those muthafuckers sent me an invitation. They pulled my name off the computer 'cause I give a lot of money to charities and stuff.' Predictably, the event had not gone smoothly: 'Soon as I got there CBS and other news stations were all there askin' how you guys gonna let him get in there. It was a whole big mess, on every station. I just wanted to go, see what they was talking about, just to see. I get home, everybody was like, "Oh so you're a Republican, blah blah." Hell no, I ain't no Republican.' And Eazy hadn't even had much of an enjoyable evening: 'They was talking about the fuckin' war [the Gulf War against Iraq, which had been in progress since January 1991] and how this and how that, it was bullshit.'

However, Ice Cube wasn't buying any of this, and made sure that 'No Vaseline' made his point clear. But the anti-NWA sentiments and the Eazy-baiting weren't what made the song such a thorn in many listeners' sides – it was Cube's apparently anti-Semitic stance inspired by Jerry Heller. 'Get rid of that devil, real simple,' he advised, adding, 'Put a bullet in his temple' and 'You can't be a nigga-for-life crew/With a white Jew tellin' ya what to do'.

The combined impact of 'Black Korea' and 'No Vaseline' was considerable. Some critics refused to condemn or support Cube – James Bernard, senior editor of the *Source*, wrote: 'I'm not arrogant enough to wag my finger at someone for stridency or incorrect language when many of *his* friends are dead and many of the rest are either in prison or standing on the corner surrounded by burned-out and dying dreams.' Others observed that Cube's apparent intolerance was letting him down: *Washington Post* writer Geoffrey Himes wrote on 3 November 1991 that 'Cube spreads a thin veneer of political correctness over his writing, but his ringing endorsement of gun ownership, male superiority, and Asian-bashing makes him sound much more like a right-wing Republican than he'd ever admit.' More seriously, the Guardian Angels (a voluntary organisation in the US that provides security for citizens in public areas such as the urban subways) tried to persuade MTV not to play Ice Cube's videos and compared him to David Duke, the Republican politician who was once a Ku Klux Klan Grand Dragon. The writer R J Smith made a similar comparison in the *LA Weekly*. In a sinister turn of events, the KKK themselves wrote to Priority Records, congratulating Ice Cube on a job well done.

However, many critics were also in favour of the funky flavour of the music on the record: *Entertainment Weekly* awarded *Death Certificate* an A grade and labelled it '20 tracks of the most visceral music ever allowed in public', and *Spin* pointed to the album's 'big, slap-happy beats' (although the reviewer was less happy with the lyrics). A single, 'Steady Mobbin'', was released on 11 November and kept Ice Cube's name in the popular press.

But the biggest press storm of all was created by *Billboard* magazine, which took the unprecedented step of discussing *Death Certificate* in its editorial column on 23 November. It advised that stores 'protest the sentiments' of the album, although (despite various inaccurate reports) it didn't support a specific ban on its sale by retailers – a ban that had been suggested by the Simon Wiesenthal Center and the Southern Christian Leadership Conference. As it turned out, the majority of record shops continued to display and sell the album, although a Midwestern chain called Camelot refused to stock it and the state of Oregon made it illegal to display Ice Cube's image in a retail outlet. In the UK, Island Records (Priority's distributor) removed 'Black Korea' and 'No Vaseline' from versions of the album.

James Bernard wrote to *Billboard* in response to its editorial, asking why the magazine had not run a similar comment protesting against NWA's early lyrics (which mentioned 'taking niggers out in a flurry of buckshot') or mention that Cube also described a potential hanging and burning of Eazy-E in 'No Vaseline' as well as targeting Heller. Robert Christgau of the *Village Voice* also wrote an article on 17 December under the headline 'Ice KKKube's Aesthetikkk Merit: Big Fukkking Deal', which was to be one of the last major pieces written about *Death Certificate* in the immediate aftermath of its release. He concluded: '[the album's] Good Qualities still don't come close to making up for its Offensive Content. As you've probably read, the worst of it is slurs against Asians and Jews, though its ingrained, ideological contempt for homosexuals isn't really any better.' Cube had defended himself to a certain extent with the words 'I respect Jewish people because they're unified; I wish black people were as unified', but Christgau observed that this comment 'feeds off the myth of conspiratorial power at the heart of anti-Semitism'.

Death Certificate had caused a storm, all right, but the problem was – and remains – that the opposing viewpoints of his supporters and detractors both hold some water. There's no denying the intelligence at the heart of the record, for one thing: the song 'Alive On Arrival' depicts the story of a visit to the emergency room (casualty) at Martin Luther King Medical Center in South Central LA, where conditions are so primitive (and the funding is so insufficient) that the staff allegedly have to resort to stealing medical supplies to treat the endless flow of patients. The fact that so many people bought *Death Certificate* – I repeat, *not* a record that glamorises violence like *Efil4Zaggin* or, to a lesser extent, *Straight Outta Compton* – must indicate that Cube has his fans, and although many of these would have bought the record for its sophisticated music alone, and many more wouldn't care either way about Cube's political stance, many thousands of people must have agreed with his sentiments. How many of them were Jew-haters or anti-Korean is not known – but we can assume that they are in the minority.

The debate gradually slipped from public consciousness, although calls of 'anti-Semite' and 'racist' would haunt Ice Cube for a long time. After all, the early 1990s were aglow with activity on many levels other than that of mere popular music, and the listener had more to think about than the work of one rapper. Even Eazy ultimately dismissed the taunts of 'No Vaseline', saying: 'That's business. If it was personal you would know about it... [Ice Cube] wanted to do his own thing... I was doing my own thing. We talk once in a while.' One small consequence of the *Death Certificate* controversy was that St Ides Olde English 800 malt beer – which had been using Cube as a frowning presence in its urban advertising – dropped the campaign entirely. Not that Cube was too distressed, it can be assumed, for the *Wall Street Journal* ran a feature in December 1991 on the worst advertising of the year, and included his St Ides slots, in which he told the viewer that the drink would 'get your girl in the mood quicker'. The article also pointed out that 'posters in poor neighborhoods showed Ice Cube making a hand sign sometimes used by gangs'.

The St Ides Olde English 800 malt beer (star of the '8-Ball' song that had featured a memorably drunken performance by Eazy) is a strong drink aimed specifically at ghetto kids. Chuck D sued its makers for £3.5 million ($5 million) in the early 1990s for sampling his voice – a case which was ultimately settled out of court the following year – and Cube himself felt some unease at being associated with it. Mary Ellison explains: 'Ice Cube was uncertain about the amount of commodification that was happening through the St. Ides publicity campaign. Notice that in the final scene of *Boyz N The Hood*, he empties out his beer bottle – almost as if he's washing his hands of it.'

However, in *Source* magazine in December 1991 he came to the conclusion that his involvement in the advertising campaign would be a stepping stone in the fight in which he was involved: at about the same time the rock band Rage Against The Machine (a famously anti-corporate, anti-capitalist, anti-imperialist outfit) was taking a similar stance, defending its association with a major record company – in this case, Epic – by claiming that the broader distribution which Epic afforded them would be a way of spreading their message.

But, as 1991 became 1992 and the spring approached, the critics were still arguing about *Death Certificate*. It seemed after several months of debate that a consensus would never be reached, as the sides were too far apart to find any common ground. Could the liberal white press accept that the violence in these raps was at least partially justified? Unlikely. Would Ice Cube admit that his gory tales of hood life could be judged immoral by white middle-class standards? Never.

But on 29 April 1992, all of this argument was suddenly made both irrelevant and obsolete. Both Cube and his detractors sat down at the end of their working day to watch the TV news, as usual – and noticed that one headline, and one headline only, was dominating every single channel.

The announcement came that a jury in Simi Valley in California's Ventura County had come to a verdict after almost 14 months of trial and deliberation. The case centred on the alleged brutality of four police officers to a motorist in northern Los Angeles, and the jury had returned the verdict that all four cops were not guilty. The motorist's name was Rodney King; the four policemen were Sergeant Stacey Koon, Officer Larry Powell, Officer Theodore Briseno and Officer Timothy Wind.

The Los Angeles mayor, Tom Bradley, said, 'We must express our profound anger and outrage [at the acquittal], but we also must not endanger the reforms that we have made by striking out blindly.' He continued: 'We must demand that the LAPD fire the officers who beat Rodney King and take them off the streets once and for all.' California State Senator Ed Smith said that he was also shocked, and was quoted by the United Press as saying, 'It's hard to believe that there was no sustaining of the charges at all... [The] world saw the videotape, and if that conduct is sanctioned by law in California, then we have to rewrite the law.' Executive Director Ramona Ripston of the American Civil Liberties Union labelled the verdicts 'a travesty of justice'.

And it seemed that many of the residents of Los Angeles agreed. As the nation watched, transfixed, reports of the biggest civil disturbance in history began flooding in.

Ice Cube went to his bedroom, took his guns from the closet, loaded them, put them on the bed and sat down to wait.

6 LA Under Siege

The greatest act of riotous destruction in American history is not explained easily. Too many factors contributed to the riots that levelled sections of Los Angeles for the six days following 29 April 1992 for any brief explanation to be accurate. However, consider the following well-documented phrases as a fairly useful introduction:

> *'I believe we are on an irreversible trend toward more freedom and democracy – but that could change.'*
> *'We are ready for any unforeseen event that may or may not occur.'*
> *'The global importance of the Middle East is that it keeps the Near East and the Far East from encroaching on each other.'*
> *'I want to be Robin to Bush's Batman.'*

The last of these famous statements may give you some clue as to who made them all. Yes, they all came courtesy of Dan Quayle, Vice-President of the United States of America at the time of the riots. A man such as this, one would presume, would have a perceptive, analytical mind. Coupled with a deep desire to serve to the fullest the country that had chosen him to deputise for its leader, Quayle would therefore waste no time in searching for the causes of such a terrible event and use every grain of his resources to ensure that it never happened again.

The conclusions of this mighty brain were revealed on 19 May 1992 during Quayle's Commonwealth Club speech: 'When I have been asked during these last weeks who caused the riots and the killing in

LA, my answer has been direct and simple. Who is to blame for the riots? The rioters are to blame. Who is to blame for the killings? The killers are to blame.' But this penetrating analysis from one of the West's most powerful politicians was not his last word on the matter. His comments on plot-line developments in a popular TV show were just as informed. From 1988 until 1998, Monday evenings on CBS focused on screenings of the popular situation comedy *Murphy Brown*, in which the eponymous television journalist (played by Candice Bergen) was depicted moving in media circles to much cult popularity. In 1992, a series of episodes depicted Brown, an unmarried woman, giving birth to a child and living life as a single mother – and, of course, the federal government couldn't let that pass. In May that year, Quayle identified Brown's motherhood as 'symptomatic' of the causes of the LA riots. Three months later Bergen won an Emmy for the role – the latest of several awards that the show scooped during its ten-year run – and in her acceptance speech, thanked the Vice-President for helping her to win it.

This, then, was the political environment in 1992, as well as the background for the decision of thousands of Los Angelenos to turn on their own city. Ten years later, it seems to many who remember the disturbances that it was primarily the beating of Rodney King which caused them – but in retrospect his involvement was merely the last in a long line of incidents, each of which raised the temperature of inner-city LA (and, most prominently, in poorer areas such as South Central) until the anger felt by many of the city's oppressed residents reached breaking point.

More serious indications of the state of the nation – which had endured a decade of Republican policies – could be seen in the decay of the city ghettos, a direct result of the deprioritisation of the urban poor by the federal government under Reagan, and now Bush. Although the global recession that had plagued so much economic growth in those dark years had affected everyone (not just the residents of the run-down city districts), its impact on suburbs such as Compton had led to a measurable increase in crime and a quantifiable rise in poverty. Couple this with the often overzealous reaction of the police to the increased urban crime levels in these areas, and all the explosive atmosphere required was a spark to ignite it. In this case, the spark was Rodney King – but the broader picture is that years of reduced domestic spending had prepared the ground for the rioters. And the looting that took place? Simply the instincts of a generation educated in Reaganomics: the children of Republicanism had come home to roost at last, it seems.

Washington Times journalist Lou Cannon wrote an excellent book about those days of April madness, entitled *Official Negligence: How Rodney King And The Riots Changed Los Angeles And The LAPD*, in which he analysed the roots of the conflict and the riots themselves. In the book, he revealed facts that Ice Cube and other rappers (such as Ice-T) had been discussing in their recorded work for years before the riots – for example, the Los Angeles Police Department is portrayed as riddled with institutional dysfunction, embracing racial bias wholeheartedly and applying those principles to the execution of their work. John Singleton was telling the truth, it seems, when the cops arrived hours too late to be of any use after the burglary in *Boyz N The Hood* – and when Public Enemy said that '911 Is A Joke', they knew what they were talking about.

Although the Department contains many honest, principled men and women (for the benefit of any disgruntled police officers reading this), Cannon's findings were largely endorsed by the independent Christopher Commission, which undertook an extensive survey of the LAPD after the riots had died down. The Commission's report stated that 'there is a significant number of officers in the LAPD who repetitively use excessive force against the public and persistently ignore the written guidelines of the Department regarding force... [Complaints] filed in recent years show a strong concentration of allegations against a problem group of officers... Graphic confirmation of improper attitudes and practices is provided by the brazen and extensive references to beatings and other excessive uses of force in [police communications].' The report goes on to conclude that the failure to control these officers indicates 'a significant breakdown in the management and leadership of the Department', and that 'the

Police Commission, lacking investigators or other resources, failed in its duty to monitor the Department in this sensitive use-of-force area'.

On *Amerikkka's Most Wanted*, released two years before the riots, Ice Cube had proven to be a prophet, and a deadly accurate one at that. Remember 'Every cop killing goes ignored... To serve, protect, and break a nigga's neck'? Ice-T had also painted the picture of an LAPD made malignant by racism a dozen times – and, of course, NWA hadn't written 'Fuck Tha Police' out of boredom. The primary (but not the sole) cause of the LA riots was the racism of the police. Just read the right books and listen to the right music, and it all makes sense.

But let us not hand all the blame over to the cops, who (especially in the ghetto) often do a fair, unbiased job in harsh circumstances. And the facts speak for themselves: many of the victims of the riots were Korean shopkeepers, not police officers. As Cannon explores, the Korean community had seen the arrest for murder of one of its members, a grocer called Soon Ja Du, just two weeks after the beating of Rodney King.

On 16 March, Du had accused a 15-year-old girl, Latasha Harlins, of trying to steal a £1.25 ($1.79) bottle of orange juice. A security camera in the store showed Harlins slapping Du repeatedly, Du throwing a stool at her, and then (after Harlins had turned to walk away) Du raising a pistol and shooting her in the back. She was found guilty of voluntary manslaughter and the Compton Superior Court judge sentenced the shopkeeper to five years' probation, 400 hours of community service and a fine of £300 ($500). This came as a shock to many – the initial expectation was that Du would get an 11-year sentence. This caused protests among LA's African-American communities, and the fact that many Korean businesses were attacked during the riots (in fact, 75 per cent of the businesses attacked were Korean-run) can be directly attributed to the bad blood between the blacks and the Koreans that had arisen from this single case.

And then there's the media. Like some outlandish science-fiction film, the TV cameras had come out of the woodwork as the first cars were torched and the first bricks thrown, in some cases even beating the police to the scene of the crime. From the very beginning of the

King case, the infamous beating that Rodney endured from the four police officers subsequently put on trial was run and rerun by several TV networks – and, most importantly, edited and re-edited to fit broadcasting schedules (and, dare we say it, to keep outrage levels high by omitting less violent segments). Might the public have been artificially enraged by the constant replay of the tape, re-spliced to indicate a harsher beating than had actually occurred?

The second manner in which the media played a role as instigators, avers Cannon and other commentators, is by televising the violence itself. The constant flow of images depicting the police as powerless to defend against the rioters might well have encouraged more citizens to join in, and those already involved to redouble their efforts. However, this is a double-sided coin – on one occasion on that first afternoon of rioting, a live broadcast of the beating of a truck driver (Reginald Denny) at the intersection of Florence and Normandie caused four local residents to run out of their houses and assist him.

Whichever ancillary causes are identified as the roots of the riots, however, it's the malpractice of the LAPD that remains its root instigator. A little-known fact about the events of April 1992 is that, of the many people detained by the police, 51 per cent of the people arrested were Latinos, 'only' 38 per cent were African-Americans, 9 per cent were white and 2 per cent were Asians or of other ethnic background. Although the riots are widely regarded as a black uprising, much of the violence that occurred took place between the Latin-American population and the police. The Latinos themselves claimed that the Latino-Chicano population of the city, rather than the African-Americans, were more likely to suffer police malpractice in the form of aggression, harassment and racially biased policing – and factual evidence bears them out. In the autumn of 1991, a Latino gang member was shot and killed by LA County sheriff's deputies at the Ramona Gardens housing project – just another reason for public dissatisfaction with the police force.

Despite this fact (that it is the LA cops and the Latino-Chicanos who are most likely to clash at any given time), a report prepared by the district attorney in 1992 stated that, after studying the LAPD's gang database, it had discovered that 'The police have identified almost half of all black men in Los Angeles County between the ages of 21 and 24 as gang members. That number is so far out of line with other ethnic groups that a careful, professional examination is needed to determine whether police procedures may be systematically over-identifying black youths as gang members.' There are conclusions to be drawn from this – and Ice Cube had drawn his as a teenager, from bitter experience. As he waited for the rioters to come on that April day, he knew better than most of us how far events might go before the authorities regained control.

He wouldn't have been impressed by the first response of the LAPD to the riots. LAPD chief Daryl Gates had chosen to attend a political fund-raising party in the wealthy beach community of Pacific Palisades, 30km (20 miles) from the centre of the riots. The Department was understaffed and unprepared for an insurrection of this scale and pulled out of one of the hot spots (the aforementioned Florence and Normandie intersection) on the first day. This didn't help matters – the area quickly became a war zone. Fidel Lopez, a Guatemalan immigrant, was beaten to within an inch of his life, with the attack being captured on video. His assailants smashed a stereo speaker into his forehead, his genitals were spray-painted black and his body was doused with petrol, presumably in order to set him on fire. However, his life was saved by a black clergyman, who threw his body on Mr Lopez's, persuaded the attackers to leave and then drove him to a hospital, when it had become clear that no ambulance crew would enter the area. Earlier that day, Choi Sai Choi, a Chinese bookkeeper, had been dragged from his car, then beaten and robbed at the same intersection. After some hours of destruction without a police presence, the National Guard was called in.

However, within hours of the first reports of violence and theft, the Bloods and the Crips entered the fray, bringing a degree of motivation, organisation and firepower that was far beyond the scope of the average street thug. At one stage no fewer than 22 members of a Crips set were arrested after they had systematically removed over £56,000 ($80,000) worth of products from electronic-goods stores. Reports of arson came flooding in as building after building was set on fire, and an unceasing flow of panicked phone calls from citizens reporting assaults, murders and looting continued through the night. Even the National Guard began to feel outgunned as weapons stores reported the theft of over 4,000 guns over the six days. Worse, the gang members had started to paint anti-police graffiti on walls, including 'Open Season on LAPD' and '187 LAPD' (187 is the California Penal Code section for homicide).

But things would get worse before they got better. The Los Angeles Fire Department reported that nine large shops were ablaze and that numerous cars had been deliberately torched in order to block the roads. A LAPD sergeant told reporters that the police department had called for a tactical recall, cancelling leave for all officers. Many cops were patrolling the streets in full riot gear by this stage.

As the sun rose on the second day of violence, news teams were shocked to report that 40 of 140 fires were still burning and that over 130 people were injured, with nine fatalities. Shockingly, many firefighters had reported sniper fire as they tried to extinguish the flames of burning buildings. Mayor Bradley was calling for calm among the city's black community every few hours, but his office was confounded by reports that many of the looters were Latinos and whites – many of the latter decidedly middle-class. Commentators revealed with genuine shock that some of the looting was being carried out by entire families, who were entering shops and exiting with armfuls of merchandise. Far from being a riot of black people against their white oppressors, this appeared to be a free-for-all in which people of all ethnic origins simply took what they wanted when the cops' attention was diverted elsewhere.

Bradley wasn't standing for this, of course, and declared a local state of emergency, with a night-time curfew in effect that would make a lockdown from dusk till dawn mandatory. He also prohibited firearms sales, banned petrol sales (unless it was loaded directly into vehicle fuel tanks), closed down all schools in southern LA, called in 2,000 extra National Guardsmen and arranged with President Bush for federal assistance to be invoked if required. At the end of the second day, an unidentified police officer commented to the news crews, 'Things are totally out of control here...and we expect it to get worse when it gets dark. I hope we all live to see tomorrow.'

By the time the riots in LA died down (4 May), the violence had spread to other cities, notably San Francisco, where 1,400 people were arrested, with a state of emergency and curfew also in effect. In Las Vegas, 200 rioters embarked on an arson-and-drive-by rampage. Downtown Seattle was struck by mobs of up to 100 people, looting cars and attacking property. In New York, groups of as many as 400 people stormed shopping malls. In Atlanta, police clashed with hundreds of black rioters. And in Tampa, Pittsburgh, Birmingham (Minnesota), Omaha and several other cities, black and Latino protestors demonstrated their sympathy with the LA rioters – either that, or a quick eye for an opportunity.

By the time the smoke had cleared, damage assessors were announcing that around £700 million ($1 billion) worth of damage had been done to Los Angeles. Many thousands of arrests had been made, over 500 structures had been destroyed by fire, about 2,500 people had been injured and between 40 and 60 citizens had died (even ten years later, the official body count varies, according to its source).

Clearly there were investigations to be made – and, while the aforementioned Christopher Commission was uncovering the LAPD's institutionalised racism, another investigation was held into the Department's management practices. The latter was headed up by ex-FBI chief and sometime CIA director William Webster, who advised that community policing should be set in motion and that police officers should 'treat all individuals with equal dignity and respect'. Webster's team also found that the lack of leadership both in the police department and in city government had led to the lack of riot strategy, leaving no coherent decision-making structure in place and allowing the rioters to spread with little restraint. Following the report, LAPD head Darryl Gates resigned his post and was replaced by Philadelphia Police Department chief Willie Williams.

As for the city itself, a salvage party called Rebuild LA was formed, headed by LA Olympic Committee head Peter Ueberoth, to help regenerate the economy in those parts of the city that had been damaged. On the streets themselves, an unexpected bonus in the form of a Crips/Bloods truce was announced, with some members even wearing articles of red and blue clothing simultaneously. A rumour spread that the united gangs were joining forces to present a cohesive front against the cops, but little aggressive action was noticed. In fact the truce itself turned out to be a temporary one – the hostilities resumed more or less as soon as the dust settled.

As for Rodney King, his trial dragged on as far as the Supreme Court, which found some parts of earlier sentences acceptable and other aspects unacceptable. The officers who had attacked him each received varying penal sentences and King himself was awarded $3.8 million (£2.7 million) in compensation for loss of work, medical costs, and pain and suffering.

To this day no one has come to a simple conclusion about the LA riots – whether they represented the will of the people and were overall A Good Thing, or if they were the acts of an antisocial mob and therefore A Bad Thing. Too much information in favour of both arguments is available for either side to make total sense, but what we do have now is a sense of perspective on the riots. As a phenomenon that grew from the LA ghetto, which had only recently gained a populist voice thanks to the rise of the gangsta rappers, it's logical to conclude that the riots were at least partly influenced by the cultural events we have examined so far – specifically, the rise of NWA, Ice Cube, and Dr Dre, who would shortly break away from NWA and launch a stellar solo career. To be even more specific, we can pin down the three most 'gangsta' events of 1991 – the opening of *Boyz N The Hood*, the release of *Efil4Zaggin* and the appearance of *Death Certificate* – as definite forewarnings of those six apocalyptic days in April 1992. Looking back, it's all too easy to ask why they were ignored.

Many of the nation's more conservative politicians took this view, too – although not quite in the positive way that I mean it here. For example, the *Washington Times* of 28 May 1992 reported that Pat Buchanan (who was at the time a candidate for the Republican presidential nomination) gave a speech to a college in the LA area on 9

May, asking his audience: 'But where did the mob come from?... It came out of rock concerts where rap music celebrates raw lust and cop-killing.' Even if you ignore the fact that rock and rap are not interchangeable (for cultural and demographic reasons, if nothing else), the aspiring Republican was so far off base with this pathetic comment that it's not even funny.

On the other hand, the phrase 'cop-killing' *was* in the news at the time. On 30 March 1992, Ice-T released the self-titled debut album of his heavy metal side-project, Body Count, on the Warner Brothers label. Metal fans were mildly interested (although it was neither as heavy nor as exciting as Ice had fondly imagined) and hip-hop fans were slightly bemused, but it didn't make many waves with either audience, and rapidly slipped out of the chart. Ice-T had a knack for giving good sound bites, and his fans had looked to him for comment on the riots. (He duly told the *LA Times*, 'I'm not saying I told you so, but rappers have been reporting from the front for years... Black people look at cops as the Gestapo... People saw that justice is a myth if you're black. Of course people will riot.') However, no one could have expected the enormous wave of controversy that would rise up just one month after the riots had subsided, proving that the ghetto battles might have finished, but the world war was still in progress.

The problem was the song 'Cop Killer', which had caused two police organisations – the Dallas Police Association and the Combined Law Enforcement Association of Texas – to campaign Warners to remove the song from the *Body Count* album. After the protest gained support from police associations in California and New York, word began to spread. Alabama governor Guy Hunt asked Alabama record shops not to stock the product, Dan Quayle labelled the song 'obscene', 60 members of Congress signed a letter addressed to Warners describing the song as 'despicable' and 'vile', and the California State Attorney General followed the Alabamans' example by asking the state's retail outlets not to sell the album. The final straw came when President George Bush spoke out, denouncing any record company that would release a product of this nature, and when Warners shareholder Charlton Heston made a bizarre appearance at a meeting on 16 July where he read out the lyrics of two Body Count songs. Two weeks later, Ice-T publicly announced that the song would be removed from all future copies of the album. 'In a war,' he later explained, 'and make no mistake, this *is* a war, sometimes it's necessary to retreat and return with superior firepower.' Seven months later, Ice-T and Body Count terminated their contract with Warners.

The 'Cop Killer' issue has been endlessly debated and, as it also affects Ice Cube's career, it's worth a brief examination here – although only a full Ice-T biography will unravel the complex causes and consequences of this most controversial of records. Suffice it to say that mainstream culture, especially in America, had spent 1991 and most of 1992 being brutally jolted awake to the reality of gangsta rap and how it fitted (or didn't fit) into the world of most music fans. Looking back on the painful way this virulent brand of hip-hop insinuated itself into the mainstream (where it now looks to be in permanent residence, albeit in radically evolved form – as we shall see), it's tempting to look upon this trying time as the birth pains caused by the meeting of two different cultures. Ask yourself this: Would 'Cop Killer' or even *Straight Outta Compton* cause much offence in the 21st century, unless you happen to live in an unusually conservative country?

Talking of the crossing of two cultures, summer 1992 saw Ice Cube take up a slot on the second Lollapalooza tour, travelling the length of the United States to bring his message to the white rock masses. Ice-T had broken new ground by appearing on the inaugural Lollapalooza the previous year, and in fact showed up once or twice to share some stage time with Cube (with whom he had become firm friends). Kicking off on 18 July in San Francisco, and taking in a mighty 37 dates right through to 13 September back in LA (with plenty of East Coast, Canadian and Midwestern shows in between), the tour line-up was an impressive one indeed. The Main Stage acts were Red Hot Chili Peppers, Ministry, Ice Cube, Soundgarden, the Jesus And Mary Chain, Pearl Jam and Lush. The second-stage line-up was more fluid, with appearances from dozens of acts including Porno For Pyros (the new band of the festival's founder, Perry Farrell), Cypress Hill, Boo-Yaa T.R.I.B.E., Stone Temple Pilots and the aforementioned Rage Against

The Machine – an eclectic festival, all right, but one skewed firmly towards the hip-hop-influenced rock and grunge direction that was in full swing at the time. The WEA label also released a tour sampler, simply called *Lollapalooza '92*, featuring 'Amerikkka's Most Wanted'.

As the third headliner, Cube had some privileges, among which was the chance to play a full hour-long set. The tracks he chose were selected more or less equally from his albums and one EP to date, including the showstoppers 'The Wrong Nigger To Fuck Wit'', 'I Wanna Kill Sam', 'True To The Game', 'Here's Your Money', 'I Kill You', and a collaboration with Porno For Pyros called 'The Devil In Me'. Another advantage of being so high on the bill was that Ice could employ a few stage tricks denied to other acts – he had two minders with fake guns on stage with him to provide a suitably grim presence, but countered this by firing streams of water at the crowd from a pump-action water gun.

Not that the festival needed any on-stage trickery to make it more interesting. Perry Farrell, a veteran of the alternative-rock scene (he had for years fronted the almost insane Jane's Addiction), had made sure that plenty of hands-on action would be made available for America's slacker youth, including a 'crush cage' where audience members could smash up TV sets, and a metal scaffold for people to hit with sticks, along with standard 1990s festival attractions such as political-action booths, tattoo tents and a market.

After the tour was completed, Ice Cube found time between his various commitments to marry his long-time girlfriend, Kimberley. Little is known about the ceremony or the nature of their relationship, which is presumably exactly how Ice wants it to be – Kim, a beautiful, slightly built woman, has appeared with her husband at one or two film launches, but rarely if ever speaks to the press, and the couple keep their lives commendably private. Their first child, O'Shea, had been born in 1990, and by all accounts is a protected and much-loved boy.

As if a sell-out tour and a marriage wasn't enough, Ice Cube had signed up for another film, which would open at the end of the year. Shooting had been completed before he embarked on the Lollapalooza tour, which itself was due to finish before recording sessions for another Cube album were scheduled to begin, in autumn 1992. Already his life had become almost incomprehensibly full – he would later point out to a curious interviewer that 'That's the way I like to work' – with commitments of various kinds. This drive to succeed in a variety of fields is one of the most interesting aspects of Cube's personality: the instinct to exit the ghetto is an understandable one, but one whose power is often underestimated.

Lucky that drive was a strong one in Ice Cube's case, then, because the album that appeared on 17 November 1992 was destined to be his most successful (and hotly debated) for the next decade. It was the album that saw Cube evolve in the public's eyes from a mere rapper and occasional actor to an all-round media figure and political orator, as well as a sophisticated social commentator and business operator. Its title was *The Predator*.

7 The Predator Stands Up

The greatest works of art are those that both reflect and inform the spirit of the age in which they are created. When Ice Cube assembled the songs that would make up his third full-length solo album, the strongest emotion that drove him was anger – anger at the casual brutality by the police which had led directly to the LA riots a mere seven months before the album was released; anger at a society that had allowed such brutality to exist and flourish; and anger that such a society denied the right to exposure of commentary phenomena such as 'Cop Killer'. Most of all, he felt a burning anger that he and the others like him had been reporting from the ghetto front line for years, warning of an imminent conflagration just like the one which had eventually occurred – but had been ignored (or, worse, merely dismissed as exploitative rhetoric). Little wonder, then, that the power of *The Predator* endures to this day, making it a vital, gripping listen from start to apocalyptic finish.

Commercially, the album surpassed Cube's previous work by an unimagined distance. It was the first rap album ever to enter the *Billboard* charts at No.1, and repeated this feat on the R&B charts, too. It was the first album to do so since Stevie Wonder's *Songs In The Key Of Life* had topped both charts 16 years previously. Musically, it was also a change of step for Cube: while the old-school beats were in place, and the vitriol of the raps was as powerful as ever, Ice had explored funkier territory, unearthing smoother samples than before for a rounded, even mellifluous sound on several tracks. But there was no sense of softening up here – rather, *The Predator* was at the forefront of a whole new movement in hip-hop, whereby the gangsta-isms of before were combined with a new melodic awareness for a far more sophisticated sound. Rappers such as Cube and Dr Dre were digging deeper into the vaults of 1970s soul and R&B for their musical inspiration these days, a process which had been started all those years before by the Sugarhill Gang and which NWA had aided with their use of Charles Wright's 'Express Yourself' on *Straight Outta Compton*. Significantly, Cube claimed in an interview at the time of *The Predator*'s release that his favourite song of all time was Funkadelic's 'Knee Deep' – a perfect blend of the funk, psychedelia and soul influences that would suffuse his best work.

As *Los Angeles Times* critic Robert Hilburn put it, *The Predator* was 'the first post-Rodney King/LA riots collection from the most powerful rap voice in the hood' – and he wasn't simply suggesting that it was the first album to appear after the upheavals. Hilburn meant that it was the first album of the new post-riots hip-hop, as distinct from the pre-riots brand that had existed before. After all, one listen reveals a simple truth: that the record was born, shaped and evolved from the flames that engulfed LA in that strange, violent week in April and May 1992.

The evidence for this is copious. First, it's an invaluable document and social commentary, created with precision by a mind that knew exactly which emotions he wanted to evoke. Future civilisations will be able to gauge the mood of black America from listening to *The Predator*, not least from the spoken-word inserts that Cube placed between many of the tracks. For example, he sets the scene in 'The First Day Of School' with harsh instructions from a military instructor telling the new recruits how to present themselves for a humiliating physical examination: 'Ain't nobody talking while I'm talking, fellas, so shut the fuck up... Open your mouth, stick out your tongue, do your ears one at a time, bend your heads over, shake them out with your fingers... Look down and lift up your nut sack, drop your nut sack and skin back your dick... Bend over, grab your ass, spread your cheeks and give me two good coughs...' With this merciless narrative, Ice is both telling the listener to prepare to undergo a harsh self-examination as well as describing the coldness with which he, as a ghetto resident, is treated.

Immediately after this section, Cube rips into the opening song, 'When Will They Shoot?' – a paranoid, fast-moving barrage of samples and percussion – with his breathless rap of 'What is the outcome?/Will they do me like Malcolm?' The song is laced with ambient noise, crowd sounds and the bustling noises of traffic, and at the end Ice is gunned down in an extended shoot-out. The message is clear.

To illustrate that he isn't playing games on *The Predator*, Cube later uses an excerpt of an interview (with radio presenter Carolyn Bennett-Speed) carried out a few months before the album's release:

BENNETT-SPEED: Do you think that sometimes [your violent] lyrics help white folks justify their continual racism against us, this continuous racism against us?

CUBE: ...[What] we need to do is look in the mirror. I do want the white community to understand our community more and see what's going on... The reason I say it is because...anything you want to know about the riots was in the records before the riots. All you had to do is go to the Ice Cube library and pick a record, and it would have told you, you know, I've been warning...

BENNETT-SPEED: So in other words it's almost like a warning or a prophecy?

CUBE: I've given so many warnings on what's gonna happen if we don't get these, these things straight, in our lives, the clashes, and you know, Armageddon, is near.

But it's not just his own words that Cube employs to get his message across so efficiently. Nothing less than the words of a preacher will do to broadcast the message of this album. And in Cube's world, in the absence of actual words from the Islamic God, those of the Nation of

Islam will suffice instead. Some of the rhetoric he uses for the insert 'Integration' comes from the speeches of none other than Malcolm X, who in one section draws parallels between America and South Africa: 'South Africa preaches separation and practises separation. America preaches integration and practises segregation. This is the only difference... I have more respect for a man who lets me know where he stands, even if he's wrong, then one who comes up like an angel and is nothing but a devil.'

Second, X observes, 'Whenever a black man stands up and says something that white people don't like, then the first thing that white man does is run around to try and find somebody to say something to offset what has just been said.'

The most indicative of the spoken-word samples, however, is a collage of words from news reports broadcast at the time of the riots, including these sentences: 'The jury found that they were all not guilty' (with the last two words repeated several times), 'Yes, we have sporadic fires throughout the city of Los Angeles' and 'Not guilty verdicts for Stacey Koon, Laurence Powell, Timothy Wind and Theodore Briseno, the four officers accused of beating motorist Rodney King'. In other inserts, a raging debate about racism is sampled, while a black man accuses another of having given up on the idea of black equality.

But Ice isn't just using real-life sources for his inspiration. In a mad twist of humour, he plunders Hollywood sci-fi as well. 'The Predator' itself is accompanied by samples taken from the film *Predator 2*, the sequel to the Arnold Schwarzenegger film in which the 'Austrian Oak' overcame a well-armed extraterrestrial opponent by means of native cunning. The film's second instalment lacked the presence of the mighty Arnie, but scored by transferring the action from the Latin-American rainforest to an unidentified ghetto battlezone dominated by gang warfare.

As 'The Predator' begins, the hoarse, fearful voice of the voodoo-practising Caribbean gang leader is heard intoning, 'There's no stopping what can't be stopped. No killing what can't be killed', and another voice warning, 'There's something out there waiting for us.' As the song starts and Cube begins his rap, promising dire retribution at the hands of the Westsiders, the listener is forced to ask who this predator actually is. At first sight you might think it's supposed to be Cube himself: his pensive but forbidding face on the album cover, wreathed in smoke from a death's-head pipe, is hardly a friendly sight. But after a while it occurs to you that the predator may be the white race, with the blacks as victims – after all, Cube has referred to the black man as 'endangered species' before. Then there's another *Predator 2* sample which seems to be an eerie reference to the LA riots: '… [When] trapped, the creature activated a self-destruct device that destroyed enough rainforest to cover 300 city blocks.' Perhaps Cube's concept of the predator is a double one.

The predominant emotion on the album is anger, with promises of injury and death for various interfering parties. In this respect the record's most powerful song is 'We Had To Tear This Motherfucker Up', a simple story of what might happen to the cops who beat Rodney King if they ever set foot in Cube's hood, and how the jury that voted them not guilty might not relish a visit from Cube and his associates. The venom which the rapper directs at each police officer is unmistakable and unforgettable: he details individual fates for Koon, Powell, Wind and Briseno ('introduce his ass to the AK-40 dick') and warns how the news of the officers' acquittal is going to be received when it reaches South Central. Musically, the song is among the sparsest on the album, with Cypress Hill's DJ Muggs providing a simple bassline and a brutal beat, requested by Cube with the words 'Make it rough!' twice in each chorus – effectively a white-noise collage of confusing crowd noise to indicate the chaos of the riots.

But alongside the rage there is humour, with the album's most memorable song – 'It Was A Good Day' – one long sideways wink at the listener. The song was released as a single on 15 February 1993, and became Cube's biggest hit to date. Its popularity stems on first listen from the beautiful soul loop on which it rests, a calming, undulating bass, and organ sample with a cooing female vocal and a childlike, almost Disney-style vibe. In fact, the sounds are lifted from the Isley Brothers' 'Footsteps In The Dark' and the Moments' 'Come

On Sexy Mama' – two silky-smooth soul cuts on which Cube's slow, almost hesitant rap sits perfectly. But it's the sentiments of the song which sold it to the American public: Ice is telling the story of a day in the South Central hood on which everything goes right, everyone has a good time, no one gets killed or injured and everyone is happy. For a while, it seems that he's having the day every young man dreams of: he gets up, eats the perfect breakfast, plays a game of basketball at which he is the king of the court, has highly satisfying sex with a girl he's been chasing for years ('and my dick runs deep, so deep, so deep/put her ass to sleep') and gets happily drunk. Needless to say, the whole thing is a straight satire, nailed by Cube's devastating closing comment, 'I didn't even have to use my AK: I'd have to say it was a good day'. The absence of cops ('no helicopters looking for murder') and car-jackers gives it away early in the song, but Ice doesn't keep us hanging around: after a few bars of the coda he cuts in, telling his DJ, Pooh, to stop playing it with the words 'What the fuck am I thinking about?', and cutting straight into the untrammelled wrath of 'We Had To Tear This Motherfucker Up'. The contrast between the two songs is almost unbearable.

Other songs on the album are less heart-stopping but just as memorable, with 'Wicked' (a duet featuring the toasted Jamaican rapping of Don Jaguar) as close to a made-to-measure radio hit as Ice had yet produced. 'Check Yo' Self', meanwhile, came close to the rolling, funky barrel-house template which House Of Pain would later pioneer – thanks to expert DJing once again by DJ Muggs – and had a deeply catchy 'Check yo' self before you wreck yo' self' chorus.

The full set of songs – 'The First Day Of School', 'When Will They Shoot?', 'I'm Scared', 'Wicked', 'Now I Gotta Wet'Cha', 'The Predator', 'It Was A Good Day', 'We Had To Tear This Motherfucker Up', 'Fuck 'Em', 'Dirty Mack', 'Don't Trust 'Em', 'Gangsta's Fairytale 2', 'Check Yo' Self', 'Who Got The Camera?', 'Integration' and 'Say Hi To The Bad Guy' – covers all the bases, which may be one of the reasons why the album was so successful. And it was wrapped up in some more wise words: in the sleevenotes Cube had included props to black fighters such as Marcus Garvey, Malcolm X and the ministers Farrakhan and

Muhammad, and included a scathing nod to 'America's cops, for their systematic and brutal killings of brothers all over the country'. He winds up his commentary with these words: 'I see myself through the eyes of an African and I will continue to speak as an African. I will become an African American when America gives up oppression of my people. Keep rap legal!' Powerful words from a man who – let us not forget – was still a mere 23 years old when the album was released.

The critics were quick to knock out rave reviews for *The Predator*, while his fellow musicians weren't slow to add their praise – Lollapalooza organiser Perry Farrell even labelled Cube 'a black Bob Dylan' in an interview at this time. *Entertainment Weekly's* Greg Sandow awarded the album an A–, saying that 'what's most striking here are songs – Ice Cube's strongest, most cohesive work yet – about the perils of everyday South Central life', although Robert Hilburn's review in the *Los Angeles Times* actually castigated Cube for 'failing to deal more directly with the events of last spring' – in other words, the LA riots. This is hard to fathom – the entirety of *The Predator* can be seen in some way or other as spawned by the disturbances. Still, reviewers must write what they feel is the truth – Cube would want nothing less.

Evidence of a certain maturing in Cube was starting to be visible, despite the rage that had sizzled from the grooves of *The Predator*. Ice told *Daily Variety* in late November 1992 that 'I'm not pissed off 24 hours a day' and that his technical development was as important as his spiritual and political sides: 'I don't want to be stuck in the same mode. I'm a rapper and I wanted to demonstrate my skills as a rapper.' This last comment was a direct response to one or two commentators who thought that the mellow grooves of songs such as 'It Was A Good Day' were a sign that Cube was losing his drive – his point was merely that he wanted to progress, and if that meant slowing down and kicking back in places, so be it.

According to various media sources, including the November issue of *Reflex* magazine, Cube made a large donation to charity at this time. This has never been substantiated by Cube or his production companies, but along with Eazy-E and other rappers who had come up from the ghetto such donations had become part and parcel of the more socially concerned performers' operations. Furthermore, there's good reason to suppose that Ice Cube, like Ice-T before him, puts his money into ghetto-friendly projects, as he had included a phone number on the sleeve of *The Predator* which raised money for LA's rebuilding after the riots.

But there were more important issues for the hip-hop community to consider at this time. As 1992 drew to a close, *Rolling Stone* magazine noted that NWA had apparently ceased operations. After some investigations by the press and a handful of interviews by Dre, Ren, Eazy and Yella, it emerged that the rumours were in fact correct – the band had split. The causes were many, but as usual the primary cause was that old devil, money. And this time the move to split hadn't come from one of the rappers: it had come from the group's biggest remaining talent, Dr Dre.

Like Ice Cube before him, Dre had fallen out with Eazy-E and Jerry Heller over his cut of the royalties. His extracurricular production work outside NWA had made him wealthy and in demand, but his main job wasn't paying off well enough, it seems, and as he had plans for a solo album his logical choice was to leave the band in mid-1992. No official statement was made by NWA for some time, who were considering the way forward – but with Dre's departure it was apparent that the band's driving force was gone, and Eazy, Ren and Yella each decided to draw a line under their controversial act and embark on solo careers. As for Heller, he has rarely spoken to the press since the demise of NWA but remains a successful mover in rock management, looking after the business affairs of artists such as ex-Guns N'Roses guitarist Slash.

Dre's decision to go solo was a controversial one, not so much for its reasons as for the method in which it was implemented. He had formed a partnership with the sometime Vanilla Ice publicist Marion 'Suge' Knight, and the pair had planned to launch a new record label devoted to gangsta rap called Death Row. However, Eazy-E was allegedly unwilling to release Dre from the contract that bound him to Heller and Priority, and Knight – equally allegedly, m'lud – persuaded him to think otherwise at gunpoint and with the assistance of several armed henchmen. However, neither Knight nor Dre has confirmed these reports, and neither man seems likely to, given the well-documented years of controversy that subsequently rocked Death Row throughout the 1990s, in which Ice Cube would sporadically appear.

The news of NWA's split was almost immediately overshadowed by the enormous impact of Dr Dre's first solo album, *The Chronic*, which appeared on 15 December 1992 and which was just as influential as *The Predator*. A super-slick collection of slow, funky tunes, the album was as laid-back as its name ('chronic' is a powerful strain of marijuana) which pilfered samples from old soul tunes to make an entirely new sound which both Dre and critics were soon labelling G-Funk, a pun on Parliament-Funkadelic's 'P-Funk' and the ubiquitous 'G' for 'gangsta'. *The Chronic* was an even bigger seller than *The Predator*, entering the R&B charts at No.1 and rapidly going triple platinum, boosted by the sales of Dre's single 'Ain't Nuthin' But A "G" Thang' and an earlier release called 'Deep Cover'. Within weeks of its release, Dre and Death Row were suddenly the right names to drop in West Coast hip-hop circles.

The album's impact was long-lasting, and launched the career of a young rapper named Calvin Broadus, among others. Broadus had got to know Dre through contacts in LA and, having demonstrated a laid-back, lilting rap style that sat well with Dre's relaxed beats, was invited to appear on *The Chronic* under his *nom de rap*, Snoop 'Doggy' Dogg (the 'Doggy' was dropped soon after). Snoop later said of *The Chronic*: 'Death Row put the West Coast on the map – *The Chronic* was the album that did it. We put gangsta rap on a worldwide scale. If it wasn't for Suge Knight in this industry, there wouldn't be no Snoop Dogg, there wouldn't be no *Chronic*, 'cause he was the business behind this. Without the business the music wouldn't be respected.'

The album's title was no joke, as Snoop explained to journalist Devin Horwitz, when he asked the rapper if weed had mellowed out the thug mentality of hip-hop: 'On the real – when me and Dre put chronic on the map, we took crack out of the black community. It's erasing the crack that was killing a lot of our people and sending homies to the jailhouse. Now it's more controlled, civilized and more about money and bitches and just smoking. That's the cool shit. Before that, the crackhead niggas was just running wild out there.' Dogg has gone on to lobby for the legalisation of marijuana along with celebrities such as actor Woody Harrelson.

Meanwhile, *The Chronic* dominated the American album charts into 1993, with *The Predator* its more violent but equally funky wingrider. These two albums came to be regarded as the vanguard of a new type of hip-hop, lumped under Dre's G-Funk umbrella but with a wider resonance than that label: the music and lyrics were simply more thoughtful than the brutal sentiments of gangsta-rap classics like *Straight Outta Compton, Amerikkka's Most Wanted* and *Efil4Zaggin*, reaching deeper into the sampling vaults and valuing melodic textures over straightahead beats. The mood of popular music had changed – remember, a similar revolution was overtaking the rock world at this time, with the hordes of heavy-metal bands decimated by the tidal wave of grunge led by Nirvana, Pearl Jam, Soundgarden and Alice In Chains – and, as time passed, gangsta rap seemed more and more likely to be replaced by the new mellow sound.

It's interesting to note that some observers believe *The Chronic* to contain various negative references to Ice Cube, although these have never been confirmed. At one point Snoop claims that he's on a 'street knowledge mission', an apparent hint towards Cube's production company. Elsewhere Dre points out that he's 'mobbin' not lenchin'', which may be a snide reference to Da Lench Mob – and, most explicitly, Dre says, 'Got my chrome to the side of his White Sox hat' (Cube had famously worn this hat in his 'Steady Mobbin'' video and on a cover of the *Source* magazine). But this is mere conjecture – until Dre himself explains the lyrics, that is.

The face of hip-hop was changing elsewhere, too. As the West Coast movement grew, helped along by Cube, Dre and Snoop (and soon to be bolstered by the recordings of the sometime Digital Underground roadie and Death Row signing, Tupac Shakur), the East Coast-based scene, where hip-hop had been born in the mid- to late 1970s, began to take notice and seize commercial ground with its own movers and shakers. Prominent among these was a unique collective from Long

Island called the Wu-Tang Clan, a group of nine rappers and producers (leader RZA plus GZA, Ol' Dirty Bastard, Method Man, Ghost Face Killa, Raekwon, U-God, Inspecta Deck and Masta Killa) who based their philosophies on the teachings of the Shaolin Temple and who had made a 'pact of artistic and financial community' with each other, sharing financial profits from all their group and solo albums. Their first single, 'Protect Ya Neck', had made an underground impact before its official release attracted attention away from South Central and back to the equally intimidating streets of New York.

Around this time, the first use of the term 'East–West rivalry' was noted, with the idea being that the two equally powerful hip-hop communities were beginning to take offence at the other's success. How much truth was in this idea is still a moot point, but one or two insults were exchanged and the more intelligent members of the rap scene prophesied violence. One rapper who voiced his unease was Cypress Hill's B-Real, who warned that internal strife within the hip-hop world was a wrong move: 'Individual competition is good, because that's how rap started back in the day. Showing your skills. As an alternative to violence…[but] the East Coast–West Coast shit can only take away from rap because that's what a lot of these muthafuckers want us to do – destroy ourselves. Blacks, Mexicans and even whites on the street fighting each other. Just like in gangs. They're fighting their own people. If we're going to battle for little stupid shit, we're killing our own culture off by even submitting to this type of fight that other motherfuckers are instigating. They love to see us going at it like this. We have to stick together.'

The two sides simmered but held back, eyeing each other across the continent. Meanwhile, arguments of a more local – but just as vehement – nature had erupted back in Los Angeles between Eazy-E and Dr Dre, who had embarked on a slanging match. Eazy had not been resting on his laurels since the allegedly violent poaching of Dre by Suge Knight and his associates, and in December 1992 released an EP, *5150 Home For Tha Sick*, which went on to sell over half a million copies. His company, Ruthless, was in the process of suing Death Row for racketeering (the case would ultimately be dismissed in August the following year), but neither he nor Dre had allowed this to stop them insulting each other on record, with Dre's 'Dre Day' video depicting a money-grabbing character called 'Sleazy-E'.

Eazy responded by claiming that *The Chronic* was a mere copy of the laid-back style of a recording that the two men had co-produced for the rap act Above The Law in 1990. He also sampled 'Dre Day' for his own song, 'Muthaphukkin' Gs', to which Dre responded, 'He can make a million records about me if wants to. He's keeping my name out there.' Bizarrely, it later emerged that Eazy was still due a royalty on Dre's solo work – the two men were helping each other every time they exchanged verbal blows, it seems.

While Dre and Eazy warred, MC Ren also released an EP, with the sophisticated title of *Kizz My Black Azz*, with two singles, 'The Final Frontier' and 'Behind The Scene', keeping his name in the public eye for some months. However, his career wasn't destined to take off and he spent some years in obscurity, only emerging to make occasional appearances on Eazy-E's albums. As for Yella, his fall from the spotlight of publicity was even more rapid than Ren's, although he did participate in one late 1990s interview with *Props*, in which he pondered on the Dre-Eazy feud with the words: 'Deep down, [Eazy] was kinda hurt when Dre first left... I think deep down, they didn't really want to do it but he just had to do it. They did have real beef, but over the years, it just wore out.'

As for Ice Cube, he watched these goings-on between his old bandmates with a wry amusement, when he had time to observe at all – late 1992 saw him divide his time between promotional duties for *The Predator* and a role as executive producer on his friend Yo-Yo's debut album, *Black Pearl*. The former Yolanda Whitaker was a skilful rapper and composer, but the album didn't make much of a splash among the many new acts that were surfacing at the time, although it bore ample evidence of Cube's new, funkier direction. However, it served both to launch Yo-Yo's career and demonstrate Ice's competence in the studio as well as on the mic.

The most successful project Cube was involved in at this time was his next movie, *Trespass*, which appeared in American cinemas on

Christmas Day 1992 (although it's unlikely that many people went to the cinema on that day, of course) and co-starred none other than Ice-T. The film's original title had been *Looters*, but was changed by its production company in response to the LA riots of seven months before, for obvious reasons (the *most* obvious of which is the film-makers' reluctance to be seen as exploiting those events for material gain).

The gangsta-rap connotations of the movie are clear, however. After the successful appearances of Cube in *Boyz N The Hood* and Ice-T in *New Jack City* (released just months apart in 1991), it was a marketing masterstroke – although perhaps also a predictable one – to place the two frowning rappers in a film side by side. The *Trespass* script had reportedly been in development for some time, perhaps waiting for the right actors to appear (Cube and T certainly form an ideal combination), or (as cynics might have it) waiting for an event like the riots to instil some gangsta awareness into the movie-going public.

The story is based squarely on that of *The Treasure of the Sierra Madre*, a romantic swashbuckling adventure yarn directed by Hollywood veteran John Huston (father of actress Anjelica) in 1948. *Trespass* updates the story by focusing on a scenario in which two white firefighters from Arkansas find a map leading them to an abandoned factory in a run-down area of St Louis. By coincidence, a black gang is executing one of its adversaries there at the same time. One of the firemen witnesses the killing, the gang chase him, and the scene is set for a violent, hour-long, hide-and-seek drama, with the hook being that it's a white vs black situation. The subplot is that Ice-T (aka King James, the gang's experienced leader) is in conflict with the aggressive young pretender Cube (whose character goes by the oddly soap-like name of Savon), who adheres firmly to shoot-first-ask-questions-later principles. 'It's time to start thinking with your brain, not your trigger finger,' Ice-T warns Cube – which is about as accurate a synopsis of the film's moral stance as you can make.

Trespass wins on several levels. Visually, it's stunning, with director Walter Hill (who had demonstrated his chops on slick action tales such as *Streets Of Fire* and *48 HRS*) pulling out all the editing-suite stops at his disposal and making much of the fetishisation of technology (mobile phones, then an uncommon accessory, are glamorised, for example). The casting was exemplary, too, with the adman's dream of Ices T and Cube foiled by the partnership of Bill Paxton (who had stolen the show in recent films such as *Aliens* and *Predator 2*) and William Sadler (who had played a quirky-but-classic role as a Teutonic grim reaper in *Bill And Ted's Bogus Journey*). And the acting is spot-on, too, with the scriptwriters (Robert '*Back To The Future*' Zemeckis was one of them) giving Ice-T a reason to reveal a human side to his merciless gang-leader role by allowing Paxton and Sadler to kidnap his brother. Cube, too, is on excellent form, showing more decisiveness than he did in *Boyz N The Hood* (Doughboy was a resentful slacker rather than a quick mover) and backing up the threats of *The Predator* with evident confidence.

But this is a boys' film, with all that implies: there's the requisite special effects budget (the final explosion is one of the biggest ever), plenty of graphic violence (for example, Ice-T's kidnapped brother will have his arms torn out if his rescuers force the doors to which he is attached) and gun battles, jump-cut edits and X-rated language aplenty. But there's little social analysis here, which would have disappointed movie-goers hoping to see a John Singleton-style 'Increase The Peace' conclusion. As Robert Ebert said in the *Chicago Sun-Times*: 'Does *Trespass* have any lasting significance? No. Does it do anything particularly well? No, only skillfully. Do the actors find depth in their characters? There is none to find.' Although he clearly enjoyed it for what it was – a simple action movie – and this is a good way to approach it: as a bit of harmless macho fun, like the *Terminator* and *Rambo* series before it.

Not that everyone looked on the film that way. Many critics objected to *Trespass*'s apparent stereotyping (the good white heroes against the *very* bad black villains, presumably) with reviewer Hal Hinson describing it in the *Washington Post* as 'a stale and routinely numbing exercise in SWAT-team cinema – men, guns, gold, blood and death', and concluding that it is 'mindlessly violent, profane and insultingly racist', 'relentless, repetitive and tiresome' and that it 'leaves us feeling that a once-great director has run out of ammunition'. Again, this is a point of view which holds some water, especially in the light of the riots and the cops vs immigrants scenario, which most of the public had concluded (and still conclude) had been the riots' sole cause.

The wider picture is that *Trespass* was one of a short-lived series of films that focused on the terrorising of citizens by urban gangs. One of the earliest had been 1990's *Bonfire Of The Vanities*, which had touched on the subject by depicting a yuppie financier straying accidentally into gang territory – with dire circumstances – while the most successful was probably 1993's *Judgment Night*. Like *Trespass*, this was an ultimately disposable film in which a gang of preppy youths led by Emilio Estevez (and – coincidentally or otherwise – *Boyz N The Hood*'s Cuba Gooding Jr) witness a gang killing and are forced to flee. However, the issue of race is less prominent, as the gang leader is played by white comedian Denis Leary. There's a unifying theme running through all these films – that is, paranoia at what the ghetto can do to the unwary visitor – and a sense that early 1990s gangsta themes lie just beneath the surface. For example, the appearance of Ice-T on the *Judgment Night* soundtrack, in a duet with the thrash-metal band Slayer, surprised nobody: his presence and that of Ice Cube on the *Trespass* soundtrack had made it a successful seller worldwide.

It's possible (and tempting) to regard the career of Ice Cube, in parallel with those of hip-hop contemporaries such as Ice-T and Dr Dre, as evolving in line with the change in the white public's awareness of black culture – and specifically hip-hop culture – across America and to a lesser extent other Western countries. In 1987, for example, the nascent NWA, Public Enemy, Wu-Tang Clan and the other seminal acts hardly troubled the consciousness of white America, while the concept of 'black film' extended to one or two early Spike Lee movies and the abysmal *Breakdance* (released as *Breakin'* in the US). As 1992 came to a close, however (after a mere five years of activity), a whole new musical movement, gangsta rap, had risen, fallen and been supplanted by G-Funk; directors such as John Singleton had won the film world's most prestigious awards; the nation had been in outcry over *Efil4Zaggin* and 'Cop Killer'; and artists such as Cube had attained the status of actor, musician and political commentator with a degree of influence, and (more importantly) a platform for expression that had never been dreamed of. Great things were afoot, it seemed, in the state of the nation, and they all hinged on one crucial issue. The issue that has plagued American consciences for centuries – race.

Public Enemy's Chuck D defined racists as 'People that are imbedded in a certain belief structure who are unwilling to be objective' and that racists must necessarily be selfish, because 'People that are imbedded in a certain belief structure have to be so at the expense of others – and really could care less.' By 1992, the American 'belief structure' Chuck mentions was being challenged – not for the first time, of course (think of figures such as Martin Luther King and Malcolm X), and certainly not for the first time via popular music (remember Aretha Franklin, Nina Simone, James Brown, Stevie Wonder, Marvin Gaye and Sly Stone, to name but a few) – but for the first time via mainstream, chart-topping popular music that the public could hear in McDonald's or WalMart and in primetime TV ads. The rise of hip-hop was nothing less than a cultural education for America.

As always, Ice-T described it well. 'You hear it being said over and over that if rap music only stayed in the ghetto, nobody would be screaming about it. The liner notes of [my album] *Home Invasion* say "We've been in your house a long time, moms, you don't know". The parents are sitting there talking this racist shit, and the kids are sitting there listening to Public Enemy on their Walkman right at their dinner table. And the parents don't know.' The consequences of this, Ice added, were nothing less than catastrophic for the white racist community: 'For so many years the white family structure was able to tell their kids to hate everything, and now it's not working anymore. The kids are like, "Why? I'm not going to carry this fucking luggage. Why? What is the problem with having another race at the country club? Why are we so scared?" It's a very tough scenario for them to deal with.'

The kids are the key to the change, it seems. Hip-hop was embraced by all age groups, but popular music is always primarily a teenage phenomenon, and it was the children who listened hardest to the rappers' messages. When a *Spin* journalist told NWA in 1991 about a teacher who taught her students to spell using their lyrics, Eazy-E cackled in response: 'That's good! Teach the little bastards how to do they ABCs in rap form, the muthafuckas'll learn faster.' Dre added 'A...B...muthafuckin' C' and Eazy remarked, 'They'll remember shit like that! Who the fuck wants to learn about Africa?' – although perhaps this says more about Eazy himself than the nation's schoolchildren.

The roots of this change, which would slowly unfold throughout the 1990s and beyond, lay in certain key albums released at the time. One such was Public Enemy's *Fear Of A Black Planet*, which appeared in 1990 and which was the clearest statement to date of the hip-hop community's anger at the racism they perceived in their society, although its predecessor, *It Takes A Nation Of Millions To Hold Us Back*, had set out the PE stall in no uncertain terms. As we've seen, Ice Cube had appeared on *Fear Of A Black Planet*'s 'Burn Hollywood Burn', which became one of the album's high points. Chuck D explained the philosophies behind the album with the words: '*Fear Of A Black Planet*, in a nutshell, is a counterattack on the system of cultural white supremacy, which is conspiracy to destroy the black race... [The] people who have designed European culture, their vision is forced upon everybody living in the world today. It means that every other culture or way of life or understanding is deemed inferior to their standard of living, especially in the western world.'

As D explained, the white fear of the black race is a primal one: 'The fear is that if the world was to come together through peace and love, then, by white supremacist standards, the whole world would be black eventually... There's this belief that the white race is pure, and this was set up by white world supremacists setting their vision through Eurocentricity, and that's false, because everything evolves from black, which means that everybody's from the same seed.'

And this fear is widespread, and in the world of entertainment it's as prevalent as in any other arena – it just looks less dangerous. In a discussion about basketball with *ESPN*, Ice Cube pointed out that a white supremacist agenda even exists in sport, leading to an overpopulation of white basketball coaches: 'a lot of people in the back of their minds think the league is *too* black anyway. That's why you get an onslaught of European players that aren't as qualified to play as the kids over here in the CBA or whatever. The league has to keep some kind of face. Maybe they're scared they're going to lose their audience... Not sayin' the white kids aren't good or aren't qualified to ball, but that's why you see so many white coaches – because there's so many black players.'

As *The Chronic* peaked, *Trespass* pulled in the crowds and more and more people realised how far black culture had penetrated the mainstream, *The Predator*'s most memorable song, 'It Was A Good Day', was released. It rapidly went gold, assisted by its video, which MTV played on an almost-hourly basis, it seemed. Ice-T had earlier said, 'Let's be honest: MTV just has way too much power. The record labels all depend on them to sell records', but in this case the TV channel was unstoppable, broadcasting Cube's message of an unlikely day of harmony in the hood into the households of America.

After 'It Was A Good Day', nothing would be the same for Ice Cube. It had been a bloody year, with his career in the ascendant from the start of 1992: after three albums, two films and many guest appearances, some pundits were predicting a fall from grace – but all good predators adapt in order to survive, and Ice Cube would prove to be no different. The next phase in his story is a strange one, all right, and one that would provide him with challenges greater than any he had faced before.

8 Violence, Silence And Tragedy

As 'It Was A Good Day' finally fell from the charts, Dre ruled the hip-hop airwaves despite Eazy-E's slurs, and the concept of the gangsta movie was finally becoming an accepted commodity, Ice Cube had time to take a breath and consider his progress since that fateful day in 1990 when he had decided to abandon the bad ship NWA. Looking around him, it's clear that what he saw was not entirely to his satisfaction: one or two accusations of selling out had been heard from the relatively few critics and fans who had not been won over by *The Predator*'s deft fusion of funk, soul and hip-hop. Cube knew better than to take these seriously (after all, every artist who achieves even a modicum of success has to handle some flak from the underground) but they evidently bothered him enough for him to address them in studio sessions for his next album.

What that album would be was a matter for some conjecture among those who had been following Cube's career. The hardcore beats of *Amerikkka's Most Wanted* and *Death Certificate* had made him an uncompromising ghetto prophet, but it was the silky textures of *The Predator* that had given him a commercial platform, and in doing so had changed the face of popular music. Would he abandon his new-found mainstream style (and, in doing so, lose much of his audience) or would he stick to the new G-Funk formula?

In true Cube fashion, the result confounded both predictions. *Lethal Injection* was released on 12 July 1993 and was his most multifaceted work to date, bearing a grim cover image of a needle being introduced into the shoulder of an unidentified black youth and listing production credits for Sir Jinx, Laylaw, Derrick McDowell, QD III, Brian G, The 88 X Unit, Madness 4 Real and Ice Cube himself, who also executive-produced the record. The track-listing was 'The Shot (Intro)', 'Really Doe', 'Ghetto Bird', 'You Know How We Do It', 'Cave Bitch', 'Bop Gun (One Nation)', 'What Can I Do?', 'Lil' Ass Gee', 'Make It Ruff, Make It Smooth', 'Down 4 Whatever', 'Enemy' and 'When I Get To Heaven'.

It turned out that Cube had squeezed in some studio time in early 1993 after all, *Trespass* promo work notwithstanding. 'I started working four months after *The Predator* was out,' he told *ROC (Rock Out Censorship)* magazine in an extended interview. 'Initially, I was going to get this one out next summer, but I started bearing down the last two months.'

This self-imposed pressure may be the reason why critics to this day are divided about the merits of *Lethal Injection*. Although the consensus was largely positive, with most reviewers praising Cube for avoiding the sell-out trap of a *Predator Vol. 2*, many thought that the stress of matching up to the previous album was one that caused Cube to record *Lethal Injection* in too much of a hurry – leading to a drop in quality as a result. Kevin Powell at Quincy Jones' *Vibe* magazine warned that it was 'not the masterpiece it could have been', although *Time* stated that 'Cube's raps about police brutality and white immorality enter the ear and expand in the brain like a Black Talon bullet; his lyrics are sometimes inexcusable, but his logic is often inescapable. Ignore his high-caliber insights at your peril.'

Despite the negative claims, the album is a powerful one, as anyone would expect. Cube and his producers had mined some unexpected sources, including the Pointer Sisters' 'You Gotta Believe', Slick Rick's lascivious 'Lick The Balls', Evelyn 'Champagne' King's 'The Show Is Over' and, most memorably, Funkadelic's 'One Nation Under A Groove'. The presence of the bevy of producers, including the long-serving Sir Jinx, underlines Cube's preferred studio method. As he put it, 'Once [the producers] get the track fat, I come in with my sugar and spice' – the sugar and spice being both his raps and the production touches which he, as executive producer, would lay over the producers' work. Add to this his decision to use more live musicians than he had previously employed, and it's evident how much his composing skills had evolved.

Commenting on each track to *ROC*, Cube made it clear that those claims of sellout had made an impact – and that he himself had been aware of the dangers of straying too far into mellow, G-Funk-derived territory. Of 'Really Doe', which is an uncompromising percussion and vocal tune, he said, 'After the success of "It Was A Good Day" and "Check Yo' Self", I wanted to do a hardcore back-to-the-underground street song, and let everybody know as long as they try to push me pop, I'll never go that way. I just say, "Let me do beats and rhymes" and I think it worked.' 'Ghetto Bird' stays with hardcore themes, as a graphic evocation of the police helicopters that patrol the skies of South Central at night: 'They make the neighborhood seem like Saigon,' remarked Cube. The ever-growing East–West opposition was clearly on Cube's mind, too. 'You Know How We Do It' is a clarion call to the East about the West Coast modus operandi: 'That's a real laid-back West Coast record,' he said, 'talking about the neighborhood and what's really going on in 1994.'

It was 'Cave Bitch' that caused problems this time round. Cube explained the thoughts behind this song: 'A guy I know told me once you get successful, you'll have to find a blonde white girl to be your wife or girlfriend... It blew me away. I had to do this song and see if the critics who don't complain when I use the word "bitch" about a black girl will complain when I talk about a white girl.' The track starts with a speech from Nation Of Islam minister Khalid Mohammad, who recites: 'No stringy haired, blonde haired, blue eyed, pale-skinned, buttermilk complexion, grafted recessive depressive, ironing-board backside, straight up and straight down, no fills, no thrills, miss six o'clock, subject to have the itch, mutanoid, caucasoid, white cave bitch.'

What to make of this song? Clearly Cube is trying to offend white people and women. On the other hand, he states that his aim is to stir up controversy deliberately in order to compare the reactions between listeners' concepts of a 'black bitch' or a 'white bitch'. If his point is simply that a double standard shouldn't apply, then fair enough – it's a valid point and one ably demonstrated here. In fact, the song didn't raise quite as much comment as he perhaps hoped it would: by 1993 the public had had over six years of gangsta rap in the headlines and a certain heard-it-all-before attitude was developing (even among critics, many of whom displayed a positively blasé attitude to the song). But it would be the last time Cube would ever base a song on a deliberately misogynistic point – a sign that his thinking was becoming more profound, perhaps.

'Bop Gun (Under One Nation)' is the album's classic Cube tune, an 11-minute epic featuring the vocal talents of P-Funk singer and renowned eccentric George Clinton. 'It's about giving respect to the man who started it all,' explained Ice, and indeed the song is as much a Clinton creation as a composition by Cube, with the veteran funkmaster's vocals high in the mix and an unforgettable appearance by him in the video.

There's a touch of philanthropy in the next two songs: 'What Can I Do?' is 'the story of a lot of guys who dropped out of school when crack was the only employer of our young black kids,' explained Ice. 'Then it dried up, and now they don't know what to do.' Meanwhile, 'Lil' Ass Gee' is 'dedicated to the youngsters coming up, on the road to destruction and who won't realize it until they get life in the penitentiary'. Now that Cube was entering his mid-twenties, it's natural that his thoughts would return to his youth in Crenshaw, where his family kept him out of trouble as much as they could – although so many other parents could not. But, despite this, Cube doesn't preach: his job is to describe rather than to proselytise at this point, with the message of the album only made explicit in overt rants such as 'Cave Bitch'.

'Make It Ruff, Make It Smooth' is a duet with K-Dee, in which the two rappers battle it out for lyrical supremacy in an almost old-school style, but the playful mic-boasting doesn't last for long: with 'Down 4 Whatever', Cube is on vengeful form once again, revisiting the anger of 'We Had To Tear This Motherfucker Up' in a direct call for revolution. 'I'm down for making records, I'm down for making revolution,' he said. 'Whatever the people call for, then that's where I'm rollin'.'

Finally, 'Enemy' consolidates the passion of 'Down 4 Whatever', firing some well-aimed shots in the direction of the white race and its forces: 'It's no secret that the powers that be have been against us since we stepped foot in this country. So don't look to the white man to help your situation, because he *put* you in the situation.' Then there's a change of pace with the almost mellow 'When I Get To Heaven', which closes *Lethal Injection* with a quasi-religious elegy: 'I don't think Jesus ever put himself equal with God, but *people* put Jesus in front of God and I don't think that's right. This song's about the bullshit we go through here on earth, what's the real deal and who put the whammy on us.'

As we've seen, there's a hell of a dose of anger on *Lethal Injection*, but for a change Cube is talking about spreading universal love in an almost hippie manner: 'We need to love and respect ourselves before we can love anyone else. That is the key. Love does what a gun cannot. Love makes you run into a burning building to save a baby. It's a lack of love for the next man that keeps the world poor and raggedy.'

Of the many mentions of racial inequality on the record, Cube pointed out: 'We need that medicine. My records give information to whites and blacks. A lot of my shit isn't easy to swallow, but I do records about black folks that aren't too easy either. I did a record called "Us" that was telling us how stupidly we act. So I don't just attack certain people or say it just to hurt muthafuckas' feelings. I say it because, for one thing, it's true, it needs to be said. For another, I need to educate everybody on what we're going through here in 1993. If someone's going to get mad because you tell them your pain, then fuck them.'

Some of the love that Ice Cube was invoking would not have gone amiss in the more sinister niches of American society. As 1993 wore on, the FBI announced the discovery of some documentation, thought to be sourced from right-wing white supremacist organisations. The documents turned out to be lists of names of public figures who had been targeted for assassination, and both Ice Cube and Ice-T's names appeared on them. To this day it is not known who was responsible for compiling these lists, how close the organisation behind them was to carrying out their plans, or (most importantly) who these people were and how much influence and resources they had.

Someone was clearly taking Cube seriously, and not just as a musician. Like many outspoken public figures, black or white, his prominent stance towards – and intolerance of – social ills such as racism had been deemed powerful enough to warrant his inclusion on a list of assassinations. This says more about America, perhaps, than about Cube himself: even back in the days of NWA, Ice and his associates had described themselves variously as 'reporters', 'journalists' or 'messengers', but never as activists or political players; yet what he reported was enough to get him targeted for murder. No clearer testament to the power of his words has yet been made.

Ironically, it was at around this time that a more relaxed, even comedic Ice Cube began to emerge. A seam of black humour had always been present in his work and that of NWA for those who cared enough to search for it, but this was becoming more obvious as time passed and he matured as a person. In March 1993, as Cube was managing the jump from *The Predator* to *Lethal Injection*, he had appeared in a third film – the asinine comedy *CB4*, a deliberately no-brainer comedy focused on the motormouth slapstick humour of *Saturday Night Live* actor Chris Rock. A more abrupt switch from the urban horror of *Boyz N The Hood* and the slick drama of *Trespass* could hardly be imagined: *CB4* was billed, *Spinal Tap*-like, as a 'rockumentary' following the progress of the eponymous spoof rap trio made up of three middle-class boys who adopt the personalities of three incarcerated gangsters in order to appear credible. Ice Cube played himself in a small role in the movie, along with cameos from Ice-T, Flavor Flav, Eazy-E, actress Halle Berry and basketball star Shaquille O'Neal. It's tasteless, juvenile and very funny, and doesn't mean a thing.

Conversely, Cube also appeared in a film that stands at the opposite end of the seriousness scale shortly after the release of *CB4*. This was an independent release made by Stephen and Grant Elliott and viewed mostly by educated, even academic audiences, but which was also freely available to the wider public. Titled *Rap, Race & Equality*, the hour-long movie was billed by its makers as 'exposing the music that is rap and placing it within its political and social context'. Once again, Cube's role was a relatively small one, contained within an interview in which Cube expressed his opinions about hip-hop and its place in the community and the problems encountered when white and black cultures met. Ice-T, Chuck D, KRS-One, Rakim (of Eric B & Rakim), Queen Latifah, the band Naughty By Nature and Def Jam co-founder Russell Simmons also appeared in the film, as well as journalist Jon Pareles of the *New York Times* and Temple University professor Molefi Asante. Opposed diametrically to the slack-jawed humour of *CB4*, *Rap, Race & Equality* was a movie to invest time and concentration in.

As gangsta rap (and then G-Funk) moved steadily into the cultural mainstream, more and more academic studies of the phenomenon were being undertaken, and more than a few rappers were choosing to expose their views in film, in print or in any other available medium. A notable example was Ice-T, whose book *The Ice Opinion: Who Gives A Fuck?* appeared in 1994. Co-written with author Heidi Sigmund, the volume was a series of treatises from the rapper on sex, drugs, religion, rap and related subjects. Although critics largely dismissed it, due to Ice-T's untutored style and perhaps disjointed reasoning, for one important reason: it remains a valuable tome for anyone interested in the life of Ice Cube and the ghetto-raised artists like him – it's authentic. Ice-T pulls no punches, but doesn't glorify gangland violence or aggression in any way, painting a picture of the hood as a grimly mundane place where no one wants to be.

However, in the wake of all this self-expression, Ice Cube chose to withdraw from recording new music for a while, partly because his second son, Daryl, was born near this time. The spring of 1994 saw three *Lethal Injection* singles keep his profile healthy, however, with MTV and terrestrial TV rotation for each of the 'Really Doe', 'You Know How We Do It' and 'Bop Gun (One Nation)' releases. The last, released on 8 March, was a radio edit of the epic George Clinton collaboration, and was accompanied by a near-psychedelic video in which Cube attends a surreal house party hosted by the dreadlocked

P-Funk frontman, and remains a music-channel staple to this day. But apart from these three releases, no new solo Cube material would appear until 1997.

There are many reasons for this. For four years Ice had steered a solo career to heights to which hip-hop had never previously risen. In the meantime he had honed two parallel careers: that of producer (Yo-Yo had been one of his first clients, and he had of course helmed his own albums) and actor (as we have seen). His talents had become in demand from several quarters and it's possible that he feared that he would soon begin to spread himself too thin. Add to this the fact that *Lethal Injection* – while a big-selling album – had not received the critical praise *The Predator* had enjoyed, and it seems appropriate that Cube chose to draw inward rather than continue to expand his oeuvre.

But the primary reason for Ice Cube's hiatus from solo recording is that he had developed into a more rational (even cerebral) individual than before. Where the angry young man of 1990 had stuck firmly to his NWA-honed themes of murder and misogyny with a grim determination, this older man had recorded 'Cave Bitch' to test the waters of critical reaction – and had warned listeners that his intention had been exactly that, rather than making the song a genuine expression of anti-white hatred (not a stance from which the Uzi-toting Ice of the 1980s would have balked). Cube's mid-twenties had ushered in a period of thoughtfulness, as the boy became the man at last.

Many of the world's greatest musicians have chosen to undergo a 'silent period' – Miles Davis and John Lennon are just two that come to mind – and their motive to do so is often from one simple cause. These creative minds need calm to grow, after their energies have been expended – and Cube had certainly done just that, with several careers beckoning and the world at his feet. Compound this with the fact that Cube's chosen field – hip-hop – had recently exploded under his feet, carrying him and some of his compatriots (like Dre) to previously unimagined heights, and it's apparent why some rest and recuperation was in order.

But this is not to say that Cube stopped working. His first move was to write and produce the majority of an album, *Guerillas In The*

Mist, for his associates Da Lench Mob. Shorty, J-Dee and T Bone had already learned their chops on *Amerikkka's Most Wanted* and had become a powerful rap unit in their own right, matching the talents of their composer and producer with their own set of incendiary rhymes and beats. Standout tracks on *Guerillas* were 'Lost In Tha System' and 'Freedom Got An AK', both untrammelled hardcore tunes that owed an obvious debt to the West Coast pioneers, and the title song itself, which was accompanied by a video based on that hood favourite, *Predator*. Although the record wasn't a commercial smash hit by any standards, it had its loyal fans and remained a B-list choice for some months.

More of an impact was made by Cube's second production commission of this period, the debut album for his protégé, Kam. The 22-year-old rapper, whose real name is Craig Miller, called his album *Neva Again* and made a smooth job of combining his own baritone delivery with Ice's silky console work. But the textures weren't too smooth for some serious vitriol to be heard: Kam had, after all, appeared on both the *Boyz N The Hood* soundtrack and on *Death Certificate* ('Colorblind'), to devastating effect. The younger man's Nation of Islam-based philosophy was even more pronounced than in the work of Ice Cube, and the overall impression was one of a young street prophet – especially on tracks such as 'Drama', with its clean gospel edge. He also denounces gang warfare on 'Peace Treaty', white racism on 'Stereotype' and conventional religion on 'Holiday Madness'. Cube himself steps up to the mic on 'Watts Riot', which revisits the subject matter of *The Predator*'s 'We Had To Tear This Motherfucker Up'. It's a powerful work, and one that sits well alongside Cube's own albums.

Late in 1994, the rapper slipped away from production duties on other people's albums and booked a surprise lecture at Locke High School in South Central, Los Angeles, to take place on 6 December, as students were in the process of winding down for the Christmas vacation. Like Ice-T before him, Cube addressed the students on the subject of self-improvement, the value of not succumbing to the traditional ghetto mentality and the importance of self-awareness – but the most interesting part of his speech on a wider level was his introduction. The school principal informed him that the only students who had been permitted to attend Cube's lecture were those who had shown 'academic improvement'. Although the teacher's stratagem will be viewed with some sympathy by anyone who has ever tried to control a group of teenagers – let alone a school full of hood-raised youths – Cube wasn't pleased, and opened his speech with the words: 'I'm here to talk to everybody outside – everybody who's ditching school today.' And his words were well chosen: it was the students with no hope of academic prowess who were most in need of his hard-earned wisdom, not those who had worked hard in order to earn the right to hear him speak.

The Cube release schedule was not going to remain inactive for long, despite his retreat from new work – and it says much for the talents of its creator that the next album, a rarities collection, would go on to be one of his most-admired works. *Bootlegs & B-Sides* was released in early December 1994 and brought together 13 rarely heard or remixed songs: 'Robbin' Hood (Cause It Ain't All Good)', 'What Can I Do? (Remix)', '24 Wit An L', 'You Know How We Do It (Remix)', '2 N The Morning', 'Check Yo Self (Remix)', 'You Don't Wanna Fuck Wit These', 'Lil' Ass Gee (Eerie Gumbo Remix)', 'My Skin Is My Sin', 'It Was A Good Day (Remix)', 'U Ain't Gonna Take My Life', 'When I Get To Heaven (Remix)' and 'D'Voidofpopniggafiedmegamix'. And, in case this might seem like a ruse to entice fans to buy in a different format the songs they had already purchased, rest assured that Ice Cube is one of the few artists whose remixed work is sufficiently different from the original versions to make them virtually new songs. For example, 'What Can I Do?' is re-tweaked to take it from its original melodic roots to a harder, more funky zone altogether, and 'Check Yo Self' lifts its central sample from one of rap's Holy Grails, 'The Message' by Grandmaster Flash.

Hardly had Cube's fans assimilated the fresh grooves of *Bootlegs & B-Sides* than news of another Ice Cube film came through. After the smooth moves of *Trespass* and the throwaway humour of *CB4*, many listeners were glad to hear that Ice had returned with a new project directed by none other than *Boyz N The Hood*'s John Singleton. The movie itself was to be called *Higher Learning* and was scheduled to hit American cinemas on 11 January 1995.

Higher Learning was a film that suffered from the outset from the burden of its own importance. Singleton had described it as the final part of his South Central trilogy, after *Boyz* and *Poetic Justice* – the latter had been a moderately well-received drama focusing on the tragic relationship between a couple played by Tupac Shakur and Janet Jackson – but the expectation that *Learning* would be a powerful social commentary was perhaps a hindrance to its makers. Singleton set the narrative this time on a fictional university campus, filming part of the shoot at UCLA and naming the film's college Columbus University (a thinly veiled reference to the Eurocentric stance that fuels much of the conflict within the story).

The plot is driven by the progress of three freshmen, all charismatic actors and all played so that their stories overlap several times with unpredictable results. The first, Malik (Omar Epps), is a black athlete, attending Columbus on a sports scholarship and full of naive enthusiasm for his own talents. He becomes a proponent of black self-awareness after tuition from a senior student, Fudge (Cube), a professor (Laurence Fishburne) and his girlfriend, Deja (Tyra Banks). Next is Kristen (Kristy Swanson), a wide-eyed innocent California girl whose sexual confidence is destroyed after a harrowing date rape and who becomes confused about her sexual orientation as a result. Finally, there is the film's most chilling character, an engineering geek called Remy (Michael Rapaport), who is recruited by the local skinheads and becomes a violent, racist thug. The story is accompanied by a soundtrack featuring evocative music from Rage Against the Machine, Liz Phair, Tori Amos and Ice Cube himself.

Unfortunately, the movie was a mixed success. The broad contrasts that Singleton had drawn in *Boyz* (gang versus gang, good cops versus bad cops, keen student versus ghetto thug, life or death) didn't fit well in this scenario, because the interwoven paths of the characters were too complex. Many critics praised the movie for its message (which is that racism exists, visibly and otherwise, in every situation, and reveals itself in a multitude of unpredictable ways) but scorned the oversimple stereotypes that populated it.

Chris Hicks of *Deseret News* concluded: 'An extremely mixed bag, combining lyrical images and sharp-edged drama with dull clichés and contrivances that border on the ridiculous… Singleton tackles some courageous themes and isn't afraid of taking risks, but he seems overwhelmed by his own material, as far too many characters remain underdeveloped, and the film gradually loses its focus.' Still, he added that Cube, Epps, Banks and Fishburne had managed to bring emotional depth to their roles, and that Singleton 'remains a talented filmmaker who will undoubtedly make some fine movies in the future' – the only problem being that the director is 'young and unfocused, and like so many of the characters in this film, perhaps a bit too naïve'. Reviewer James Berardinelli thought that 'Perhaps *Higher Learning* tries to cram too much into two hours… The tragic, ironic twist that punctuates the film is anything but surprising. In fact, most of what happens in the final 15 minutes is easily predicted.'

Others were more upset about Singleton's apparent dismissal of the film's white characters. Pete Croatto at Filmcritic.com complained: 'The one subject Singleton seems to know a lot about is that white people simply can't be trusted, which is alarming considering the movie's goal toward understanding', while John Hartl of Film.com was even more specific: 'It's a given in Singleton's movies that black kids will be roughed up by white police, who will then treat even a raving, gun-toting white skinhead with more sympathy. But the idea is hammered home so often in *Higher Learning* that it almost becomes a running gag.' Hartl also added that, 'in his zeal to create moral breathing space for his black characters, Singleton seems to have forgotten about everyone else'.

Possibly these reviewers are missing the point in part. If John Singleton had wanted to create a brittle interplay of characters, brimfull of subtleties and barely evidenced hints, presumably he could have done so – many of the critics noted his gentler touch from time to time (the scene when Kristen clutches her purse protectively when entering a lift with Malik is a case in point) – but that may not have been his aim. In fact, this can't have been his aim: *Higher Learning*, like *Boyz N The Hood* before it, is a brightly painted, almost hyperreal exaggeration of campus life – there's little middle ground in this set of extremes, with characters and events all bigger, louder, angrier or faster than real life ever is. The broad brushstrokes that Singleton uses in the film are the tools he uses to expedite this, and shouldn't be construed as a simple misjudgment on his part.

Whether or not the story of the film is any good (its ending was widely disliked, for example) is a moot point, of course – but where most reviewers agreed was that Ice Cube delivered a topnotch performance as the driven student Fudge. Less apathetic than Doughboy (*Boyz*) and just as full of venom as Savon (*Trespass*), Fudge's character could have played as well by few other actors, with Cube's brooding presence suiting the part perfectly. Its mixed reviews notwithstanding, the movie took a respectable £27 million ($38 million) in box-office entries and about £14 million ($20 million) more in home-movie rentals – not a bad score for a so-called 'ghetto movie'.

As 1995 progressed, Ice Cube's profile remained healthy, thanks to the *Bootlegs & B-Sides* album and the *Higher Learning* film. Clearly 'ghetto culture', the somewhat patronising term some mainstream critics were applying to hip-hop movies and records alike, was flourishing – and, in line with this, the hip-hop scene across the nation was beginning to undergo some rather ominous changes.

First, the West Coast *enfant terrible* of rap, Tupac Shakur (whose story only overlaps superficially with that of Ice Cube, despite his enormous importance to the development of hip-hop) had got himself into serious trouble. He had exchanged a few insults with certain members of the rapidly rising East Coast scene (which had begun to reassert itself against West Coast hip-hop dominance with the emergence of skilful rap acts such as Notorious BIG – aka Biggie Smalls – and the aforementioned Wu-Tang Clan), but this had been a mere irritant. Shakur's real problem lay in his physical safety: he had been shot five times on 30 November 1994 in the lobby of a Times Square, New York recording studio, and his assailants had also reportedly relieved him of £28,000 ($40,000) worth of jewellery. Surviving the attack, he checked himself out of hospital less than three hours after surgery – possibly wishing to keep as low a profile as possible, as he was on trial for sexual assault and weapons charges at the time. Two weeks later, he was acquitted of all charges except that of sexual abuse, which would lead to a sentence of four and a half years in New York's maximum-security prison on the infamous Rikers Island.

So much for rap's new wave (although Shakur would not remain incarcerated for long). The second major upheaval in the hip-hop world came courtesy of the Nation of Islam, to which so many rap artists had devoted themselves. On 10 March 1994, Nation of Islam leader Louis Farrakhan had appeared at Boston's Strand Theater as part of his 'For Men Only' tour. At the venue he addressed 2,500 men, asking them to perform a variety of spiritual tasks, including the restoration of God at the head of their lives, the relinquishing of drugs, alcohol and crime, and the assumption of more responsibility for their wives and families. Not an unusual sermon to preach in any church, one might imagine – but in this instance Farrakhan's words sparked a chain of events that would lead (a year and a half later) to the Million Man March, an enormous pilgrimage of black men to Washington, DC, on 16 October 1995.

Cypress Hill rapper B-Real told *Addicted To Noise* magazine: 'That thing was about getting ourselves together. In order to live with everybody else without problems, you gotta have your own community living amongst themselves with their shit together. And that's what it was for. To say, look, this is where we're fuckin' up. We're not complaining about anybody else. First, we just need to get ourselves together. And then we'll deal with the outside.'

On whether the march was a separatist move by the Nation of Islam, the rapper mused: 'I don't think it was about separatism. We just needed to be able to respect ourselves and have our shit down so we can make something of ourselves. And then our relations with everyone else will fall into place.' It's the old problem of the culture turning on itself, it seems: 'It's not black gangbangers killing off white gangbangers. These fuckers are killing off each other. And that's what has to stop. It's the muthafuckers dealing drugs to their brothers.

That's what has to stop. The gang problems, the badass drug problems. That's how it relates to us; it relates to everyone in a different way.'

Although the political motives behind the Million Man March were complex (too much so to be fully explored here), it's clear that hip-hop culture would be affected profoundly by it. But the overarching reason for the music and its attendant culture entering a state of flux at this time – which may lead to a greater understanding of why Ice Cube chose to withdraw temporarily from it – is a simple one: it was a controversial time for hip-hop. At the forefront of the headlines was none other than Eazy-E, Cube's old nemesis, who, like some crazed, cackling goblin had been involved in a series of publicity stunts promoting his solo career since the fall of NWA in 1992, of which his infamous Republican dinner attendance was a minor blip.

In April 1993, Eazy took the wholly unexpected step of publicly supporting one of the police officers that had attacked Rodney King, providing the spark which ignited the highly charged atmosphere in LA. The cop, Timothy Briseno, was (according to Eazy) the only officer who took no active part in the beating – although why exactly this merited the rapper's respect was never fully clarified. Ex-Geto Boy Willie Dee was one of many hip-hop artists who took offence at this – Dee labelled Eazy a 'sellout' in an interview with the *Los Angeles Times* the following month.

Why would Eazy-E take this almost inexplicable step? Simply because he was that rare thing – a true rebel, and one with the courage (although some might call it suicidal insanity) and vision (again, some might say arrogance) to follow through his plans. Furthermore, he had found himself in the position that so many ghetto residents dreamed of – that is, with wealth and its attendant power – and used this position to its maximum, in this case to shock people profoundly in the belief that all publicity is good publicity. It's tempting to conclude that Eazy looked around him for the most unexpected avenue, caught sight of the Rodney King beatings and deliberately allied himself with Briseno in the sure knowledge that heads would turn everywhere.

It worked. His business interests flourished. In August 1993,

Ruthless signed a deal with the Relativity label in which the latter would use its considerable marketing muscle to promote and distribute Ruthless artists. Two months later, Eazy released his second solo album, the threateningly titled *It's On (Dr Dre) 187um Killa*, which depicted Dre on its inner sleeve wearing makeup and woman's clothing. Despite the record's obvious agenda (187 means 'homicide', while the intended target of the attack wasn't hard to divine), it eventually sold over 1.5 million units. Clearly nobody had told Eazy's fanbase that gangsta rap was supposed to be dead and buried...

Ice Cube took a break from solo recording in 1994 and G-Funk continued its apparently inexorable rise (Snoop Dogg was the hottest name to drop in West Coast hip-hop circles, while the Wu-Tang Clan were becoming the most powerful force in the East), but it was no more peaceful for Eazy than 1993. Brushing aside the small matter of a child-support lawsuit which left him paying an annual sum of £41,000 ($58,000) for a Nebraskan daughter, Eazy took the mic on *The Ruthless Radio Show*, a Saturday-night radio slot broadcast by LA's KKBT station and on which Eazy's faithful companion Yella co-hosted. The rest of the year was all about building Ruthless, and met largely with success (although an October lawsuit from the hip-hop crew Po' Broke & Lonely was a minor setback).

All seemed to be going well for Eazy at this stage, and he had become regarded as something of an example of black business initiative. When asked by journalist Brian Cross how he felt about the possible future of black record companies, Eazy replied: 'Imagine if there was one black record company, one major company, and everyone went over there – imagine how powerful that would be? People have power and they don't even know they have it. 'Cause a lot of the records put out are black rap, R&B, if you take all that away and build one big black owned and run company it would fuck everybody else off. A lot of people don't trust black people. A lot of black people steal, it's sad but it's true. Fuck this black-white thing.' When Cross asked Eazy about his white audience, he added: 'They like listening to that "I don't give a fuck" attitude, the Guns N'Roses attitude. They buy something like 70 per cent of our stuff. They wanna really learn what's going on in different parts of the neighborhoods – they wanna be down, just like I want to be down too.'

Ice Cube, whose feud with Eazy had not extended as long as Dre's or been driven by such anger, had buried the hatchet to the extent that the two men spent some time together in January 1995 at a New York nightclub called The Tunnel, where the rappers talked for most of an evening. Eazy was accompanied by Ruthless's latest signings, a group called Bone Thugs-N-Harmony who combined R&B and gangsta rap, and Cube by the newly emerged rap artists Biggie Smalls (aka the Notorious BIG) and soon-to-be producer extraordinaire Puff Daddy/P Diddy (Sean Combs). Cube later said, 'We talked for two hours, just me and him. He looked just like he always looked. Actually, he looked a little fat.'

The reference to Eazy's looks is a grim one. In mid-January, Eazy had started to experience flu-like symptoms and difficulty breathing, although he initially dismissed it, as he had been prone to sporadic attacks of bronchitis since childhood. As this became worse, however, his bodyguards Jacob T and Big Man insisted that he see a doctor, and on 16 February took him to Norwalk Community Hospital. He was diagnosed with bronchitis-related asthma and ordered to rest after a three-day spell in hospital.

However, his health didn't improve and Eazy was admitted to the well-known Cedars-Sinai Medical Center under the alias Eric Lollis. His personal assistant Charise Henry and his bodyguards visited him, as did his mother, who brought him food while the rapper underwent a series of antibiotics for a lung infection that had developed. Henry later recalled: 'Me and one of his girlfriends would get him to sit up and move around, but he couldn't walk much because it was hard on his breathing. His spirits went up, then down, and we'd try to cheer him up. I did the running man to Montell Jordan's "This Is How We Do It" and he laughed.'

The bombshell came on 1 March, when Eazy and his longtime girlfriend Tomika Woods were informed that he was suffering from full-blown AIDS. Woods informed his friends, while Henry and Eazy talked over the implications of the news. 'He told me it wasn't fair,' remembered Henry later. 'That he didn't want to die. He said he wouldn't care if he didn't have a dime; he said he wouldn't care what anybody said, if he could just drop the top on his car and ride up the coast one more time.' After the diagnosis was made, it was noticed that Eazy's lungs were beginning to fill up with liquid, and surgery was scheduled for 15 March. But there was some doubt over whether Eazy – whose condition was rapidly worsening – would survive the procedure.

Arrangements were made for Woods and Eazy to marry the day before the operation, and the evening before he was due to go under the knife the couple were married, with the rapper's parents, brother and sister in attendance. His recital of the wedding vows, plus the alleged signing of a will naming trustees of his estate, were the last things he did before his condition became critical: the lung-draining operation was cancelled, as he grew weaker later that night. A statement was released to the press through Eazy's attorney Ron Sweeney, in which he disclosed his illness and claimed to have fathered seven children through six different women – it was presumed that he had contracted the HIV virus from one of these partners. Tomika and their son Dominick both later tested negative for the virus.

Eazy remained on life support for a few more days as his strength slowly decreased. On 17 March, he was visited by Dr Dre and, although the content of their conversation has never been disclosed, it is widely thought that the two men made their peace. Cube is also said to have visited Eazy, although he has said several times that he and Eazy had been at ease with each other for some time. He later spoke to Dre about the fate of their ex-colleague, observing: 'Dre saw him in the hospital, hooked up to all that shit, and said Eazy looked asleep. He looked like nothing was wrong with him at all.'

While the ailing rapper may have appeared tranquil as he lay *in extremis*, the hospital's administrative staff were far from relaxed. 'We've been overwhelmed with thousands of phone calls asking about Eazy-E,' reported Paula Correia, the Cedars-Sinai public relations officer. 'Lots of young people – emotional, upset, concerned. We've had a high volume of calls for other celebrity patients – Lucille Ball, George Burns, Billy Idol – but never this many.'

Charise Henry last saw Eazy on 24 March, and recalled: 'I was talking to him but he didn't respond. It looked as if he was asleep. It was the first time he looked comfortable in a while. He looked peaceful.' Yella, meanwhile, had been a constant presence in his friend's hour of need, and spoke at length about Eazy's illness in an interview with *Props*, revealing that rumours of Eazy's condition had been circulating for a few days before the official press conference, but that E had kept it to himself as long as possible. 'We were just talking normally about business and joking around. He didn't sound down or nothin'. He was talking like he was gonna be out next week and that's what we thought. We knew he had bronchitis, but we didn't think nothin' about it. Then, our buddy Big Man called me and told me that it was true that he got [AIDS]... I was shocked because I had already been hearing rumors for the past two weeks.'

The most memorable feature of that press conference was the reading of Eazy's last message to his fans, which ran as follows:

'I may not seem like a guy you would pick to preach a sermon. But I feel it is now time to testify because I do have folks who care about me hearing all kinds of stuff about what's up. Yeah, I was a brother on the streets of Compton doing a lot of things most people look down on – but it did pay off. Then we started rapping about real stuff that shook up the LAPD and the FBI. But we got our message across big time, and everyone in America started paying attention to the boys in the hood. Soon our anger and hope got everyone riled up. There were great rewards for me personally, like fancy cars, gorgeous women and good living. Like real non-stop excitement. I'm not religious, but wrong or right, that's me. I'm not saying this because I'm looking for a soft cushion wherever I'm heading, I just feel that I've got thousands and thousands of young fans that have to learn about what's real when it comes to AIDS. Like the others before me, I would like to turn my own problem into something good that will reach out to all my homeboys and their kin. Because I want to save their asses before it's too late. I'm not looking to blame anyone except myself. I have learned in the last week that this thing is real, and it doesn't discriminate. It affects everyone. My girl Tomika and I have been together for four years and we recently got married. She's good, she's kind and a wonderful mother. We have a little boy who's a year old. Before Tomika I had other women. I have seven children by six different mothers. Maybe success was too good to me. I love all my kids and always took care of them. Now I'm in the biggest fight of my life, and it ain't easy. But I want to say much love to those who have been down to me. And thanks for your support.'

These words have struck an emotional chord in many people – but Yella is doubtful about their reliability: 'I don't know who actually wrote the letter. Those aren't his words because he would've cussed in his regular way. Once I heard the first couple of lines I knew that it wasn't him.' Seven years later, it's still not known if Eazy's final words came from his own hand or not – but the evidence seems to suggest that they were genuine, despite Yella's instincts.

Eazy-E finally died on 26 March 1995. In the 1992 interview he appeared in with Howard Stern and LA police chief Darryl Gates, he had said that he didn't wear condoms because the women he slept with were 'clean'.

Tributes began to pour in as the news of Eazy's death spread. MC Ren said, 'He was first, before all of us. He had a record on the street and his own label. That changed everything. He hyped us up to want to make street records... Back then, rap was only New York groups with big strong voices. Eazy wasn't like the typical B-boy. He had a distinct, little laidback voice and nobody could copy it.' Jerry Heller remembered his 'playa' habits – 'Eazy loved women. He had lots of them. Lots of kids. They were a big part of his life' – but also that he had been a truly professional businessman. 'He was driven by the thought that when he was sleeping, he was missing something. He worried that people were getting ahead of him. He just never slept.' And, in his most evocative statement, Heller – who has rarely spoken to the press about Eazy – added: 'He was the most Machiavellian guy I ever met. He instinctively knew power and how to control people. And his musical instincts were infallible.'

In a truly surreal move that could – as they say – happen only in America, the LA mayor, Omar Bradley, declared the day of Eazy's funeral to be Eazy-E Day, calling him 'Compton's favorite son' and stating: 'Eric made Compton famous not just in California, but all over the world. I recognize Eazy as a young man who grew up in the streets of Compton.' Bradley finished with – wait for it! – 'And brothers and sisters, we know it's not "easy" growing up in Compton.' In a last flourish of gangsta style, Eazy was buried in a gold-plated coffin, wearing the traditional NWA uniform of a check shirt, jeans, sunglasses and a black Compton baseball cap.

When the next instalment of Eazy's KKBT radio show came round, both Snoop Dogg and Ice Cube phoned in to speak on air. Snoop said that he was praying for Eazy, while Cube, in his pragmatic way, explained, 'Me and Eric worked out our differences... I had just seen him in New York, and we talked for a long time. We was laughing and kickin' it about how NWA should get back together.' On a more prosaic level, a street vendor was observed selling T-shirts on the corner of Florence and Crenshaw boulevards in South Central. The garments were adorned with the words 'Aids Is Ruthless. So Take It Eazy. RIP 3/26/95'.

Back at Ruthless, the lawyers had gone to work immediately after Eazy's death, with disputes over ownership of the company escalating between rival parties to the extent that the LAPD had to shut down the offices until the legal disputes could be resolved. Eazy had left a personal fortune of approximately £25 million ($35 million) to various benefactors, but the legitimacy of some of the documentation was in dispute and it would take several months before any resolution could be reached.

Yella (who had been signed to Ruthless until his contract expired in 1994, but had remained at his friend's side anyway) had the last word on the subject of Ruthless, largely because he had been entrusted with the task of finishing and releasing Eazy's last album. This appeared in 1996 under the old-school title of *Straight Off The Streets Of Muthaphukkin' Compton*. Of the legal arguments, he said: 'By the time they finish, I think the company will be broke. The only people who will be making money will be the lawyers. That's why the last thing I did over there at Ruthless was his album. I didn't want nobody else to put it together... All Ruthless Records is now is just a name. The real ruthless person is not here so I'd rather not be stuck up with a bunch of court-appointed people, I'd rather be on my own and do my own thing.'

Meanwhile, more than one of Eazy's ex-lovers appeared with a claim for a share in his wealth. It was apparent that, perhaps because of the speed of his illness, many of his business affairs had not been resolved. Maybe the rapper would have gained a certain dark satisfaction from knowing the havoc his passing had caused.

The whole affair of the passing of Eric 'Eazy' Wright had a profound effect on the hip-hop community (although relatively few commentators outside that scene had much to say about it), with Yella musing: 'When [basketball star] Magic [Johnson] got it, people thought about it for a minute. But everybody knew Eric; he's right there in the streets. His dying from AIDS has got a lot of people thinking, "Now that's close, it can't get no closer but me getting it."'

An epitaph for Eazy that he might not have wanted might be the slogan 'Real Niggaz Don't Die', the title of one of NWA's most throwaway songs. Real niggas did, it seems, die like everybody else. Perhaps this was the lesson which spelled the end of gangsta rap as it had been since the late 1980s, when five ghetto boys named Eric, O'Shea, Lorenzo, Andre and Antoine had thought it a good idea to invent this apocalyptic music.

RIP Eazy-E and, with him, the Compton era. A new way was coming.

9 Caught In The Middle

Despite all the grimness that had surrounded Cube for the last few months, his most surprising career move yet was about to be revealed. On 26 April 1995 – one month to the day after the death of Eazy-E – a new film appeared in American cinemas. Its title was *Friday*. Subtitled 'A lot can go down between Thursday and Saturday', posters advertising its launch showed a surprising range of images of Cube laughing, putting on a dopey, over-the-top expression of shock, or grinning in a bug-eyed, insane way into the camera. The movie, it seemed, would be a comedy.

Imagine the struggle that entered people's minds when this fact registered: Cube had now made three movies which exploited his sulking, almost smouldering presence to the full. It was difficult to digest that he might now be joining Eddie Murphy, Martin Lawrence and Danny Glover in the echelons of black movie comedy – but such an idea did not remain strange for long. *Friday* would be Cube's most-praised movie since *Boyz N The Hood* – which reveals much about the viewing preferences of his audience.

The film was based on a simple premise – events occurring over the course of a single Friday at the South Central LA house of Ice Cube's character. Craig (Cube) is a fairly conservative character, who has been unfairly fired from his job and chooses to spend the rest of the day with his friend, Smokey, a slacker played with absolute genius by the comedian Chris Tucker. The story line's parallels with Cube's 1993 hit 'It Was A Good Day' are obvious – in fact the song's video director, F Gary Gray, was also the man commissioned to helm *Friday*.

The scenario is satisfyingly effective. Craig and Smokey sit on Craig's parents' porch and are visited by various people, including local bully Deebo (who tries to rob them), Craig's possessive girlfriend (who happens to visit just as Craig is entertaining another girl, Debbie), leering Pastor Clever (played by comedian Bernie Mac), and comedian LaWanda Page as a cursing Jehovah's Witness. Most memorably, they are paid a visit by Big Worm, the local drug baron, who has entrusted dealer Smokey with £140 ($200) worth of weed to sell and wants to see some payback. Unfortunately, Smokey has consumed the goods (sharing a joint with Craig after much persuasion) and is given an ultimatum to come up with the cash. The rest of the film covers the chasing of this sum, which ultimately comes after Craig is involved in a fairly brutal fight with Deebo and wins Debbie's admiration by knocking him unconscious. Smokey steals the comatose thug's cash and repays his debts, escaping execution by the skin of his teeth.

Standout scenes are many – if you're not put off by toilet humour, that is. After finally being persuaded to take a hit on a joint (Smokey says, 'Weed is from the earth. God put this here for me and you. Take advantage, man, take advantage'), Craig begins to hallucinate. Later, a more serious angle develops when Deebo and Debbie argue after the bully has hit the latter's sister. Craig steps in and pulls a gun on the enormous thug, but is persuaded to fight him with his fists by his father, a moronic dog-catcher with a bathroom fixation.

The script was written by Ice Cube, with help from his *Predator* collaborator DJ Pooh, and was his first attempt to author a film. In many ways it is similar to his first raps (produced almost a decade before at Dr Dre's skating-rink rap parties), in that both creations focus on lowest-common-denominator issues such as sex, toilet skits and violence. Its messages are also pretty blunt: weed is a way of life, but drug dealing can get you killed; violence against women is wrong; fist fights are more noble than gunfights; and that if you live by ghetto values, you may die by them. Not that *Friday* has any heavy, didactic purpose, like the two John Singleton films Cube had already starred in, but there are certain similarities between it and *Boyz N The Hood*, for example, of which not the least notable is the final drive-by shooting.

Note, however, that *Boyz* sees one of its central characters killed in this scene, while in *Friday* everyone is still alive and uninjured after the smoke settles.

Ice Cube and Tucker make an excellent partnership, carrying the film forward effortlessly. Cube's unpretentious performance (he never seems to *try* to act) meshes with the hyperactive, machine-gun delivery of Tucker to make the centre of the film an unpredictable force, especially when combined with the off-the-wall lunacy of the more eccentric characters. In this film Cube proved that his acting skills weren't limited to portraying trigger-happy gangstas – a useful development, given that the ghetto-movie wave had now reached its peak and that he himself was evincing signs of wanting to break away from the genre. He told Ira Robbins in *Newsday* that 'I like to do projects like *Friday* and stuff like that to kind of show the other side of who I am, because I'm not serious 24 hours a day... I have a sense of humor, it comes out every now and then.' The script for *Friday* came from 'events that happened in my life, friends' lives, things I've seen. The movie was actually written before I started writing. In my head.' As for the wider impact of his films on his career, he remarked that 'A lot of doors are opening because of the rap records that I do, and I would be a fool not to step through them. The movies have taken my career to a whole new level. I'm going to take advantage of it.'

Many reviewers liked the film's combination of juvenile gags and hood threat, although others found it too banal to take at all seriously (David Keyes of *Cinema 2000* mused that 'This stuff is not funny. Someone in the studio must have a mental deficiency, because any normal person who saw the film being made would have pointed out that this stuff isn't funny'), but most were united in their praise of director F Gary Gray, who had engineered a remarkably good-looking film despite lack of funds. Gray's budget was a mere £2 million ($3 million), but by basing much of the action, *Reservoir Dogs*-style, in one primary location, Gray eked out every penny of this to good effect. The film would ultimately gross ten times this meagre sum – a mighty achievement for this genre.

Gray's rise to success paralleled that of John Singleton and says much about mainstream America's new-found acknowledgment of hip-hop culture. Born in 1972 in New York and raised in South Central – but moved to live with his father in Highland Park, Illinois, after the mean streets of the hood started to have an undesirable impact on his education – Gray seized the opportunities offered to him, as he told *The Source* magazine. 'I went to a predominantly white, rich high school, [with resources] much better than anything I had ever seen. I knew I had to take advantage of this situation.' Learning the basics of filming, editing and directing, and then compounding his studies at an LA film school, his break came when he was working as a camera operator at the Black Entertainment Network and *Pump It Up* for the Fox Channel. Meeting rap act the Madd Circle, which numbered among its ranks the then-unknown Coolio, he persuaded them to let him direct a video for them. As he later recalled, 'The first thing I did was use my director's fee to shoot the video in 35 millimeter, like actual films are shot' – a more ambitious format than the standard 16mm frame.

This led to clips for Mary J Blige, Coolio, TLC and Dr Dre, and when the video for Ice Cube's 'It Was a Good Day' made it into *Rolling Stone*'s Top 100 Videos Of All Time, the awards began rolling in. Gray picked up several trophies at the 1995 MTV Video Music Awards and the step into feature-film directing was an obvious one to take. *Friday* was the perfect vehicle for him – with its Cube-authored script – although tensions were running high at first, as he told *High Times*: 'I knew that I had to deliver something that was high-quality. There was a lot of pressure, because with making motion pictures, when you're a first-time film-maker, if the dailies don't look good the first week, [or] if the performances aren't good the first week, the director gets fired.'

An interesting point about the making of *Friday* was that Gray – highly impressed with the spontaneous humour of Chris Tucker and John Witherspoon (who played Craig's father) – instructed them to improvise each take. He told *High Times* that '[They] are so funny on the fly and right off the cuff that I didn't want to miss any of that, so I said, "Stick to the script for the first two takes, and on the third take, do it how you want to do it." When I got to editing, I used most of the third takes because they were so funny, especially Chris' facial expressions.'

Gray was also full of praise for Ice Cube, whose experience of acting in three prominent roles had clearly been beneficial: '[He] has a lot of discipline. It helps me as a director for him to have that much discipline and be the star of the movie, because if everybody wanted to run wild, then it would just be a big babysitting session and you lose a lot of time. Cube doesn't play that whole "I'm a star" trip.'

Hollywood was changing, it seems, in line with the whole rise of hip-hop culture. Gray told the *Los Angeles Times* that 'I appreciated New Line Pictures giving me a shot. How often does anyone write a check like that to an unproven 23-year-old?', and that having a low budget isn't necessarily a problem – 'Any other comedy would have three times the budget and [take] twice as long to shoot.' After *Friday*'s success, however, it seems that the production vultures came out of the woodwork – he later stated in *USA Today* that he 'was offered every regurgitated action comedy idea that Hollywood has done' and, in *Vibe*, said that 'I didn't want to be pegged as an in-the-hood-type director. It's just too easy to get that title.'

Such is the fate, perhaps, of anyone who pioneers a new, big-selling trend in show business: the mainstream craves underground success and, in doing so, cheapens it. The similarity between the rise to glory of F Gary Gray/John Singleton (young film-makers get popular after making big-selling ghetto movies that lead to wider black awareness) and Ice Cube/Dr Dre (young rappers get popular after making big-selling ghetto albums that lead to wider black awareness) does not need to be stressed.

In this case, however, Gray (and Singleton before him) was not naive enough to presume that his success was here to stay. 'These people will put you on a pedestal,' Gray said of the movie industry's movers and shakers, 'and then knock your ass down.' Rarely were truer words said, especially in the context of American hip-hop, which was now undergoing something of a crisis.

The years 1995 and 1996 were primarily memorable in US hip-hop terms because of the depressing evolution of the East Coast/West Coast rivalry, which escalated by the end of this period into a tragic situation of unforeseen proportions and which would inform the work of Ice

Cube to a significant degree. The story of the rift revolves around the career of the East Coast-born, San Francisco-raised rapper Tupac Shakur who, as *Friday* appeared, was incarcerated in Riker's Island prison for a variety of offences. However, this hadn't stopped him from straddling the public consciousness, almost like a political prisoner, for his third album, *Me Against The World*, entered the *Billboard* chart at No.1 on 1 April 1995, while a single, 'Dear Mama' (devoted to Shakur's mother, ex-Black Panther Afeni Shakur), helped it score a double-platinum status inside the next six months.

It didn't stop there. *Vibe* magazine interviewed Shakur in jail the same month, and in the article Tupac showed a curiously split persona. On the one hand, he renounced his motto of 'Thug Life' (the letters were famously tattooed on his stomach as an acronym for The Hate You Give Little Infants Fucks Everybody), committing himself to spreading a positive message in future works. Simultaneously, however, he implicated rappers Biggie 'Notorious BIG' Smalls, Sean 'Puffy' Combs, Andre Harrell and Randy 'Stretch' Walker in his New York shooting, which had taken place the previous November. Four months later *Vibe* ran a feature in which Smalls, Combs and Harrell denied any involvement in the shooting.

The saga stepped up a notch in October, when Death Row Chief Executive Officer (CEO) Marion 'Suge' Knight posted a £1 million ($1.4 million) bond to release Shakur from jail, who immediately flew to LA, signed to Knight's label alongside Dr Dre, and began recording an album, *All Eyez On Me*. With the Death Row backing behind him, the situation appeared to be more than simply Shakur versus the Puffy/Biggie axis – it had become a case of Death Row against Combs' label, Bad Boy, with all the corporate power this would imply. The concept of East vs West seemed more plausible as a result, although it shouldn't be forgotten that the whole situation had arisen after Tupac had been shot by still-unidentified assailants, whose affiliations (whether to East, West or otherwise) remains unknown and cannot be presumed.

The summer had been an eventful one on a political level, then. But on the surface the hip-hop industry was flourishing, with the presence of key players never far from most media platforms. Least of all Ice Cube, who was rumoured to have entered the recording studio with a new project – not another solo album, but with a band (his first since the sporadically active Lench Mob, which had finally parted ways in 1994). A release was still some months away, according to industry insiders.

However, a select coterie of fans was able to content themselves in early June with the release of another Cube-featuring movie, *The Glass Shield*, although this time the rapper's role was even smaller than the supporting part he played in *Higher Learning*. Inexplicably, this film has hardly been seen, although its budget (£2.2/$3.13 million) was adequate and the production company (Miramax/Ciby 2000) and distribution company (Miramax) are all well-known movie industry names. Possibly the film's lack of impact was due to its international status (it had premiered in Switzerland and Canada in the summer/autumn 1994, perhaps because Ciby 2000 is a French company) or because audiences perceived it as an art-house or independent movie – which might make it seem too challenging for the average viewer.

It's certainly no smooth, effects-laden ride: this film requires some intellectual effort, and even then repays with a mixed dividend. It's the story of a young black police officer, JJ (played by TV actor Michael Boatman) whose first assignment on graduation is a posting to the LA Sheriff's Department. Initially full of naive enthusiasm for the cop life (the film opens with a series of colourful comic-book frames, indicating the character's idealistic love of the thin blue line), JJ tries hard to fit into the racist, lawless department, even to the extent that he perjures himself while testifying to the lawful arrest of an innocent man (Cube). However, the constant prejudice of his fellow officers towards him (and towards Deborah, a Jewish female officer played by Lori Petty) eventually opens his eyes and he makes the right decision, Justice is ultimately served, and the lesson is clear.

It's based on a true story – that of a real-life black officer called John Eddie Johnson – not that this fact made audiences any keener to see the film. Reviewers weren't crazy about it, either, blaming its lack of cohesion, the unnecessary complexity of the story line and the lack of detail given to the white officers (who are uniformly thuggish) for its failure as a box-office draw. Critic James Berardinelli wrote: 'One of the problems with *The Glass Shield* is that it settles for stock villains... the bad guys here are pretty much one-dimensional from start to finish. This lack of character depth blunts the film's impact. With the exception of the two protagonists and one token veteran officer, every cop is like the next: nasty, crude, and bigoted.' However, it's a worthy effort otherwise, he says. 'The film clearly has something worthwhile to say, and does so in a manner that, while not ground-breaking, is at least engaging. There just should have been a little more gray amidst the black-and-white.'

Mike Clark at *USA Today* was more impressed, commenting: 'This modest sleeper presents a marketing challenge to rival the movie year's significantly worthier tough sells... Though no masterpiece, the film is an interesting sidebar for moviegoers who try to keep up; it's like a '50s film noir oddity you catch on 3 a.m. TV, only to find that it's become a more scintillating view than *Ben-Hur*.'

The *Washington Post*'s Hal Hinson gave it the ultimate condemnation by comparing it unfavourably with TV police dramas, pointing out that 'It's a buyer's market as far as cop dramas go, and with shows such as *Homicide*, *Law & Order* and *NYPD Blue* around, Burnett's contribution can't compete with what's on television. That's because there is so little real electricity in the filmmaking and no special insight into police life.' But he showed a little charity by adding that '*The Glass Shield* certainly isn't brainless or empty; it has both ideas and a point of view. But the ideas are far from new, and the point of view is blatantly knee-jerk.'

Along with *Higher Learning*, this makes two Ice Cube movies panned by many critics for their too-brusque depiction of white-to-black racism: it seems that the reviewers (and possibly the public) had tired of street-perspective finger-wagging in the wake of the LA riots, and were preferring their anti-racist films to be a little more restrained.

How best to respond to this? Simply by accepting, perhaps, that they were at least partly right. As we have seen, the LA riots were not caused by one simple incident of racial injustice (although that was certainly their immediate precursor), and to continue dealing with the race issue with broad strokes was simply no longer an accurate way to depict the subject. On the other hand, it might be argued that the LA riots had highlighted societal ills to an unforeseen degree but, once they had died down, white America didn't want to be told about the problem any longer – which is clearly hypocritical.

The problem was compounded on 4 October 1995, when the nation was informed of the final decision of a US grand jury that one of the nation's sporting heroes, OJ Simpson, was not guilty of the murder of his ex-wife (Nicole Brown Simpson) and her friend (Ronald Goldman). Millions of Americans and Europeans had followed the case for several months, with no clear idea whether the ex-footballer turned actor was likely to have committed the crime or not. When the verdict came, many snorted in disbelief, while others rejoiced. Some commentators at the time noted that the dismissal was taken by some black communities as a victory against the legal system, with all that this implies. Oddly, Simpson was found 'liable for the deaths' of Smith and Goldman and ordered to pay over £5.6 million ($8 million) in damages – a situation which leaves most of the world not sure whether he committed the crime or not.

At the time, Ice Cube was interviewed by the journalist Jack Chance, who asked him: 'You've never shied away from the spotlight on issues, so what's your take on the OJ Simpson verdict?' Cube responded thoughtfully: 'OJ was found innocent in his criminal trial of killing these people, but he's still hated more than any serial killer I know of. For what? If you think he did it, OK. But evidently, this whole thing is nothing but a game.'

Warming to his theme, Cube continued: 'If you feel he has a lot of money, and that's what got him off, that's the game that's been laid down. Don't get mad at him for playing the game within the rules and winning – regardless of whether he did it or not. He played the game everybody has to play when they sit in that courtroom.'

It would appear that the truth has little part to play in Ice Cube's opinion on the legal system: 'Truth – really, who gives a damn about truth? It's all about *winning*. That's America. For all the good things about America, it's like a nice mansion that's filled with termites.'

The evocation of an outwardly gleaming, but inwardly corrupt society was appropriate. On 30 October 1995, Randy 'Stretch' Walker (one of the men whom Tupac Shakur had claimed was involved in his own shooting, exactly one year to the day before) was murdered in an execution-style shoot-out in the Queens district of New York. His killer remains unidentified, but his death was widely assumed to be a revenge attack for the shooting of Tupac, largely due to the significance of the date on which it occurred. Shakur's camp denied any involvement, but it was clear that the stakes had been raised and that the East–West situation might turn more bloody at any stage.

Tupac stayed in the news when *All Eyez On Me* was released by Death Row in February 1996, said to be the first double album released by a rap artist. Shakur then issued what has now been construed as the challenge which led to his ultimate downfall in a *Vibe* interview the same month, when he suggested that he had been sleeping with Biggie Smalls' wife, Faith Evans – who immediately dismissed the idea. Tensions between the two camps were made evident when, after the Soul Train Awards in Los Angeles the following month, some verbal sparring between the Death Row and Bad Boy retinues led to a gun being pulled.

Things had now got out of hand, it seemed, with observers comparing the current atmosphere with the gang warfare situation in LA that had prompted KRS-One to launch his Stop The Violence campaign in the late 1980s. Calls for a truce were ignored or dismissed and, in April 1996, Tupac even went on air in a radio interview with KMEL (radio station) to explain the situation.

He said: 'I can't change. I can't live a different lifestyle... [This] is it. This is the life that they gave and this is the life that I made. You know how they say, you made your bed, now lay in it? I tried to move... [Can't] move into some other bed. This is it. Not for the courts. Not for the parole board. Not for nobody. All I'm trying to do is survive and make good out of the dirty, nasty, unbelievable lifestyle that they gave me. I'm just trying to make something good out of that.

It's like if you try and plant something in the concrete... if it grows and the rose petals got all kind of scratches and marks, you're not gonna say, damn, look at all the scratches on the rose that grew from the concrete. You're gonna say, damn! A rose grew from the concrete! Well, that's the same thing with me. Folks should be sayin', damn! he grew out of all that?'

On 25 April it was announced that *All Eyez On Me* had gone quintuple platinum, an astounding achievement for a rap album or a double album, and especially a rap double album. But it seemed that Tupac was hell-bent on arousing yet more trouble: teaming up with Snoop Dogg, in May he released a single entitled '2 Of Amerikaz Most Wanted', which was accompanied by a video featuring caricatures of Biggie and Puffy being punished for their alleged role in Shakur's late 1994 shooting. The following month's 'Hit 'Em Up' single was even more explicit, attacking Biggie, Bad Boy, Mobb Deep and other associated acts.

By this stage, many American hip-hop fans had begun to tire of the constant bickering between the two camps and the column inches that the feud was taking up on the pages of the nation's more impressionable publications. Few, if any, listeners really understood the reason for the rivalry, and many of the hip-hop scene's veteran acts were urging both sides to withdraw before more blood was spilled. But it was to no avail – and thousands of music fans in many countries were profoundly shocked to hear, on 7 September 1996, that Tupac Shakur had been shot four times in the chest after the Mike Tyson–Bruce Seldon fight in Las Vegas. Shakur was sitting in the passenger seat of Suge Knight's black BMW when a white Cadillac drew up alongside and an unknown attacker sprayed the car with automatic fire.

Tupac was rushed to the University Medical Center and underwent immediate surgery, including the removal of his right lung. Knight was treated for a minor injury and released, but Shakur remained in critical condition.

While Tupac lay on life support and his family gathered at his bedside, a gang war had erupted in Los Angeles, focused primarily on the Compton and Lakewood areas. The reason for this is alleged to revolve around Blood and/or Crip involvement in the shooting. It's also rumoured that Knight had Blood connections, although neither report has ever been confirmed. Whatever the truth, a Compton man whom police said was associated with the Crips was the first victim, executed on 11 September. Snoop Dogg was asked by journalist Eric Berman if there was any truth to news reports that the war had started because Shakur's shooting broke a previous truce. The rapper replied, 'Fuck the news. They're gonna tell you what they want you to hear any motherfuckin' way.'

Two days later Tupac died, at the age of only 25. His death caused an explosion of conspiracy theories and fake-death rumours greater than any since the death of Elvis Presley 19 years before, with some fans claiming that a mass of evidence points to his continued survival – one of these is the fact that his middle name, Makaveli, can be rearranged to form 'mak alive' and sounds a bit like 'Machiavelli', the name of the devious Italian politician.

Many observers hoped that with Shakur gone, the East Coast/West Coast problem might go away, and for some time it seemed that this might prove to be the case, especially as Suge Knight was imprisoned shortly afterwards on charges of racketeering. Death Row wavered for some time (just as Ruthless had done after Eazy-E's death), but it was clear that the label was in trouble.

In Tupac's KMEL interview he had made several pronouncements that are now somewhat poignant in the light of his subsequent murder. His first point was to address his fans, saying, 'I love y'all... [Don't] let this East Coast–West Coast thing get to you.' He took pains to explain that his anger was not directed at the East Coast in its entirety, which had been his original home in any case, but with Biggie Smalls, who had been elected unofficial leader of the scene. He explained, 'I worked hard all my life...to bring about East Coast–West Coast love and make everybody feel comfortable. I dreamed of the day when I could go to New York and feel comfortable and they could come out here and be comfortable', and that 'As soon as the East Coast separate themselves from Biggie we will do shows in the East.'

He had concrete plans for East Coast business, it turned out. 'Now let's go to the table. Let's talk. Let's make peace. Let's work it out. Let's give the community the money... We're about to start Death Row East with Eric B and all the OG niggas out there. We got Big Daddy Kane, Christopher Williams, we're trying to get Bobby Brown.' Tupac's (and presumably, Suge Knight's) plans for national domination might have created a network of unprecedented proportions – *exactly* as Eazy-E, Tupac's predecessor in many ways, had prophesied back in 1994.

Shakur went on: 'We're trying to get the East Coast Death Row to be like the West Coast Death Row and make it major. We're not doing that until we get this business settled. Even while we're doing this, we're trying to get Wu-Tang. I feel as though they represent the East Coast the way we represent the West Coast, and I love them.' Once again he reiterated that he wanted the struggle to be resolved: 'I'm calling for dialogue. I'm gathering attention for dialogue which is what you do in a struggle for power.'

Most resounding was Tupac's answer to the question, 'Five years from now, what do you see yourself doing?' The rapper paused before answering, 'I see myself having a job on Death Row...being the A&R person and an artist that drop an album...every five years. I'll have my own production company which I'm close to right now. I'm doing my own movies. I'm starting to put out some calendars for charity. I'm gonna start a little youth league in California so we can start playing some East Coast teams...some Southern teams... I wanna have like a Pop Warner League except the rappers fund it and they're the head coaches. Have a league where you can get a big trophy with diamonds in it for a nigga to stay drug free and stay in school. That's the only way you can be on the team. We'll have fun and eat pizza and have the finest girls there and throw concerts at the end of the year. That's what I mean by giving back.'

With these words Shakur sounded not like a man with a vendetta to accomplish, but like a philanthropist with goals for his community: his assassination was a shocking, pointless waste of a life and one which should have shamed the hip-hop community into action. But the West and the East were far from reconciled, and one of the reasons why the feud was prolonged came (entirely inadvertently, it should be stressed) from none other than Ice Cube. Ice confirmed rumours of a new beginning by surfacing from his self-imposed exile in Hollywood in November 1996 with a new group called Westside Connection, who released a single and album of the same title – *Bow Down*.

The reasons for the presumption that Ice was adding to the East–West feud are simple to understand. It's all in the name – Westside. But Cube's choice of name for his new band wasn't a simple allegiance cry in the bicoastal war: he told various members of the press that the patented cry of 'Westside!' that populated the grooves referred to his origin in the West Side of LA, and wasn't a reference to the country in general. The band was a trio – Cube was joined by Mack 10 and WC (of WC and the Madd Circle, Coolio's old band) – all of whom had Western roots, it emerged.

Cube told journalist Billy Jam of the *Bay Guardian* that the whole thing was a misunderstanding: 'Doing that record it looked like we were siding with Death Row and Tupac against Puffy and Bad Boy, but that's not the case. And never did we want to see any brothers get hurt or killed. We was throwing the W sign long before that feud.' He also told *Music Monitor* that 'The Westside Connection project was the most misunderstood project that I've ever released, because it got caught in a whirlwind of Death Row versus Bad Boy, and it seemed like we were all in cahoots, all together on those issues, like we were down with what was going on at Death Row and not down with Bad Boy. That's not true.' It was also pointed out at the time that West Coast stalwart Snoop Dogg (who is from the east of LA) had a habit of making E gestures with his fingers, and had even formed a band called the EastSidas. The same misunderstanding may well have been made in the tense atmosphere following Tupac's death.

Yet there *was* a clear element of anti-East Coast feeling in the record, too – one of the songs was called 'All The Critics In New York' ('Fuck all the critics in the NYC/And your articles trying to rate my LP') and another, 'King Of The Hill', slammed Cypress Hill with the words 'You hip-hop hippies/How you fuckin' junkies/Think you gonna punk me?' No wonder people were confused when Cube disowned any rumours of adding fuel to the fire. But he later explained it more clearly with these words: 'I'm not really tripping on straight being from the West Coast. But when I was doing it, I heard a lotta shit being said about the West Coast, so I stood up for the West Coast.'

In other words, the band was formed and already recording in 1995 and 1996 when the coasts starting warring. Angered by the anti-west sentiments coming out of the East, Cube included a couple of songs relating to the rivalry even though the original intention of the band had not been associated with it.

Cube explained the anger he had felt towards the hypocrisy of certain media players in the East: 'If [the East Coast media] diss a DJ Quik record but praise a Biggie Smalls record, and say gangsta rap is over and played out, and then a dude comes out and does the same [kind of music] and gets all the praise, well then we gotta stand up and say, hold up! We see what's going on here! Someone's trying to pull the rug out from under us and basically shut us out of the market.' He later observed: 'Our whole purpose from the beginning was to make sure that people wasn't gonna just snatch our style from under us and give us no credit and no props.'

It sounds as if Cube was concerned that the East was trying to steal the West's trademark laid-back sound: 'The record was put in place because I felt that we were not only starting to get dissed for the kind of music we were doing, but they would diss us for using "bitch", "hoe", whatever we would do, and praise East Coast artists for doing the same thing. And I felt that we were getting the music stolen out from under us,' he told *Music Monitor*.

Even his cherished position in the East (gained back in 1990 when he chose the Bomb Squad to produce his first album) couldn't stop him from attacking the NY critics: 'I just couldn't sit back, even with my status on the East Coast. I don't have a problem, but my fellow rappers do. And I was sick of the potshots being taken with records like "Fuck Compton" and stuff like that, for no reason. I felt like it was on my shoulders to represent the West Coast, tell everybody we love the West Coast, and then people took it so personal, like just because we love the West Coast we aren't down with the East Coast. But we all grew up on East Coast music, all bump it. Still bump it to this day, we just wanted people to give credit where credit was due.'

The roots of Cube's feud with Cypress Hill are complex – but it's clear why he chose to record 'King Of The Hill'. In 1995 the East Coast trio had released their third album, *III: Temples Of Boom*, a funky, well-crafted album which contained a song called 'No Rest For The Wicked'. This stated in no uncertain terms that Cube was not among Cypress Hill's favourite characters – some lines accused him of stealing their style ('Doughboy rolling down the Hill 'cause it's all steep/Jackson, lemme figure out the name/Jack 'cause you be stealing other niggaz game' and 'Yeah nigga, my homie thought he had a homie in you/He let you listen to our muthafuckin' cut, and you turned around and put some old Friday shit out'); others accused him of being merely a 'studio gangsta' ('You put a pipe on your cover, even though you don't smoke buddha' and 'Never used to bang 'til you hit the microphone/I got Cube melting in a tray/Pulling up his card and fucking up his good day'); others pointed to his disrespect to fellow artists ('Talk about Eazy, correct yourself/Cube better sit back and check himself'); and still others resorted to simple threats of violence (('I got a can of kick-ass wit' your mothafuckin' name on it Cube. You wanna come collect it, or should I bring it to you? 'Cause all that bullshit you doin', ain't shit fly about that shit' and 'Don't trust that nigga named O'Shea/Fuck him, and send him on his way').

Asked to explain their vendetta by *Addicted To Noise* magazine, Cypress Hill's B-Real said: 'What we're trying to do with Cube is make him an example. This is the typical muthafucker you have to look out for, because not only will he steal from you, he's slowly instigating this East Coast–West Coast rivalry which is slowly going to deteriorate the whole rap community. He's one of a handful of platinum artists from the West Coast who have a lot of say-so in this rap industry among the public, fans and all that shit. A lot of people listen to him. We're not taking either side; we're just saying, don't take this muthafucker seriously. All he's trying to do is separate the coasts while we've been trying to get them together.'

This was no mere rivalry, B-Real continued – the future of the hip-hop scene was at stake: 'For us, it ain't about West Coast or East Coast; the hip-hop community needs to stick together. We're getting under fire by Congress, by Dole, by Gingrich... [When] they see us do this ignorant shit, they're like, see...they're fighting amongst themselves.' However, there was a personal beef here, too: 'We're dissing him for what he's done to us. But now it's like a snowball... [It's] been rolling and building up. It's not just a ploy to sell records. Fuck that... We're not the only one he's stolen from. He's stolen from people who don't even have a deal, who can't even get a deal. They were just kicking ideas to him, he takes 'em, doesn't give them the money or credit.'

DJ Muggs continued the story in an interview with *Cypress Hill Connection*. 'All that Islam shit was fake, man. Cube's a real smart, intelligent man. All the concepts on his first album came from JD of the Lench Mob. I was bugging one day, 'cos JD was talking a lot of shit about Cube. He was saying that Cube took his song titles. At that time I didn't really trust JD, 'cos I had just met Ice Cube and he seemed cool. So when Cube got down with the Nation on his *Death Certificate* album, that was all Kam's shit. That was Kam's whole idea. Kam put him down with the Nation. I guess Cube ran out of ideas, so on his third album he jumped on the Cypress Hill dick. I say that because he called me and asked me to do about six songs. I said that I was only going to give him three, because I had the rest for the Cypress album.'

The accusations got worse, and more specific. 'Cube flows with whoever's hot,' continued the DJ. 'When Ice-T was hot with "Six In The Morning", he wrote "Boyz In The Hood" for Eazy-E. Chuck D was hot, so he jumped on that. The funk shit was hot, so he jumped on that. We was hot, so he jumped on that.' Muggs then recounted a story that had taken place around the time of the *Predator* album, on which he had assisted Cube: 'Now I had this skull pipe that a girl had given me, that I'd been smoking for the last three days. He kept asking me for the pipe, so I gave it to him, it was only about five dollars [three pounds] anyway. All of a sudden his album cover was him on the front with my pipe. I thought, man, this nigga's phoney!' He also claimed that Cube or his associates had tried to do him out of royalties on his work and that the feud between Cube and B-Real had led to the two having a physical confrontation and ultimately a phone call from Cube, who said: 'Yo, we rich, man. I ain't got nothing personal about you. I just had to do a song about you because you did a song about me. I think we should be cool.' The argument was then resolved, according to Muggs.

And so Westside Connection found an uneasy niche. But many interviewers wondered why had he formed a band at all. 'I was tired of doing solo albums. I wanted to feel the group thing. With me, Mack 10 and WC, our chemistry was so tight that the Westside Connection was born,' he said in an interview with *Throttlebox*, while he told writer Jack Chance that 'It's hard hitting that stage by yourself every night – especially when you come from a group. You miss that. The competition between each other is unsaid, but you can feel it. You're competing at something that takes skill. It takes skills to rhyme. If you don't polish them skills off people that can do it as good as you, you might lose touch.'

The album itself is a solid, rather than scintillating, listen. Its high points are undoubtedly the title track and a cover of Funkadelic's 'One Nation Under A Groove', featuring a guest vocal from George Clinton. It's the beats that drive this album, rather than the samples (although the record notably features a fragment from the Nine Inch Nails song 'Hurt' on 'The Gangsta, The Killa And The Dope Dealer'), making it a favourite listen for the old school but less so for those more enamoured of Dre/*Predator*-style G-Funk. Reviews were mostly positive, with *The Source* of December 1996 awarding it 4.5 out of 5 and stating: '*Bow Down* is the best Ice Cube-related project in years – 10 tracks and three skits of well-executed and tightly produced songs... All three Westside Connection MCs put their all into this.' *Rolling Stone* gave it 3.5 out of 5 and explained: 'Ice Cube is one of the few rap artists... [Still] capable of making you think, even if you don't agree with a word he says.'

And so Cube accidentally rocked the hip-hop boat at one of its most fragile moments. Although the scene would gradually regain some stability, a couple of players were still to fall before the war would be over – and one of these was Death Row Records, which lost the jewel in its crown, Dr Dre, at around this time. With Tupac dead, Knight in prison, Snoop's second album not selling as well as its predecessor, and now Dre away, the label was a shadow of its former self, although it remains active in some form or other to this day.

Dre left to form a new label, Aftermath Entertainment, which suffered a little at the outset from two less-than-stirring releases – one a Firm album and the other a compilation bearing the label's name. However, his fortunes (and that of the label) were to reverse dramatically the following year, after he witnessed the closing rounds of the Rap Coalition's 1997 Rap Olympics competition. The silver-medal winner had shocked everybody who had seen his performance – because he was a geeky, dark-haired white kid from Detroit. The youth, named Marshall Mathers, was a diminutive, whiny-voiced father of one, and was struggling to stay above the breadline, but had managed to scrape enough cash together to record a cassette EP and send it to the office of the Interscope Records chairman Jimmy Iovine. Dre happened to be visiting Iovine and wandered into the industry mogul's garage, where the cover of the cassette caught his eye. He picked it up, slipped it into a tape player and pressed 'Play'.

Or, as Mathers later reported it to *Addicted To Noise* (much later, after he'd bleached his hair and changed his name to Eminem), 'He said the cover just caught his eye, and he just picked it up and just popped it in. And was like, "Where's this dickhead at?"' This 'dickhead', apparently, had something which impressed Dre, who called him up, brought him to the studio, signed him to Aftermath, co-wrote and produced three tracks on an album called *The Slim Shady LP*, and then sat back and watched as history was made.

As well as discovering and then mentoring the most controversial rap act in history, Dre also found time to team up with Ice Cube once again. The two rappers had considered a joint project for some time and the result, created when both men had sufficient time to record it and shoot a video, was a single entitled 'Natural Born Killaz'. It was a bleak, pessimistic song, all downtempo beats and gruff raps, narrated from the perspective of a serial murderer. Dre begins with the ominous (but somehow slightly ridiculous) 'Journey with me into the mind of a maniac/Doomed to be a killer since I came out the nutsack', and goes on to promise, 'Decapitatin', I ain't hesitatin' to put you in the funeral home/With a bullet in your dome'. Cube comes in with 'So fuck how you're livin'/I'm the unforgivin'/Psycho drivin' murderer' and consolidates the grim message with words guaranteed to offend somebody: 'I'm a pull a fuckin' Jeffrey Dahmer/Now I'm suicidal, just like Nirvana'. It's a powerful, fearful song, and its accompanying promo clip was the same – all futuristic sets and faded colours.

As the song rose and fell from the charts, the primary hip-hop players from both sides of the country were showing signs of wanting to patch things up. Relations were still frayed, so the idea was conceived that the two men most involved in the dispute in the absence of Suge Knight and Tupac Shakur – Snoop Dogg and Sean 'Puffy' Combs – would appear in public together. In February 1997, therefore, the two rappers made a cameo appearance on the Warner Brothers TV sitcom *The Steve Harvey Show*. The plot ran as follows: each man requested permission from Harvey's character, a schoolteacher, to use samples from his old band, a group called the Hi-Tops, in a song. Harvey refused permission to either man, 'until you make up your differences'. Both then explained that the entire East–West rivalry was nothing but a media invention. The show was duly taped and broadcast, with both men being friendly to each other and everything going as planned.

But in the violent world of gangsta rap (and its variants) nothing can be relied upon to go smoothly and on 8 March 1997 – just six months and a day after his nemesis, Tupac Shakur, had been gunned down in Vegas – Biggie Smalls was murdered in Los Angeles. Like Tupac, Biggie was sitting in a car (in this case, a GMC Suburban utility vehicle) at the time of the attack, 12:35pm; like Tupac, he was leaving a high-profile event at the time (he had been attending a party at the Petersen Automotive Museum on the Miracle Mile in the Wilshire district, in honour of the 11th Soul Train Music Awards ceremony); and, like Tupac, he was engaged in promoting a new album – called, bizarrely, *Life After Death*. He was pronounced dead on arrival at the

Cedars-Sinai Medical Center. His estranged wife, Faith Evans, who was pregnant with his twins, witnessed the attack.

And so the last victim of the Bad Boy/Death Row feud, which had escalated to the extent where people were referring to a national civil war, met his end. The rivalry died with him. A short time later, the Nation of Islam was asked to act as mediator in a truce, which was agreed over a 'Day Of Atonement' on the neutral ground of Chicago. The injured parties met and shook hands: Biggie's family received a letter of condolence from the family of Tupac Shakur, and all those involved agreed that a similar situation should never be allowed to develop again.

It's almost tempting to add 'And they all lived happily ever after', except, of course, that we know that this is unlikely to be the case.

10 Monsters, Movies And Monster Movies

With the deaths of Tupac Shakur and Biggie Smalls, the hip-hop world had lost two of its most prominent spokesmen at a stroke – performers whose only equal in marketing terms were a select group of acts such as Dr Dre, Ice Cube, Puffy (who was now going by the name Puff Daddy), the Wu-Tang Clan, Bone Thugs-N-Harmony and one or two newcomers who were about to make their mark, like Eminem. Many of the community's most outspoken artists withdrew a little from the scene, hoping that the tension would pass.

Critics were still on the lookout for headline-worthy news, of course. Ice Cube himself was noticed to have employed a couple of bodyguards at one or two public events, but explained this to Louis Hobson of the *Calgary Sun* as an occasional decision: 'They're not with me 24 hours a day, or every day of the week for that matter. They've been with me for years. It's not something I've initiated since the deaths of Tupac and B.I.G.' His reasoning was sound: 'I don't watch my back any more or any less than I ever did. A violent death isn't something you can dodge easily.'

When asked for a statement about the murders of the two rappers, Cube replied: 'They were good friends and great artists. Their deaths are hard to take. I'm not over them yet. A lot of brothers know only too well that you don't have to sell a million records to get murdered. It's a fact of life in the ghettos.' As for the role of gangsta rap, he observed that 'It's here to stay, and that's an important thing. It's down-and-dirty but it's socially conscious. That's why it is so necessary.'

Ice expanded on the subject a little more in an interview with

Addicted To Noise, whose journalist asked him how the deaths of Tupac and Biggie had affected him: 'The impact of Biggie's, Tupac's deaths... Well, it had an impact. But I hear about a lot of death. I hear about a lot of death – not only death in the streets, but friends, family – those deaths. So I can't say it took me to where I had to go soul-searching, or that it was a big revelation in my life. It's something that's real tragic.' As for the causes of the deaths, he mused: 'They don't have anything to do with each other. I don't believe Tupac's death has anything to do with Biggie Smalls', and I don't think Biggie Smalls' has anything to do with Tupac. They were so public that when these people died, that was the effect – the perception that *rap* caused these deaths. That was really the biggest effect, that the fans took it like rap caused these deaths. And I don't think that's true. I kind of looked at that – if they think that's true – we gotta roll with it. If they believe rap caused this, then we as rappers gotta figure out how can we gain the trust of our fans.'

On 8 April 1998 Cube told Barry Koltnow at the *Orange County Register* that 'Being from the West Coast, I naturally expressed my pride in the West Coast and that hurt me a little on the East Coast. But I sometimes push unpopular opinions, so I was cool with that... But, when the murders started, I did get a little nervous. I thought at first it was a hit on rappers, and I was a popular rapper. I couldn't help but wonder if I was a target. Now that we know differently, I think it has had an impact on the rap world in a way we didn't realize in the beginning. It brought everybody down to earth. The murders showed how the real world works. It showed that no matter what you do in this life, you can't put yourself above the world. We're all mortal and I think that is something that we all need to remember.'

Always a man willing to view the wider picture, Cube himself couldn't help being pulled into a minor slanging match at this time, despite his words of wisdom. For the first time outside the NWA camp, Ice Cube perceived himself to be under critical fire from another hip-hop act – although the feud appears, with hindsight, to have arisen through a simple misunderstanding. The rapper in question was Common Sense, a Chicago resident who had released a couple of well-crafted albums in the mid-1990s and shortened his name to Common in 1995.

One of his songs, 'I Used To Love H.E.R.', included the line 'but then she broke to the West Coast, and that was cool/Cause around the same time, I went away to school'. Ice Cube is said to have heard this and, assuming that it was intended as a snub to the West Coast in general, included the line 'used to love her mad cause we fucked/Her pussy-whipped bitch with no common sense/Hip-hop started in the West' in a guest rap on Mack 10's 'Westside Slaughterhouse'. However, no anger was necessary – in 'I Used To Love H.E.R.', Common was referring to hip-hop in general and included the line about 'going away to school' simply to indicate that he had missed out on the West Coast period of dominance.

But it was too late – Common heard 'Westside Slaughterhouse' and recorded an answer track called 'The Bitch In Yoo' on an album, *Relativity Urban Assault*. The opening lines ran as follows: 'A bitch nigga with an attitude named Cube/Step to Com with a feud/Now what the fuck I look like dissing a whole coast/You ain't made shit dope since *Amerikkka's Most*'. The rest of the song cast slurs on Cube's management and rapping skills, and added a snide mention of his Hollywood career with the words, 'Get some beats besides George Clinton to rock over/Rap career is over, better off acting'. Cube didn't respond in rhyme to this specific barrage of insults but, in the wake of the murders, both parties realised that an extended feud could only lead to ill-consequences for all concerned and, once more, the Nation of Islam conducted a peace negotiation.

The wider consequences of this short-lived argument, plus the rumours that had started with the formation of Westside Connection, meant that many observers counted Cube as part and parcel of the East–West rivalry, which was now close to extinct and would have vanished had it not been for minor scuffles such as this. Worse, Cube's own unique position as an artist with a fanbase in both the East and West was suffering because of it. As Cypress Hill's B-Real later concluded, 'Common Sense came up with that one song where [he] dissed the West Coast and certain artists over here didn't take too well to that, especially Ice Cube...which kinda fucked him up in a way, because he had a lot of love from the East Coast people.'

Ironically, it was at this time that Ice Cube was tackling his first wholly serious leading role. The film *Dangerous Ground*, which opened in the USA on 12 February 1997, was a tale with a solid political message behind it and, coupled with its 'name' director – Darrell Roodt, who had made his name with *Cry The Beloved Country* two years before – it looked set to be the film that might finally establish Cube as a respected actor.

It's the story of Vusi Madlazi, a South African man who was forced to flee the country as a teenager after being persecuted by police after a demonstration against apartheid. After 13 years in America – where he has grown into manhood, shed his original accent and become a student of African literature and an inner-city teacher – Vusi returns to the post-Mandela South Africa to attend his father's funeral. Meeting one of his brothers, Ernest, he is told that their other brother, Stephen, has disappeared in Johannesburg, where it is feared that he has fallen into shady circles.

Vusi travels to Johannesburg to find his brother, only to be car-jacked in Soweto by a black gang (his query of 'Why you botherin' me?... We supposed to be brothers!' causes a round of hysterical laughter, to his bemusement). Another culture shock comes at his father's funeral, when tradition dictates that he must slit the throat of a cow: accustomed to Western ways, he can't bring himself to do it and declares: 'I left as an African. I came back as an American.'

After some disturbing scenes of the new urban South Africa (the streets are violent, racist places haunted by neo-Nazis), Vusi eventually encounters his brother's crack-addict girlfriend (played a little unconvincingly by the flawlessly made-up Elizabeth Hurley) and frees him from the clutches of a sadistic drugs baron, Muki (Ving Rhames). The rest of the plot concerns a war against the drug gangs and Vusi's eventual return with his brother.

Jack Chance asked Cube some penetrating questions about *Dangerous Ground*, and received some revealing answers – including the fact that Cube and Darrell Roodt had had initial problems working together. 'It's just basic communication. He's a white guy from South Africa. I'm a black guy from South Central. I felt that before we could make a picture together, we had to have a certain respect for each other. I fought for that... You know, I had to do some rewriting of the script, too. There were certain things in the script I wasn't going to do. I'm not going to elaborate on which scenes they were, but I told him that, and I said we were going to have to rewrite it, and that's what happened.'

Ice was also emotionally involved in his character's far-from-home situation. 'It's hard for me to be away from home. I'm not a person who has to travel, who has to be all over the world. It's cool to visit a place, but when you have to stay there and shoot for eight weeks, it's harder. I was in awe of the beauty of the place and the people, and it was very difficult for me to adjust. I was actually going through the same things my character was going through... [You] feel your soul has seen something your body has never seen. When we were coming into South Africa, we flew across Africa for about eight or nine hours, and I couldn't wait to land and see if I felt what I thought I was going to feel. And I did.'

Cube took away a clearer picture of what South Africa was actually like: 'You pick up any books on South Africa, and they'll never really show you what's going on. When I got there, and I saw that this was true, that made me attached to the part even more. A lot of people see South Africa in these apartheid movies, but they never really see the cities. The new South Africa has the old problems.' And the drugs-war theme of the film is global, of course: 'If [US drug culture] is changing, it's for the worse. Our appetite for drugs is the problem. That people even want to be on drugs, that's the deeper problem.'

As an actor, Cube was slowly beginning to find his way. Chance asked him if he was confident about his first leading role. 'Not as confident as I would like to be,' came the answer. 'As an actor, there's a lot still that I need to learn, a lot of things I need to develop. With every movie I do, I get a better comfort zone... I don't bring qualities from my music into my movies. I'm starting to take acting as serious as I take records.'

The film was a mixed success. Most reviewers lamented the fact that Roodt's portrayal of the American/African culture clash (epitomised by the cow-slaying issue, for example) was abandoned so soon in favour of a formulaic action-movie story, although many enjoyed the director's skilful evocation of modern South Africa and its terrible problems. However, many critics were divided about the performance of Cube, whose work in previous roles had always been praised as solid, even where the accompanying vehicle was not (as in *Trespass* and *Friday*). This was a worrying departure, and one that may have made Cube think more carefully about his later choice of film.

Roger Ebert said in the *Chicago Sun-Times* that '*Dangerous Ground* begins with a promising idea and runs away from it as fast as it can... Ice Cube delivers [his] lines with a bluntness that is supposed to pass for a performance, but there's little sense here that he's playing a character – certainly not a "student of African literature and community volunteer". He seems more like a tourist who has wandered into an action picture.' There's some truth to his assessment that the film tries too hard to appeal to Western audiences, too: '*Dangerous Ground* seems to be an attempt to make an American-style action film and sneak some South African stuff in sideways. That's a doomed approach... Canada could have had a much healthier film industry if it hadn't tried to be a little Hollywood, and the films of Australia and England are thriving right now because they are local, particular and about something other than canned action scenes.'

A little harsh? Perhaps. Reviewer James Berardinelli praises Cube as 'a forceful screen presence... Over a series of movies from *Boyz N The Hood* to *The Glass Shield*, Cube has carefully honed his acting abilities to the point where his off-screen persona no longer eclipses the role he's playing'. However, he is less charitable about the movie itself: 'While the film gets off to a promising start, it eventually devolves into a typical, formula-driven revenge thriller whose characters become progressively less intelligent as the body count rises.' In common with most critics, he concludes that the film's standard action-movie finish is the most disappointing part of it: 'The final half-hour could have taken place in almost any city around the globe, using stock characters.

Dangerous Ground never lives up to the promise and potential it shows during its opening moments.'

Barry Walters of the *San Francisco Examiner* found *Dangerous Ground* ludicrous, labelling it 'essentially a 90s blaxploitation film that skimps on the goofy fun essential to the genre...but this movie could have been so much funnier as a comedy, instead of a vaguely political drama that only its director could take seriously'. And its leading actor? 'Cube, however, is deadly. Not in the literal sense, like his off-screen gangsta persona would leave you to believe, but as in deadly dull. Rarely does Cube's face register an emotion, and his delivery is mostly just cranky... Now he gives the impression that what he wants most is to pick up his paycheck.' Ouch...

But Ice Cube has always split critics with his acting style. With his unlearned, almost naive approach, his on-screen moves are honest and unforced to the point where he seems almost laid-back at times. This earned him enormous plaudits in *Boyz N The Hood*, of course, when the primary emotion he was required to give of Doughboy was a kind of smouldering apathy. *Friday* was also a good example of a scenario where his brooding presence was more important than any physical dynamism – and in that film his slumped thoughtfulness added a touch of humour to his role.

This is not to say, of course, that Cube can't move rapidly with the best of them – in *Trespass*, for example, he was required to play a gun-slinging thug with plenty of speed and a certain panache. But, just as in his music, a threatening, impassive role suits him best – and *Dangerous Ground* required a different persona entirely, an enthusiastic, cocksure character whose inexperience lets him down. No wonder some critics found him too emotionless: he's a thinker, and that doesn't make for the most dynamic of actors.

In box-office terms, *Dangerous Ground* wasn't a big hit, but it wasn't a flop either, with a respectable stream of cinema-goers ensuring that it made back its budget. It's possible that the era of great world/political movies – think *Gandhi, Biko* and Roodt's own *Cry The Beloved Country* – was also in hiatus at the time. The blockbuster was king – 1997 was the year when *Titanic* famously resurfaced to make a clean sweep at the Oscars, while light-hearted fare such as *Men In Black* and *Jurassic Park II: The Lost World* swept up the remaining movie audiences. Even the action movies against which *Dangerous Ground* was competing were more glamorous than Roodt's film could ever hope to be. Pit the futuristic glitter of John Woo's *Face/Off* or the honed suavity of the Bond film *Tomorrow Never Dies* against an anti-apartheid movie set in dusty South Africa, and what do you get? An instant knockout for the special-effects wizards.

In case this sounds like too much of a protest, bear this in mind: the film was attempting to convey a message, and not an easy one at that. To dismiss Cube's performance as too stiff, or Roodt's script as falling between two stools, is to miss the wider point, which is that this movie made a valiant effort to succeed against almost insuperable odds. Perhaps it should be given a second chance.

It's ironic, then, that Cube's next project should be the most ridiculously kitsch movie he had ever appeared in – and, in fact, one of the cheesiest films ever made. On 11 April 1997, after the Los Angeles gunfire had died down, the rap scene had retreated to lick its wounds and *Dangerous Ground* had been all but forgotten, posters went up all over America with the tag lines 'You can't scream if you can't breathe', 'It will take your breath away' or simply 'It's a scream!' The text overlaid an enormous, scaly head, with inhuman eyes and a forked tongue. Alongside the names of Ice Cube, Jennifer Lopez, Eric Stoltz and Jon Voight, there appeared the movie's title – *Anaconda*.

Not since *Friday* had Ice Cube appeared in a film with so little pretensions towards significance or good taste; not since *Trespass* had he been required to perform in so many stunt sequences; and, what's more, he was finally in a film with some money behind it. *Anaconda* director Luis 'The Specialist' Llosa had £25 million ($35 million) to spend, much of which went on funding the computer-generated images of the film's central character, a monstrous snake. The cost of making the movie on location in Las Vegas, California and Manaus (in the Amazon rainforest in Brazil) was also a considerable outlay.

The story line is not complex. A film crew head into the rainforest intent on making a documentary about 'the People of the Mist...one of the last great mysteries of the rainforest'. The standard horror/action movie cast are all present and correct: there's the nerdy anthropologist, Steve Cale (Stoltz), the voluptuous director, Terri Flores (Lopez), the hard-case cameraman Danny (Cube), and secondary characters including an annoying (and doomed) British narrator, a sound man and a production assistant. On a bend in the river they rescue from his wrecked ship a mysterious snake expert, Paul Sarone (Voight), who, after Cale is rendered comatose by the sting of a giant jungle wasp, steadily assumes command of the film-makers' ship.

Sarone's agenda – a search for a legendary mega-snake, which subsequently begins stalking them – becomes apparent as the fatalities mount up, and the film becomes a struggle between the humans and the eponymous beast. I'll let you discover the ending for yourself, but be advised that Cube, Stoltz and Lopez are the sole survivors after several extremely close shaves indeed, with the scene where the snake vomits up the still-alive but semi-digested body of Sarone a particularly memorable moment. We are warned that this may occur in the opening frame of the movie, when a scientific note informs us that anacondas are in the habit of regurgitating their prey in order to consume more food.

Director Llosa was interested in the symbolism of the snake as much as its tendency to make audiences' hair stand on end: 'When I read *Anaconda*,' he said, 'I thought it had an intriguing, scary story that could keep the audience on the edge of their seats... There was also an aspect of peeking into the dark side of human beings, which interested me.' A Peruvian by birth, he pointed out that the location was no joke: 'To film in the heart of the Amazon jungle, with the hardships and all the problems that conveys, is in itself a challenge... I scouted other locations but in the Amazon you see a great variation of places, every five minutes in a boat you're seeing spectacular locations. For me, that was very difficult to reproduce someplace else.'

The filming was certainly eventful, although the veteran Voight kept the cast's mood positive, according to Lopez: 'He was always so helpful, with such incredible insight into the art of film-making. He knew so much about so many elements, from how to play to the camera to how to work stunts, the kind of knowledge that only comes with experience and from doing as many movies and winning as many awards as he has.' Yes – but even Voight had never appeared on screen covered in reptilian digestive juices before...

As always, Ice Cube had a perceptive comment to make: 'I hate snakes, to be honest... Political snakes are pretty much the same as the kind of snakes we deal with in this movie. So, I knew what I was going to be dealing with; these snakes are just coming from a different angle.' Confident words, although he later revealed that in one scene he and Lopez were caught in the coils of an enormous mechanical snake (used for scenes where computer-generated animation was inappropriate or impossible), and it started to malfunction: 'There was this power surge and for a minute, they didn't have control of this thing, which was like 2000 pounds [900kg] of momentum, moving like a real snake... It was like fantasy and reality merging. This snake is the best animatronic thing I've ever seen in my life.'

It wasn't just the machinery that kept Cube on edge, either. The pleasures of the rainforest came a little too close for comfort sometimes, as he told MTV: 'The attendants at our hotel in the Brazilian jungle caught an anaconda under the porch. While they were wrestling with it, the thing spit up an alligator it had swallowed... I love Los Angeles. I'm not a nature person. Cell phones and traffic I can deal with. Snakes, spiders and monkeys are another thing altogether.'

After five weeks of Brazilian heat and humidity, Cube and some of the others were starting to feel the strain, and even talked about making an early departure: 'The mutiny!' he exclaimed. 'Yeah, some of the young actors were getting real testy, you know... Brazil's a beautiful place, sunsets, toucans flying over your head. That part of nature was cool. But the fact was you couldn't leave, you couldn't go home, and I had so much business going on here. Trying to get through on the phone lines, some days you might get through, some days you might not. Things like that just made it so hard. And the conditions doing the movie! An action adventure movie!' Luckily, Voight was on hand to pour oil on troubled waters: 'Jon loved it. He didn't care if we spent nine months at that location... [He said] you're doing a movie, you're getting paid a lot of money, so stop complaining, you know what I mean?'

The result was an entertaining, if slightly gruesome and fully forgettable movie. In the great tradition of monster movies stretching back as far as *King Kong*, *Godzilla* and *Planet Of The Apes*, the shock-horror element of the film makes it simultaneously gripping and laughable – and this particular film is as self-parodic as it is fast-moving, with the up-puked Voight even throwing a hammy wink directly to the camera as he emerges from the anaconda's throat.

Plausibility (even outside the supposed existence of a 25m/80ft reptile) was also less than spot-on, with audiences noticing several gaffes – such as the fact that Voight manages to outswim a boat after being stabbed and beaten with a golf club, that an explosion powerful enough to take out a whole factory barely singes the snake inside it, and that an enormous tree falls on the hapless film-makers' boat but has conveniently vanished in the next scene, allowing them to sail away to safety.

More tolerant film-goers didn't care about all this, of course, but one or two reviewers couldn't stomach the film at all. The *Toronto Sun*'s Liz Braun caustically concluded that 'What, if anything, is interesting about the movie…is that it involves filmmakers and movie-making within a movie. The moral of *Anaconda* seems to be that the evil the characters encounter and the disasters that occur are all triggered by…their irreverence for, and ignorance of, the world they've stumbled into. That would make the fictional filmmakers and the *Anaconda* filmmakers just about even.'

However, the *San Francisco Chronicle*'s Mick LaSalle didn't mind that: 'To watch *Anaconda* is to get the impression that there is only one snake in the entire rainforest, and that it's been waiting its whole life for a chance to devour Eric Stoltz, Jennifer Lopez and Ice Cube', making the observation that all right-minded viewers would also make – that '*Anaconda* is so desperate and silly that here and there, it's a lot of fun.'

By any standards, *Anaconda* is a no-brainer movie, so why did Ice Cube agree to do it? It's obvious that he did it with a clear sense of its insignificance – his first line is 'No – it was a good day', for example, a little piece of *Predator* conceit that Llosa must have allowed him to get away with. He told the production company's Website that 'I am a great fan of movies like *Jaws* and *Indiana Jones*. I saw doing *Anaconda* as a chance to be in one of those kind of movies', and told Nancy Jo Sales in *Premiere* that 'It was corny. I did it because I got to kill the snake and because I want to expand my audience.'

Corny it certainly is – in abundance. But Cube was also right when he observed that it would help expand his audience: people who would pay to see what was basically a monster B-movie might not be the type of people who would be aware of hip-hop culture, whether manifested in film or music. After all, what are the unifying themes between *Boyz N The Hood* and *Anaconda*? Only Cube's presence – there are no similarities in plot, characterisation or setting whatsoever, with no sense of winning out against apparently insuperable odds in *Boyz* and no social commentary in *Anaconda*.

Although many a fan of cheesy horror movies was won over by the easy charm of *Anaconda*, Ice Cube's credibility wasn't at its all-time peak as an actor. Luckily, he was still a potent force in hip-hop (although a year had now passed since the emergence of Westside Connection, and three since *Lethal Injection*) – and it was time to reassert his rights. In hip-hop terms, the summer of 1997 had been dominated by a sickly ballad in tribute to the late Biggie Smalls, a record by Puff Daddy called 'I'll Be Missing You' that sampled the Police's 'Every Breath You Take'. Elsewhere, the Wu-Tang Clan's second album, *Wu-Tang Forever*, released in June 1997, was hailed by reviewers (although its sales had failed to match its critical response), but hip-hop wasn't the cutting-edge force it had been even a year before, with Western youth looking towards the power of alternative rock and nu-metal (the latter genre had recently spawned a band called Korn, who would soon play an important role in Ice Cube's career) for its illicit kicks.

Although Cube had dropped hints here and there that the following year might see the launch of a new and significant project (whether in the guise of a new Westside Connection album, a solo project or something else entirely, it was not clear), his fans were keenly waiting for more product. So on 16 December 1997 a compilation album of Cube material was released. It wasn't the greatest-hits set that many had expected Ice to produce at this stage, however, for the concept behind it was subtler than that. Always aware of the business opportunities in a given situation, he had selected 11 songs on which he and another artist had worked (and which had subsequently appeared on an album by him or the other partner) and called the result *Featuring...Ice Cube*. In other words, he had gathered up many of the collaborations he had recorded over the past five or six years and made them into an album – astute thinking, many would agree, and most appropriate given the plethora of acts with whom he had worked over the years.

Cube explained the concept behind the album to *Addicted To Noise* as follows: 'I've been on a lot of people's records. And there's no way to hear that, unless you buy this person's record, this person's record, this person's... I've had songs on records, and the record didn't even do nothing. The artist only sold 250,000 records, and we've got a good song on there, but it's not a single, so it don't sell. I was like, man, all these songs where I'm featured on someone else's album, I want them all on one tape. So that's where the concept for this compilation come together called *Featuring...Ice Cube*. I just kind of threw it together – it wasn't a big major project, it's kind of just something for my fans who love Ice Cube and wanted that same tape that I wanted.'

The album was a useful rundown through Cube's career, and avoided the best-of trap by including unexpected songs that might not otherwise have seen the light of day – especially when they were ones that appeared on records that 'only sold 250,000' copies, as he put it. The track-listing ran, 'Natural Born Killaz', 'Bow Down', 'Bop Gun (One Nation)', 'Check Yo' Self', 'Endangered Species (Tales From The Darkside)', 'Trespass', 'It's A Man's World', 'West Up!', 'Game Over', 'Wicked Wayz' and 'Two To The Head', and appealed to the G-Funk fans (the George Clinton track), the hard-core fans (the Chuck D and Ice-T collaborations of 'Endangered Species' and 'Trespass'), those who preferred their Ice anthemic ('Check Yo' Self') or ominous ('Bow Down'), and simply those who enjoyed his sense of humour ('It's A Man's World'). Perhaps one or two of the needlessly 'Westside' tracks could have been omitted, but if the aim of the record was to demonstrate the breadth of scope of Cube's co-conspirators, the point was made admirably.

Cube had now come to the point where his status as a kind of hip-hop 'everyman' was obvious. He had rapped on his own and other people's records, as a solo artist and as a member of a band; he had produced records for himself and other people; he had executive-produced albums, holding the whip-hand over other, perhaps more experienced producers; he had acted in movies; he had written soundtracks for movies; he had written scripts for movies; and he had altered other people's scripts for movies.

One small task he had not yet managed to fit in, however, was making his *own* movie. In late 1997 and early 1998, however, that changed. Ice Cube had been hired to direct a film, and announcements were made as the year began that it would be launched in April. The title of the movie was to be *The Player's Club*, and Cube would script, direct and star in it.

The Player's Club duly appeared on 8 April 1998 to a moderately successful opening weekend, easily recouping its £3.5 million ($5 million) budget with a take of £6 million ($8.4 million) on about 600 screens in the US. The fact that its focus was a strip club might have lured the more unquestioning moviegoer to see it rather than see other, less 'interestingly' themed movies. But it didn't take long for the word to spread that this was no idle fleshfest: body parts were only sparingly revealed and the film's focus was far more centred on the human drama played out by the characters. Cube had said during filming that 'I think I'm good with actors. I'm in a low-budget situation and I think I'm handling that well. With the kind of movie we're doing, we need much more than [the £5/$7 million budget], but that's where we're at. It's war every day. Yet, in the midst of all that, we're still getting good footage. I'm proud of it.'

The story is essentially that of a young mother and journalism student called Diana Armstrong (played by new actor LisaRaye), who leaves her home after an argument with her father and takes her son to live with her in Atlanta while she studies. To finance her education, she takes a job at a shoe shop, where she works diligently – until the days when she meets two strippers who work at a local strip club, The Player's Club, where they advise her to seek employment and boost her salary. At first Diana is shocked at the suggestion, but begins to think otherwise. After a while she follows their advice, becoming Diana Diamond for the benefit of the club's patrons and overcoming her revulsion at the job by focusing on the career and security for her son that the stripping will provide.

Complications set in, however, when her visiting cousin (an alcoholic played by Monica Calhoun, who had appeared in *Higher Learning*) leads Diana into insalubrious company. Gangsters threaten the life of the club owner (played by comedian Bernie Mac), there is a graphic rape scene (Cube plays the role of the thug responsible for initiating the assault) and an extended fight between Diana and another of the strippers. In the end the club is torched by one of the gangsters and she makes her escape.

Yet again, the critics weren't able to agree on a verdict, finding both flaws and areas of excellence throughout. This time, however, Cube hadn't acted much in the movie, meaning that the reviewers lacked the fall-back of praising or damning his performance and had to focus on the movie itself. Gene Seymour of the *Los Angeles Times* analysed the plot with an accurate eye: 'As was the case with 1995's *Friday*, for which Cube wrote the script, *Player's Club* is loosely constructed, with anecdotes flowing into each other with the ambling, hit-and-miss rhythm of a comedy routine.' Seymour also noted Cube's trick of invoking plenty of comedic talent: 'Also like *Friday*, the movie is heavily populated with an all-star line-up of comics, including Jamie Foxx as the club's caustic disc jockey; Bernie Mac as Dollar Bill, the club's slime-ball owner; AJ Johnson as Dollar's put-upon sidekick; and Adele Givens as a dancer with so much mileage on her that the club empties as soon as she swaggers onstage.'

Jane Ganahl, of the *San Francisco Examiner*, wasn't happy with Cube's approach to the stripping issue: 'any attempt at a message is clumsily obliterated in Ice Cube's backhanded glorification of the lifestyle he's supposedly out to denounce. Aside from one rape scene, which is presented seriously and actually creates some tension, the picture is played for yuks, there is wall-to-wall (slobber, drool) female nudity, no one gets hurt (translation: It's OK to live this way), and everyone has fun.' Perhaps she has a point – there's little anti-exploitation propaganda to be uncovered in this film (although, of course, Cube never claimed that there should be).

The *Toronto Sun*'s Bruce Kirkland was even more negative: 'Intended as a "serious" social comedy about a single-parent woman trying to make it through college by stripping in a sleazy sex club, *The Player's Club* plays like an afternoon soap. It's the African-American version of Demi Moore's white trailer-park-trash flick *Striptease*.' Harsh words indeed – the Moore film had been derided as one of the poorest films ever made. But Kirkland seemed more irritated than offended: 'Part of the frustration is feeling that Ice Cube, a creative man, could do more and do it better. A few scenes in the movie demonstrate that he has at least a fragmented talent for filmmaking. When Ice Cube tries too hard to be "profound" about women's issues, however, he falls into mawkish melodrama. It's not a pretty sight.'

Perhaps the story behind the film is more revealing than the politics of its director, who never bothered to respond to criticism of his directorial debut. Cube later recounted to *Movieweb* how he had visited some Southern strip clubs while filming *Trespass* in Atlanta with Ice-T back in 1991. 'I thought, there is some very interesting stuff going on here... [The] Southern black strip club industry is a phenomenon not many people know about.' In 1996 Cube wrote a draft script while on location in South Africa for *Dangerous Ground* and showed it to his manager and Street Knowledge partner Pat Charbonnet, who recalled: 'I liked the fact that the story was crafted around the complexities of the lives of young women, with an empowered heroine... I thought that would be unexpected to people familiar with Ice Cube's work. But it wasn't surprising to me. I knew from having managed the guy for seven years that he had far greater respect for the capabilities of women than the average suit.'

The script was then offered to New Line Cinema and a deal was struck, although shooting didn't start for some time, as suitable actors needed to be found. Cube said he wanted new actors for the main roles: 'I wanted the movie to be authentic... I didn't want people walking out and saying, damn, Jada Pinkett-Smith was good!' Charbonnet added: 'I knew Cube wanted new talent, and that it would take time because he was a first-time director.'

But pictures from potential actresses soon began pouring in. 'When the word first hit the grapevine, we started hearing from college girls all over the country who felt this was their story,' said Charbonnet. 'At first, the script was basically a piece of fiction to me, and I was devastated to learn that it was real. I met girls who were in medical school who worked at clubs far away in order to avoid running into classmates. I was blown away by the whole experience.'

Cube was quick to point out that the flesh-baring element was the least of the film-makers' priorities. 'This story isn't about stripping. *The Player's Club* is just a backdrop for what's going on, because everyone involved in the club is using it to get somewhere else. *The Player's Club* is about anybody who has to do something that they don't want to do just to better themselves. The message is: Make the money. Don't let it make you.'

The main actress herself, LisaRaye, said: 'Originally, I had very negative perceptions of strippers. But during the production, I learned that it's an art, and it's very hard to do what those women do. You have to be a strong individual, and you have to stay focused. I had to learn how to walk in those shoes, let alone dance in them. A stripper has to have a mindset that's awesome, because she has to make you believe that she's the baddest person on that stage. That's a confidence level most people don't have.'

Cube told *ET Online* that the newness of Raye (who had only acted in an independent Spike Lee film and a Tupac Shakur video) was crucial: 'I didn't want my movie to be "rapper directed". I wanted it to be a movie that was taken seriously, so I figured that if I'm going to do this story then I want unknown people that you have never seen before. You can get caught up into their lives and their stories...That's what I wanted.' When asked if his first directing gig had turned out as he had expected, he answered: 'In some ways yeah, in some ways no...

It was challenging, but it was something that I love, that I have done, I'm going to do it again. Yeah, but it was hard at times where I was saying, "Ugh, I can't take it no more." But I stuck it through and I'm glad I did. I'm glad that the movie came out as good as it did. And I'm happy with it.'

Cube was asked how the film and music industries compared from his perspective. He responded: 'With music, it's straight from the heart to the record. There are no people critiquing and trying to refine your work before the public sees it. It's all you. But with movies, you've got some people who really don't care about the subject or your vision and tear your work to shreds before it's even filmed. That's a part of Hollywood I don't like. What I do like is when you have smart people who know how to make movies, know how they're put together, know how the beats go, everything that makes a good movie, and they add that to what you have.'

Teri van Horn of *Addicted To Noise* and *Sonicnet* also asked Ice how the idea of a strip club came up. 'Interesting topic,' he said. 'I didn't think anyone really hit it on the head, really nailed it, or really got kinda under the large stuff. For me, it's an interesting story – the story of a girl, kind of in the pit of hell, trying to keep her head above water, and her cousin kind of jumps on her head, takes her under. And she can either be swept under, she can try to save her cousin, or she can save herself. It's that story, which I thought was kind of cool.'

There are several political lessons to be learned, it seems. 'I think that's the one thing about capitalism... [It] looks safe but what it does is kind of corrode your sense of reality, your sense of what's right and wrong, what's cool to do and what's not. And that's just a part of America, I guess. There's gonna be those low, low jobs that pay a lot of money, and it's going to tempt you, but it could destroy you in the process.' And Cube couldn't tell the story without directing the film himself: 'I just felt that if I wanted to say what I wanted to say, I had to jump behind the camera and do it myself. Rather than tell somebody how to shoot this, I gotta jump in there, and be the man and do it myself. And I'm really happy with that opportunity. I never went to film school or nothing like that, I've just watched people to see how things are done and I created my own style... I think it gives the movie a certain amount of realness, a sense of reality, because I did do all those little subtle things that gave the movie a texture to it that's real – it's not just a Hollywood production.'

Interestingly, Cube had given himself an unpopular character to play – the thug who instigates the rape of the central character's cousin. 'The reason I picked myself to be that character is 'cause it's my movie. I could have picked the role where I was like The Man – you know, I come in, save the day – I could have done all that. But I didn't want to; I wanted it to be a movie. I didn't care if you was mad at my character at the end of the movie because I put the whole thing together, so I was just playing the role. So that's the only reason I chose to be the instigator of that.'

Six weeks after its release, the movie had grossed £14 million ($20 million) – a relief for New Line, who viewed it as a resounding success. Part of its appeal lay in its soundtrack, an excellent collection of work including songs by Mack 10, Scarface, Brownstone, and Rufus Blaq with Spindarella as well as Cube's own 'We Be Clubbin'', which was released as a single shortly after the film opened. *Addicted To Noise* asked him if the soundtrack had been all his own work (he had also been its executive producer): 'Well, not completely. We were dealing with A&M Records, and I started my new record company, Heavyweight Records, and we kind of used some of their favorites, and we used my own favorites. We had a music supervisor by the name of Frank Fitzpatrick, and he's real good. We used some of his connections to get some of the people, call them in to do songs. It was kind of mixed from everybody; it wasn't just me.'

So Ice Cube made his step into the world of the director – a stage higher than actor (in terms of power) but a little down from producer. The volume of roles which he had played in the worlds of both music and film was now a full range indeed, but Ice wasn't about to turn any of them down. 'If opportunities present they self, you take them. I think I can do this from all different sides of entertainment.' In saying this he was echoing the words of Ice-T, who had agonised over playing the role of a police officer in *New Jack City*, saying: 'I didn't want to play the part of the cop. But then I wanted to act, and coming from a place where you don't have many opportunities like I did, you just don't shun opportunities like that. You don't say ah, fuck it. I talked with all my friends and they said, Ice, you hold your ideals high, do the part, don't miss the opportunity.' As Smokey had so memorably said in *Friday*, 'Take advantage, man, take advantage'...

And, in becoming a director, even one involved with an independent production studio, Cube admitted that he had become part of the establishment – that dreaded step which so often goes hand in hand with major success. He told *Premiere* magazine in April 1998 that 'Hollywood has it sewed up. With a record, you could put it out yourself and still be on a major level. But in the movie business, that road won't happen. At some point, you're gonna have to attach to the machine.'

But the machine wasn't quite ready to swallow him up just yet. One bastion of alternative culture still awaited him, and this time it was none other than the white kids who invited him inside.

11 Heavyweight Values

In 1994, a change in modern rock music had been heralded by the emergence of Korn, a five-piece metal band from Bakersfield, California. The band were notable for the angst-ridden glamour of singer Jonathan Davis, their penchant for stomach-churning riffing from seven-string guitars and the fact that they were the first band to be produced by Ross Robinson, the enfant terrible of a new kind of music – nu-metal. By the time 1998 came around, Korn had built an unusually devoted fanbase with four impressively heavy albums, and were in a position to embark on a tour with some significant pulling power.

Rather than sticking solely with metal's established recipe of riffs and roars, Korn had also distinguished themselves by including a certain hip-hop awareness in their sound, courtesy of bass player and principal songwriter Reggie 'Fieldy' Arvizu. A notable example of this hip-hop tendency can be seen in the outro to Korn's well-known song 'Blind', in which Fieldy picks out an identical bass part to that of Cypress Hill's 'I Ain't Goin' Out Like That'. Ross Robinson told *Record Collector* magazine in 2001 that Arvizu 'was a big Ice Cube fan, so he played all of Ice Cube's bass lines'. This might account for the fact that, when Korn announced the line-up in summer 1998 of their next ' – the knowingly titled 'Family Values '98' tour, named after a buzz phrase in a speech by that most streetwise of politicians, Dan Quayle – Ice Cube was the second act among the names on the bill, after the opening act, Limp Bizkit (who would eclipse even Korn the following year, so rapid was their rise at the time), and before Orgy, Rammstein and Korn. The tour was scheduled to run from 22

September to 24 October 1998, and would expose over 400,000 American teenagers to the cutting edge of rock, with a DJ called Punk-Roc filling in between acts.

But this was an unusual bill, all right. For years the metal scene had witnessed rolling festivals such as this career drunkenly around the country (Cube had even appeared on the Lollapalooza stage back in 1992). This time, however, all the other acts were much more homogenous – nu-metal and rapcore to a man – which made Cube stand out even more prominently. Orgy are a glammed-up, futuristic act who covered New Order's 'Blue Monday' in an electronically enhanced metal style; Limp Bizkit are the kings of rap-metal, with staccato riffing a trademark, and offer up a very white take on hip-hop; Rammstein are an inscrutable German act whose show has to be seen to be believed, and stand at the very forefront of chart-friendly industrial rock; and Korn, despite their hip-hop allegiance, are a metal band through and through, with guitarists Head and Munky a fearsome axe partnership. On this stage, the homeboy from Crenshaw seemed very much alone. Fans and non-fans alike asked the same question. Would Ice be able to handle a rock crowd?

Their second question was simpler. Why had Cube been chosen to appear? Did Korn fear that the bill was 'too white'? Were the metal stars trying to snatch some of hip-hop's urban cool? Some of the answer came from an interview Korn conducted with *Addicted To Noise* shortly before the tour began. Fieldy started by saying, 'We've been trying to get [this tour] together forever. We just haven't had the right bands. Or we had one of the right bands, not enough for a festival... But now we've got all the bands together, and it's so good. I love the lineup; it's like the perfect little mix-up. We've got a little bit of variety, but I think a lot of people like that.'

The interviewer, Teri van Horn, asked the key question – had Cube been chosen as a token rapper, as some had presumed at the time of Lollapalooza? Fieldy explained that the choice to take Cube along was a fan-driven decision: 'I think all our fans really like hip-hop. We're really close to our fans. We talk to them all the time, and all the fans we've ever talked to are into hip-hop... The first tour we ever did was

House of Pain. When we were doing our first Korn record, all we listened to was Pharcyde, every day. I don't know if Korn fans love them as much as we do, but we had a good time watching them every night.'

It emerged that the link with Cube was no coincidence – in fact, he and Korn had worked together on a song, 'Children Of The Korn'. *Addicted To Noise* asked Jonathan Davis how the partnership had worked out, and the singer was almost speechless: 'He's like my idol. I fucking love him. I was so scared to sing with him because he's like the one guy in hip-hop I respect. I've kind of lost it for hip-hop now, but old school – I love that shit. Him in NWA, and then him sitting there singing with me; I was freaking the fuck out. Like, singing with your favorite artist ever.'

The song had developed almost unintentionally, it seems, as Fieldy pointed out: 'It was a song I wrote called "Fieldy's Dream". I wrote the music out in the back room of the studio and laid out the beats on this drum machine and laid down the bass and some scratch guitars, and showed these guys, and they were like, that's cool... And we had this track with no vocals, so it seemed perfect. Cube's a professional, man – he's been doing it for 20 years. He came in and did his shit, took his wife home and then he came back. He doesn't do anything half-assed.'

'Working with Ice Cube was a little different than I thought it would be,' Fieldy told *Hit Parader*. 'I thought he would really kind of walk in and wonder what we were up to. I thought he would be very intimidating. But he came in and just was one of the guys. When he worked with us, it was like having a sixth member of Korn around. He was so cool.'

Korn weren't likely to change their style completely, as some fans might have feared – even though another guest on Korn's album alongside Cube was Limp Bizkit's Fred Durst, on a song called 'All In The Family'. 'The hip-hop thing has always been there in us. Those songs broke up the album in a good way, because we have these heavy songs and then we have the hip-hop heavy songs. To me, if you take out the vocals on those songs, they're the heaviest fucking three songs on the record, you know? I mean, "All In The Family" – that song is so heavy, but it gets thrown off by the rapping, which, you know, we like. We're not going to become rap – if Jon started rapping, we'd probably giggle our asses off.'

Cube himself had plenty to say about the Korn collaboration, and for similar reasons: like Korn's fans, his own followers might well have been forgiven for worrying about his intended musical direction – after all, the 1990s had been characterised in popular music terms by the collision of rap and rock. In an interview printed on the *Icecubeworld* fansite, he explained that a Korn and Cube project had been in the running for some time, as both acts shared a management company, The Firm. Matters were helped along by the fact that Korn had even covered Cube's 'Wicked' on a previous album: 'When I was getting The Firm as my managers they said that Korn really wanted to meet [me]. So I went to the studio and everything just clicked. The next thing you know I was listening to one of their tracks and they were going to put somebody else on it. I said fuck that – I want to be on it... I asked if they had ever done a song called "Children Of The Korn" and they said no. I couldn't believe it... I got down on it and they came and laid down some guitar licks on my record. I can't wait to go out on the road with them and show them how Ice Cube do it.'

Asked about the fans' likely reaction, Cube's response was as rational as always: 'Me, I've dibbled and dabbled in all kinds of hip hop. [This is] a merging of fans. My extreme fans probably have a Korn album, too. The fans have been blending more than the artists. Now the artists are starting to pick up on it, so you're going to see some new music in the future.' In fact, he viewed a collaboration such as this as the only sensible option, for 'If you look at groups like Korn who take alternative and merge it with hip-hop, it only seems right for hardcore rap to do the same thing to reach the masses. I've been in the game so long that I have my fanbase, my core audience or target audience or whatever they say. If I'm not trying to expand, then what am I doing here?'

But he was, as ever, aware of the fans' sensibilities. The spectre of rap–rock fusion was not one that many hardcore fans would welcome, and it seemed an almost daily occurrence that a once hip-hop-devoted act emerged with guitars as part of a new look – Cypress Hill, for example, were on the point of doing just this. Cube explained: 'If I do a record with Korn, I'm not going to do it like I would do a record with Public Enemy. What I like about myself is that I can do what I want to do. I can do a record with Korn, I could do a record with DMX... I'm trying to expand my horizons as a person, too.'

And it's a thankless task trying to please everybody all of the time, especially the purists: 'I can't cater to hardcore hip-hop fans. I have to cater to Ice Cube fans. If you try to cater to the hardcore, they don't like nothing that's above the street level, period. They would like for you to stay at one level and that's it... I haven't stayed at one level since *Boyz N The Hood*. People said that I sold out when I did that. I can't concern myself with the hardcore because I put it all together [with] four other dudes named NWA. So I can't concern myself with nothing that the youngsters are saying nowadays.'

Cube finished off by pointing out that he'd been in this position before, anyway: 'When I did the Lollapalooza tour in 1992, I was exposed to fans who had never gone to see a hip-hop show and Ice Cube fans who was scared to come to my [regular] show. I always looked at myself as the alternative to the alternative. It was a breath of fresh air for that tour and I think that I'll be a fresh of fresh air for this one.'

Questions, and more questions – but, as the tour approached, the issues raised by Cube's appearance as a black hip-hopper on a stage full of white metallers gradually ceased to become important. In retrospect, it isn't difficult to see why he was chosen to appear: of the rap acts big enough to warrant a slot at the time, he was perhaps the only one with a public profile that the majority of Korn's audience would recognise (due in part to his films) and, furthermore, the only one who had crossed over to mainstream white culture quite as obviously.

Perhaps Dr Dre might have been a big enough name to make an appropriate tour companion for Korn and their noisy accomplices – but the Doctor's patented recipe of laid-back G-Funk beats might have lacked the gritty edge the metal audience would demand. The 'Family Values' tour was also a solid commercial decision for Ice Cube. Where else could he get as much white exposure without sacrificing his style at the altar of rap-metal? As we've seen, many of Ice's career moves have been backed by sound business sense, be it by accepting a role in a monster movie or demanding to direct his own film. And so the tour embarked. A camera followed the players constantly (a VHS and DVD was later released), focusing on the various bands backstage and in performance. A key moment cropped up early in the tour, when Cube told the interviewer, 'The audience are loving it, man, because they're not expecting what they're getting... [They're] getting this whole multidimensional show.' Tellingly, among the backstage shenanigans that were so carefully preserved for posterity by the 'Family Values' film crew (Orgy, a new act mentored by Korn and signed to their Elementree label, almost overwhelmed by the excitement of it all; Rammstein smashing up the dressing-room ceiling; Limp Bizkit's Fred Durst racing down the venue hallways on a scooter; and even Korn putting on some half-hearted breakdancing), Ice Cube is totally absent apart from a brief appearance when he improvises a quick Westside shout-out to camera. There's a sense, intended or otherwise, that he's too wise or too experienced to indulge in such activities (or to be caught on camera, anyway).

His performance reflected this: Ice emanated a kind of dignity that was not seen in the acts of the much more frantic metal acts, whose visual impact revolves around a lot of headbanging and jumping around. Cube's image had to be more subtle, based as it was on the interplay between him and his rap partner, the solidly built WC of Westside Connection. But this is not to say that his set was static or unspectacular. On the contrary, the two men were dwarfed by the main centrepiece of the show, an enormous head and torso of Cube resembling a stone statue, with outstretched arms and a massive, Abraham Lincoln-style hat in which his DJ had his decks.

One or two reviewers made snide jibes about Cube's decision to use a statue of himself, claiming that it was an arrogant gesture – but in actual fact its use was a masterstroke, amplifying Cube's presence (he himself was dressed simply, in black shirt and trousers) to an awesome degree. In any case, he needed something dramatic: Limp Bizkit, who had finished their set just before him, had started and finished their set by emerging from, and re-entering, an enormous 'crashed' UFO.

Cube's set consisted of four songs, plus a lot of crowd interaction between songs, during which the DJ dropped in several fragments of distorted sound and beats and the two rappers exchanged a lot of banter. Appropriately, he chose to kick off with a remix of 'Check Yo' Self', an amped-up version with a grinding Korn-like guitar riff appended to it. Its intro is dramatic, with the stage bathed in blue light and the Cube statue overlaid with the shadow of the Grim Reaper – Ice had clearly been paying attention to the classic demonic imagery of traditional metal shows. Running up and down the sides of the stage and whipping up the audiences in those areas, Cube showed that he'd become a pretty awe-inspiring performer over the years. After all, when your only prop is a microphone, you need to learn about body language in your act.

The next song was a new one, which Cube introduced with the words 'I know for a fact you're gonna like this one, because the guitars on it were played by my homeboys in Korn... I wrote this song especially for this generation. They say we dying off – but we call this one "Fuck Dying".' It's a classic Cube tune all right, all vitriolic sentiments and a fistful of orchestral samples. The Korn-generated riff is unremarkable, however, and it's not surprising that a few fans' eyebrows were raised about the large number of metal influences in Cube's set.

But the show still held some surprises. After these two metallic songs, Cube took the tempo down with a shortened version of 'It Was A Good Day', with the old-school command of 'Put your pieces in the air like this/Put your pieces in the air' yelled over the instrumental intro. Now some six years old, the song was received with pleasure by the older sections of the crowd, although most of the 'Family Values' audience (who fell into the 14- to 18-year-old bracket) were inevitably too young to have heard it when it first appeared. Cube was evidently one step ahead of them, however, calling an abrupt halt to the song after the second verse and announcing, 'Hold up, man, this shit is too soft... We're on the Family Values tour, man – this is the hardcore crowd right here!'

In Chicago, Cube had told the press, 'I just want to give people a whole repertoire... From NWA shit to new shit' – and the 'NWA shit' in question turned out to be a stamping version of 'Fuck Tha Police', with the extended courtroom intro edited out (Ice went straight into his infamous 'Fuck the police/Comin' straight from the underground' line), and the focus, unsurprisingly, on his own portion of the song, although Eazy-E's voice could clearly be heard in the chorus. Purists were a little disappointed that Cube had left his own original vocal on the backing track, making for a slightly weird, karaoke-style effect, which a song of this historical calibre doesn't deserve. Perhaps Cube couldn't access the original tapes in order to remove them – although, given the studio tools available to him (and the expertise which he had gained in that area), it's probable that he simply decided that the presence of the original vocals wasn't a problem.

Still, it was a powerful set, with the audience roused into a frenzy at times and energised for the next band – the most obvious function of any support act. But Cube's involvement wasn't over: he and Korn performed 'Children Of The Korn' on the tour, which was where, finally, rock and rap met with a degree of power. While the riff-accompanied 'Check Yo' Self' remix and 'Fuck Dying' had their share of guitar input, the fact that the riffs came from the DJ in Cube's set meant that they were fairly low in the mix, losing some of their strength. 'Children', however, was a genuinely angry beast, with Cube's rap over the full power of the band a perfect complement.

Over the course of the month-long tour, each band introduced variations into its act. For example, one of the many other encores tried out live (as well as 'Children Of The Korn') was a collaboration between Korn and Limp Bizkit called 'All In The Family', which featured singers Jonathan Davis and Fred Durst sparring in an old-school rap battle. (It can be presumed that the irony of this was not lost on Ice Cube.) Each band played the song as its singer sang his respective verse, before an apocalyptic finale in which the stage equipment was trashed and the singers wrestled each other to the floor. A surreal edge was added to the proceedings by the presence of Davis's 2-year-old son Nathan, who ran happily about the stage wearing industrial-strength headphones to shield him from the volume of the music and the liberal rock'n'roll swearing that filled the air.

It's interesting to note that, once again, Ice Cube played no part in the instrument-smashing, rock-pig debauchery that characterised so much of the tour. For example, Korn told the press that the amount of alcohol consumed nightly was prodigious...but it's difficult to imagine the reformed Nation of Islam supporter Cube joining in, even if he had endorsed St Ides beer all those years before. An interview he gave to *Music Monitor* shortly after the tour shed some light on his new, mature frame of mind. Asked how his musical style had evolved since the days of NWA, he responded: 'Earlier in my career, I was pissed off about everything, with no responsibilities to anything. Now, I'm a grown man and I understand that being pissed off gets you nowhere. It's kind of like a baby crying, it's not going to help the situation. I think now I know more about the world, and I've said things and there's no reason to resay them, or no reason to go over old ground. I'm always going into new records, into new things... I feel like, I'm an artist, I can do anything I want to do without having to drag any kind of baggage. Sometimes I do records that reflect the old NWA style, sometimes I don't want to do that.'

Such a sober (one might even say 'reconstructed') world-view stands at clear odds with the youthful brashness of some of the 'Family Values' players, but it's clear that Korn perceived a vitality in Cube that overrode those concerns. With his welcome into the world of nu-metal, Cube had taken a vital step, and not one that has been repeated since: a black artist, with outspoken views about white oppression, had been asked to join a tour representing the new face of heavy metal, which has always been the whitest of musics. The world had certainly turned some way since the dark days of *Straight Outta Compton*.

A couple of weeks before the 'Family Values' tour rolled to a halt, with a riotous show in which the players dressed up as 1980s hair-metal stars to celebrate Halloween, Ice Cube was replaced by the nu-metallers Incubus. The reason for this was that he had shooting commitments on a new movie, and that nothing could get in its way – his co-stars were a cut above his previous projects and the film was said to be something rather special. He also had a new album to promote and, like the movie he was about to make, the record was unlike anything he had done before. Nonetheless, the subsequent *Family Values Tour 98* album (released by Columbia) included three Cube songs ('Check Yo' Self', the Dre collaboration 'Natural Born Killaz' and an excellent 'Straight Outta Compton'/'Fuck Tha Police' medley), as well as an Incubus song, 'New Skin'.

Rumours of the movie were soon subsumed by the release of Cube's new album, the first of a proposed set of two entitled *War & Peace*. The first, *The War Disc*, appeared on 17 November 1998 and was a significant release on many levels. To start with, the two discs were Cube's first real venture into concept-album territory, with the themes of aggression versus pacifism, anger versus calm and life versus death fully integrated into the set's 36 tracks. However, the full impact of the set wouldn't be felt or assessed until the release of the second disc (initially scheduled to appear in the summer of 1999), so *War* had to stand up in its own right. The decision not to release both albums together was an astute one for several reasons – not least because, as a solo artist, Ice had been absent from the music scene since *Lethal Injection* way back in 1993, and his fanbase might not have been immediately keen to pay for a double-CD set when Cube had produced little evidence of musical form in recent years.

Where did the war and peace theme come from? Cube told *Music Monitor* that 'The war and peace is with everybody. The reason I titled my album that is because I think that is the conflict of life. You know, you got peaceful moments and then you got moments where you gotta get down. I just looked at it as a metaphor for not only the rap game, but for the game of life.' He clarified this with: '*Peace* is more of a visionary record... [How] it should be. I'd say my *Peace* record is my conscious record and my *War* record is [a] street record.'

He also told journalist Blair R Fischer that a double album is also too much for anyone (even the most dedicated listener) to take – as recent releases by Notorious BIG, the Wu-Tang Clan and, at the forefront of the UK's drum'n'bass movement, Roni Size & Reprazent had shown: 'I've tried to listen to some rap double albums and it's just too much... I didn't wanna do that.' And the no-compromise themes of the album would make even a single disc a demanding experience: 'War & Peace is about life and living... Every day is a struggle. Today might be cool, but tomorrow might be a horror for yourself.' He also explained to *Music Monitor* that 'On *War* I deal with topics like the three-strikes-you're-in law, ex-girlfriends... I got a record on there called "Fuck Dying" because so many rappers – not rappers, people period – are so preoccupied with death. Everybody's gonna get there, it's not like you're gonna miss the boat, so why rush it?'

As before, some people thought that the new albums might be Cube's last. 'Everybody screams, Cube's about to retire,' he pointed out. 'I still think that I can rap as good as anybody. I figure, why should I quit? Why should I stop? [This] has the potential to be my biggest record ever. I take pride in myself for not doing the same records [all the time]. If you look at my records you'll see that each record can stand on its own.'

Asked if the albums were dark enough to be labelled 'Gothic', he mused: 'The attitude of the two albums *is* dark. I wouldn't use the word "gothic" because that tends to throw people off. [There is] a lot of experimental songs that we are doing. The one that I like the most is the one where I got the guy from Korn to play on which is called "Fuck Dying". It's just like a different approach. I don't know if what I'm doing is still considered gangsta rap, but I feel that it is... I got to say that [this is] my best record in years. I set everything aside – movies, producing, all of that – to focus on me, my record, what I want to do, how I want to sound. For a couple of years I lost focus, just by trying to do so many other things. This record is me grinding for a year and half to put this together.'

Five years away from the studio (in his own right, at any case) had left its mark on Cube. In purely musical and production terms, the album was a more multifaceted record than anything he had created since *The Predator*, with influences taken from a wider host of sources (the Korn riff on 'Fuck Dying' is just one example) from the standard soul and R&B canon. For instance, the title track is based squarely on the strummed guitar background and vocal melody of No Doubt's

'Don't Speak', which had been a mighty hit for the ska-rock quartet the previous year. Furthermore, 'Dr Frankenstein' and 'Ghetto Vet' (the latter a poignant, piano-led rap from the perspective of a paraplegic drive-by victim) are laced with horror-movie samples and effects which, far from the simple inserts of earlier albums, were fully fledged editing-suite soundscapes worthy of any major-studio, full-budget Hollywood movie.

Lyrically, Cube is functioning on two levels. The murderous anger of before is still present (see the intro of 'Fuck Dying', in which Death himself comes to take Cube away, but is met with the words 'I ain't goin' nowhere wit' your ass…and if you put your hands on me, we're going down, right here'). And there are the two vitriolic anti-materialist rants of 'Greed' and 'The Curse Of Money' plus the righteous wrath of '3 Strikes You In', which is more or less an anti-LAPD diatribe along the lines of 'Fuck Tha Police', albeit with a sophistication entirely lacking from anything that NWA produced before *Efil4Zaggin*.

Talking of sophistication, Cube's second level of commentary is a sombre, almost cerebral attack on government and authority. 'Once Upon A Time In The Projects 2' was a reflection on the issues he had brought up in the original 'Projects' – police brutality, the consequences of extreme urban poverty and the prevalence of addiction and violence, which those not physically present simply fail to see. Cube's conclusion? Apparently that nothing has changed, perhaps because of several years of Clintonian focus on the condition of America's middle class and the attendant impact on those in the city ghettos. See also 'Extradition', 'Penitentiary' and inserts such as 'MP' for more examples of a wider-ranging mind than the Cube of yore, but this is (after all) still an Ice Cube album, with 'If I was Fucking You' on the surface at least a simple boast of sexual prowess by Cube and his associates Short Khop and K-Mac.

In effect, *War* was Cube's comeback album, after an absence that might have been longer than originally planned – Ice Cube was not to know that his acting and production careers would take such precedence after *Lethal Injection*. In fact, the simple matter that he had managed to record two albums (*War* and *Peace* were the product of the same sessions), complete a stint on the 'Family Values' tour *and* arrange to star in a new movie – all within a matter of months in summer and autumn 1998 – is no small achievement.

Cube spent a lot of time in interviews of the period answering the simple question of how he managed to fit everything in. 'If you're planning it right,' he told Blair R Fischer, 'you can do it. Just planning it, shit starts to look haywire.' It helped, he said, that he planned his life out year by year: 'Early in my career I always had a habit of, at the beginning of the year, saying what I wanted to accomplish this year, and this just kinda gives me some guidance on what moves I need to make to make sure everything keeps a steady ride.'

This clear-headed approach had stood him in good stead, it seemed, leading to a position where – only months short of his 30th birthday, a milestone in anybody's life (and even more so in the notoriously fickle world of showbiz) – Cube could sit back a little and reflect on his life to date. 'I have a lot of ideas that I want to bring to an album and to the screen,' Cube told the *Toronto Sun*. 'I guess what would be ideal is if I can continue to do both movies and music forever. It takes up a lot of my time, but if I see that there's a story that needs to be told, I'm going to tell it. Like with *Friday*, I was able to tell a story about people hanging out in the hood. There wasn't supposed to be a big lesson learned. People were just supposed to laugh.' There was no doubt about his core activities, however: 'Besides, it's cool being a screenplay writer, an actor and a director, but my first love is music. No matter where I go, I'll always come back to that.'

This more enlightened world-view had been seen in other gangsta-rap veterans, too. Bearing in mind that the raw old-school verison of the genre had peaked in about 1990 with a handful of 18- or 20-year-olds at its forefront, by the end of the 1990s many of those who had survived (both physically and in showbiz terms) had mostly developed into socially aware thinkers. One of these was Ice-T, who talked to *Props* magazine about what he had learned from his own experiences: '[To the white mainstream], whether it's Ice-T or Ice Cube, we're all the same, their attitude is "fuck all of them"... Hip-hop as a whole will stand behind you, but to the masses, hip-hop is considered one big nigga. If 100 rappers stood behind me, it wouldn't matter.' The rapper, an older man than Cube and his contemporaries (he had recently hit 40), had seen the top and the bottom of the industry through the 'Cop Killer' controversy and over a decade at the vanguard of non-mainstream hip-hop – and, like Cube, he had learned some valuable lessons from it. As did his younger contemporary, Ice-T concluded that the social change they all yearned for would happen slowly, if it happened at all.

More and more of the ghetto rappers were taking their business affairs into their own hands. In 1998, Ice Cube added to the Street Knowledge roster by launching Heavyweight Records, which broke new ground by signing a distribution deal with a major label, in this case the respected A&M Records. One of its first releases was the *Player's Club* soundtrack, with its hit single, 'We Be Clubbin'': 'I figured, why go to a label that's got a lot of rappers when I can go to A&M and make my mark... My brains and their money is the perfect marriage,' he said.

One or two perceptive journalists later noted that the *Peace* disc contained a song called 'Record Company Pimpin'', which was an open attack on artist exploitation. When asked by *Music Monitor* whether this was a conflict, given his own status as head of Heavyweight, he reasoned that 'There's no conflict of interest doing a song called "Record Company Pimpin'" and being a record company [head] because I don't plan on dicking my artists. I plan on teaching them the music business and giving them all the money that's due them because I made a lot of money and I don't need to steal from nobody.' The point is, he claimed, that he had inside experience of the rap game: 'I can go out and make my own money, I don't need another artist to do that. But where you got a record company owner, all he has is who comes in the door and raps for him. So most of the time they're not that sympathetic to the artist, like me. I've been an artist and I've gotten kind of dicked out of my money before, so I know how that is and I don't plan to be that way.'

In the meantime, his distaste for record industry exploitation ran as far as the whole of hip-hop itself, as he told MTV: '[I don't] recognize hip-hop no more… Hip-hop's not what it was when I got in it. Now people are in it for the money and the fame. It ain't about having skills or trying to say something to make any kind of difference and that's what makes it frustrating.' Perhaps this explained his new, above-it-all stance. 'I've kinda detached myself from hip-hop. I'm like, why get caught up in it when I can just do my thing…so I'm gonna do the Ice Cube thing and let everybody else deal with hip-hop,' he said.

He had a point. So much time had passed since hip-hop had taken root, and white society had changed so much (in its appreciation – and appropriation – of black music, at least), that the whole status quo with regard to hip-hop and its role in Western culture had almost reversed. Hip-hop and its variants were now the norm (it had spread as far as soul, pop and even metal, as we saw with Korn), not the underground, with its stars as big as any that other musical genres had provided. But Cube's claim that rapping skills were no longer a priority was an incomplete one in part. After all, it was thanks to pioneers Cube, Dre, Snoop and Tupac – all of whom had specialised in a slow, G-Funk rap style on at least one major record – that the simpler, less aggressive approach was now in vogue.

In a slightly surreal twist, this turnaround was superficially illustrated by the active role played in November 1998 (just as *War* was hitting the record stores) by the Californian Police Department. Recording equipment and studio gear valued at £1.1 million ($1.5 million) had been stolen from a Redondo Beach storage facility rented by Cube, but the items were returned to him after the police tracked down and arrested the thief. According to press rumours at the time, the officers involved were 'hoping' to be thanked by Ice for their efforts – presumably they didn't hold out much hope for a 'Thank Tha Police' single…

12 The Desert King

As the years passed and Ice Cube's career extended its reach through various arenas, one consistent theme never went away – that of gangsta life. Even today, almost 15 years after the release of *Straight Outta Compton* – the most G-indebted record that Cube has ever made – people still regard him as a ghetto prophet, or at the very least as someone whose sole mission is to expose the issues that pervade black urban society. As we've seen, his remit has expanded to include so much more than that – almost every facet of modern life has come into Cube's verbal sights at some point or other.

But fans are fans – and one question they always levelled at Ice Cube, and at Dre, Ren, Yella and even Eazy before his early demise, was when – not if, but *when* – the world would witness the sight of a NWA. Even back in November 1993, not so long after the line-up had collapsed after *Efil4Zaggin*, *The Predator* and *The Chronic* all blew up big in the face of the establishment, Cube and Dre had talked about a possible reunion. Cube said at the time that the two men had even discussed potential album titles – one possibility being *Helter Skelter*, for no obvious reason.

'After he got away from that other clown, he was back to the old Dre,' Cube said (the clown in question would either have been Jerry Heller or Eazy-E, presumably; Cube's beef with both men was still white-hot at the time). 'We sat down and talked. Us hooking up was like... Have you ever jumped in a cold pool? You stick your foot in first to test the water, but once you get in you're cool. We weren't trying to bullshit each other. He was the same muthafucka I had met, and I was the same muthafucka he had met. We just clicked, started laughing about old shit.'

Some years later it was the turn of MC Ren to talk up the possibility of a new NWA. The former Lorenzo Patterson had been through a lot since the break-up of his old band, including some disputes with Eazy and the Ruthless label, and had resolved these issues by joining the Nation of Islam, straightening up his act (he eventually became a NOI lieutenant), getting married and presenting a much more responsible image than the AK-wielding 'Villain' of the 1980s. Ren told *USA Today* in 1996 that 'It won't be the same without Eazy, but it's not like he's still alive and we're trying to do this without him... You got a million NWA clones. Only a few got their own flavor. We need a new NWA album to set everyone back on the right track of being creative.'

But the road towards a reunion was far from smooth, with Cube flatly dismissing the chance of a new NWA in the *Toronto Sun* on 21 March 1998. He had clearly been in the thick of negotiations, juggling other artists' commitments with his own, and the frustration was starting to show: 'It's not worth it 'cause the magic's not gonna be there. If trying to put something together is like pulling teeth, it's not gonna be the shit,' he growled. 'Trying to put this NWA project together *is* like pulling fucking teeth. I'm so disgusted with the shit I don't want to hear nobody say shit about an NWA reunion.'

Almost a year later he was telling the same story to *Music Monitor*, although his explanation was much more rational. It seemed that the most important person to the reunion, Dr Dre, was unable to schedule time for the project – 1998 had seen the fall of Death Row and Dre's move to Aftermath, with all its attendant complications, after all. If Dre was trying to re-establish a solo career (it had been six years since *The Chronic*), the last thing he would need, it seemed, would be a new group project taking up his time: 'I think Dre, after the release of *The Aftermath*, wants to concentrate on his own career, and I think he's going to release *The Chronic II* before we talk about any projects. I think him leaving Death Row, and all the events that happened, kind of steamrolled our project, and it's not even in the air no more. Who knows if we'll ever get back on line?' Cube had retained his artistic integrity, too, refusing to bow to public pressure (despite the enormous earner that a new NWA would undoubtedly be for him) by jeopardising the quality of the music: 'I figure, why do the record if it's not going to be a great record? I don't want to throw something together just because it's going to be me and Dr Dre.'

'We're up against two things,' Cube told *Rolling Stone* magazine. 'We don't have a lot of time, and we have to do a great record. That doesn't compute. There are a lot of expectations with that record, and if we don't have time to meet those expectations, it's better not to do it than to go in and half-ass it... It's really on Dre. If he ain't puttin' the tracks together, I really ain't down to rap on nobody else's tracks. He's the quarterback.'

And there the matter rested – for the moment, at least. But, while events moved forward (in the life of Ice Cube and the figures in his circle), that persistent question kept coming, on Websites and in chatrooms worldwide... When are NWA reforming?

However, Cube had his own concerns. On 13 October 1998 he scored a US No.1 single with 'Pushin' Weight', an insightful song that remained at the top for two weeks and was accompanied by a video directed by the adult film-maker Gregory Dark. 'It's cool,' Ice Cube told MTV Radio. 'I think that Gregory Dark has become a great editor, he knows lighting, and he knows how to save money, which is a good thing for a director. He knows how to get the shot without spending for it, and that's a beautiful thing. That's why the video looks so good... [The video] is a big game hunter type of thing, [with the prey] the people that don't like Ice Cube just because he's Ice Cube.'

On 16 March 1999, Columbia released a decidedly odd record – a tribute album to the Clash called *Burning London*, which featured 12 versions of Clash songs (classic and otherwise), attempted with varying degrees of success by a host of bands chosen (it seemed) solely for their lack of anything in common. Thus the ska-metallers Mighty Mighty Bosstones' stab at 'Rudie Can't Fail' sat alongside 'White Man in Hammersmith Palais' by nu-rockers 311; Antipodean rockers Silverchair's 'London's Burning' brushed shoulders with 'Straight To

Hell', rejigged by electronic jester Moby; and a phenomenal cover of 'Should I Stay Or Should I Go?' by Korn, Ice Cube and Mack 10 was the record's standout track by a mile.

Producer extraordinaire Danny Saber remixed the Clash's finest moment, providing a vocal interplay between Cube and Mack 10 that had critics asking whether the rap partnership might not be Cube's best since the days of Eazy-E and MC Ren. But it's not a straight cover of the Levi's-ad classic: the two rappers play around with the time signatures, introducing their own lyrics, and even Korn's reproduction of that famously simple riff isn't an obvious interpretation.

Although the album was a moderate success – and the Cube track was almost universally said to be the best – the rapper wasn't heavily involved in its promotion. After spending time with his family and getting things moving at Heavyweight and Street Knowledge, Cube then devoted May and June 1999 to filming the sequel to *Friday*. This would not appear for some time, however, but in the interim fans delighted themselves with his best film yet – the unexpectedly excellent result of Ice's much-speculated-about project with George Clooney and Mark Wahlberg, filmed the previous autumn after the 'Family Values' behemoth bid Cube farewell.

Three Kings previewed on 27 September 1999 and made an immediate splash among reviewers and audiences. Let us be in no doubt here (a change from the recent mixed responses to the semi-good, semi-lame films Ice Cube had appeared in since the mid-1990s): *Three Kings* is an excellent piece of moviemaking. Superbly scripted and directed with effortless panache by David O Russell, its setting (the final chaotic months of the Gulf War) and message (partly anti-Bush, partly anti-consumerist, but intriguingly not wholly either) were entirely unprecedented – and the cast was, quite simply, to die for. Add to this a significant budget (£34 million/$48 million), plus experts in location scouting (California and Mexico), photography and special effects, and the result is truly gripping.

On first glance, though, the plot seems to be merely a beefed-up treasure-hunt movie. It's the end of the Gulf War. Saddam Hussein's Iraq has collapsed under Western attack, with the leader gone to ground, its infrastructures crushed and its people traumatised. A few divisions of American soldiers are waiting for the command to pull out and go home, although communications are sporadic and the general air of chaos that pervades the Iraqi desert communities also extends to the US military, who have no clear idea of what their role is, if a war is actually happening and even if they're allowed to shoot people (the film starts with this exact query – Mark Wahlberg kills an Arab soldier and isn't sure if he's just committed a heroic deed or a simple murder).

Four soldiers convene. Their leader is Major Archie Gates, played by George Clooney, heartthrob and recent inheritor of the *Batman* film role. Clooney's rogueish/disarmingly attractive character is typical of those which he had adopted to great effect in films like his Quentin Tarantino/Roberto Rodriguez-helmed debut, 1996's *From Dusk Till Dawn* (in which he 'emerged as full-blown film star', raved *Variety*) and, later, *Out Of Sight* and *Ocean's Eleven*. Gates notes that one of the other soldiers, Troy Barlow (Wahlberg), has found a map which seems to indicate that hidden treasure in the form of gold bullion stolen from Kuwait is located nearby. Along with Chief Elgin (Cube), a deeply religious, working-class army reserve member from Detroit, and Conrad Vig (played by director Spike Jonze in his first major acting role), a simple but appealing redneck straight out of *Deliverance* territory, the four men plan to steal the gold for themselves, with Barlow, Elgin and Vig persuaded by the charismatic Gates to play along in return for a share of the wealth.

So far, so standard adventure story – but as the film progresses several themes come into play which turn it into a fascinating social and political exposé. The soldiers come across the loot and are about to leave the scene – an Iraqi village – when the inhabitants beg them not to leave. It suddenly becomes clear that the locals will be rounded up and executed by Saddam's Republican soldiers (true to actual fact, the populace had been exhorted by President Bush to rebel against Saddam, but had received no Western support in this and the dictator's troops were exacting cruel vengeance for their rebellion) if the Americans leave. Gates' team elects to take the villagers with them, effectively turning their selfish search for riches into a humanitarian mission. Their motives have been reversed at a stroke, and a powerful criticism has been levelled at their country and its leaders.

The second major theme is explored in detail when Barlow is capured by Iraqi soldiers, tied to a chair and tortured extensively. His torturer, a young man whose family has been killed in bombings by the Western forces, makes him drink oil – both the currency and the cause of the Gulf War – after learning that his victim is a new father himself. He is eventually freed, but (suffering from shock) barely survives a sniper attack. His friend Vig dies in the same scenario.

Third, Russell cocks a snook at consumerism. The media are everywhere (Gates and his soldiers are tailed by a persistent news reporter) and throughout the film there is an amusing interchange between Barlow and Elgin about Lexus or Infinity cars and whether they are available as convertibles.

Ultimately the three men conquer all the odds and get away with it, but not before the film has been variously a farce, a grim parable and a violent horror story. Its multifaceted nature seemed to appeal to audiences (Cube later said, 'I like how the movie shifts gears. It's like going from comedy, then it goes into the heist, and then there's this action and then…it turns into a whole different thing') and it's easily the best thing Russell or any of the actors (including Clooney) have done, before or since, although some might prefer Wahlberg's stylish *Boogie Nights* for its glossy chic. All the performances were superb, with Clooney a resilient, war-torn leader (at one point he uncovers an Iraqi corpse, to silence the younger soldiers' naive complaints that they had seen little 'action'), Wahlberg a troubled everyman, Jonze a kind of doomed court jester, and Cube – at last – in the perfect role for his brooding, almost sullen acting style.

'Chief is basically from Detroit – you know, seen a lot of violence,' he explained to the *Michigan Daily*. 'Very religious man. Basically in the Army Reserves and making a little money on the side and isn't expecting to be caught up in the war. And he gets caught up in the war. He relies on the training, but he is going to rely on the same thing that got him through the streets of Detroit, his Lord and savior Jesus Christ… I think Chief is somebody you want on your right hand.'

Elgin has both gravity and nobility. A telling scene occurs early in the movie when Vig the redneck is using the terms 'sand-nigger' and 'dune-coon' when referring to the Arabs. Cube's character warns him not to use these words near him – the threat of righteous violence is tangible – before the scene becomes surreally hilarious when the two men agree that 'towelhead' and 'camel jockey' are acceptable synonyms. And when Barlow is rescued, pale and silent, from his torture session, Elgin informs him with sympathy that he (Barlow) is in shock. This short sentence is full of pity. That Cube invested these few words with so much power is an achievement worthy of a far more experienced actor.

'The first time I saw *Three Kings* I was like, this is something,' Cube told the *Daily Bruin*. 'I didn't think it would be liked by so many people.' This is perhaps due to the vision of David O Russell, who had evidently picked a subject that audiences wanted to respond to. He also knew his actors and their careers: Ice hadn't had a real chance to stretch himself as an actor since *Dangerous Ground*, after all, with the *Friday* and *Player's Club* roles amusing rather than demanding – as Russell told Student.com, '[Cube] was the first person I cast... I saw his work in *Boyz N The Hood*. He's gotten to do a lot of commercial movies, like *Trespass* or *Anaconda*, but I think this is a real chance for him to show his chops. He's quite serious as an actor, and he's very professional, and he's a no-nonsense kind of guy.'

Russell then recounted a story in which he saw Cube squeezing the contents out of a Taco Bell taco: 'We were sitting in the lobby of the Holiday Inn in Casa Grande, Arizona... [He] saw me looking at [the taco], and he said, "You think that's strange?" I said, "Well, yeah, I guess." And he said, "That's what makes me me." That is pure Cube, he's just totally, shamelessly confident about himself and his choices.'

The director was obviously delighted with Cube's seamless performance. 'He bought that character big time. To pull off that toughness combined with that vulnerability... Cube *prays* in this movie, you know, that's really vulnerable. When was the last time you saw a character pray, sincerely? It's not a joke, it's not a goof, and he pulls it off, with a lot of integrity.' The famous 'sand-nigger' scene had not been an easy one to include, added Russell: '[The US] had this alliance with the Saudis and other Arab nations, but war always makes the enemy a racist enemy, so it's very confusing. We're supposed to like certain Arabs and not like other Arabs... [The] Arab advisers said, "We don't want you to have this conversation in the movie," where..."towelhead" and "camel jockey" are perfectly acceptable. And Cube, a black man, says "Exactly". Cube's agreeing with him.' The conversation would be offensive to both Arabs and blacks, he was warned, but Russell insisted that it stay in the script for the sake of veracity: 'I said you *have* to have that in there, because that's where these guys are. It's meaningless otherwise, when they hang out with the Arabs, if they haven't started at that place.'

Although the movie was a triumph, Cube had initially been unsure whether to get involved, as he told the UK *Guardian*: 'I wasn't sure about it. Wasn't sure at all. Because it's offbeat, it's not your typical...movie. But once David O. Russell explained what he wanted to make then, yeah, I was cool with it.' The wheel had come full circle, it seemed, in one respect at least. Remember Ice-T's uncertainty at playing a cop in *New Jack City* back in 1991? It was now Ice Cube's turn to feel that he might be on thin ice: 'You know, it's funny, 'cause if you asked me back in '91 would I ever be in a movie as a soldier, a US soldier, I'd have said get the hell out of here. Hell no! But that's what I like about the film – we showed there were a lot of people on both sides who really didn't want to be there.'

The broader implication of this last statement is simply that Cube feels the desire to educate. Asked whether the film's indictment of both Saddam and Bush had attracted him, he answered with enthusiasm: 'Oh yeah... I love any time you can enlighten people to mistakes, that's how I started my career. It definitely turned me on. Plus I like the interaction of the soldiers and the Shi'ite Muslims.' Whether he says this last sentence from a Nation of Islam perspective, or simply from someone angered by the West–East imbalance of wealth, is not clear – but his global appreciation of what the film means certainly is, not least the film's title itself. As he told the German *BZ Aktuell*, the soldiers' turn from greed to good, ultimately bringing the people out of Babylon (or its equivalent), is a direct reference to the three kings of the Bible.

The political agenda of the director went deeper than a simple anti-White House attack. Russell was also targeting the American Way itself, to a certain extent, which made the film's box-office success even more unexpected. He told Michael Sragow at *Salon* that 'I knew there had been a whole side to the conclusion of that war that had been buried under a sea of yellow ribbons. I thought it was scandalous that it hadn't really been told. Many of the soldiers I met who had experienced it felt – strongly – that there was something hypocritical about the end of the war. And then, when I continued my research, I found...that some of the stuff the media had "previewed" had happened, to a degree never brought into our awareness.'

The media's control over how the war was perceived had given him a genuine desire to tell the truth about the hidden events, it seemed: 'Everybody's image from the war was of computer images, which dehumanizes the whole thing. So I wanted to show what it was like to live with a gas alarm and know that different kinds of gases are in the air. I wanted to show what it was like to meet Iraqis face to face, and what it was like to see all this stuff stolen from Kuwait. Getting the information out was a powerful motivation for me.'

Ice Cube may well have been the first person Russell cast but, as he revealed to *SplicedWire*, there was another contender for the Chief Elgin role – a very surprising choice. 'I wanted either [Cube] or Charlie Hayes, who played third base in the '96 World Series Yankees. I think now he plays for the Giants. He's not an actor, but I love his energy.' Personal qualities overruled acting experience, it seems, when it came to casting this part: '[Hayes is] very focused, quiet, solid, intense, no nonsense. Cube has that in spades, and that's how I cast him... I thought he really hadn't had an opportunity since [Boyz] to do some serious acting, which is what he wanted to do, which is why there's no songs of his here. He wants to separate himself as an actor and take it seriously... I cast people who I think feel real and think feel right for the part and have a passion about it.'

As for the anti-consumerist message, alongside which Cube's

almost spiritual role is in stark contrast, Russell was very clear about his motives: 'I knew that consumer culture was going to be a big part of the movie. Everything I read...showed that this was the first war where [they] had their CD players over there, some guys had Watchmans and they were watching the war they were in on TV. And there was a lot of stuff stolen from Kuwait, which is one of the richest countries in the world, and all the goodies of America are over there, from blue jeans to lime green Cadillacs.'

The making of the film was both tough and enjoyable, it appears. Ice Cube later told a fan during a Webchat that both Wahlberg and Clooney enjoyed plenty of female attention ('Man, that George Clooney just turns down pussy all day long'), while Wahlberg recounted how everyone wanted to watch the filming of his torture scene: 'It wasn't fun. George and Cube and a bunch of guys who were not in that scene would come to watch.' Russell explained that the others had stepped on the wires leading up to Wahlberg, managing to hurt him temporarily. Add to this the military training the cast underwent, and the learning curve must have been both steep and exhausting. Russell said, 'They had three days of going shooting, then [the military advisers] got them comfortable with the M-16 [rifle], they gave them the lingo of the war, then they had a four-day mission where (after) we built our sets, they did an assault on the town and stuff like that.' However, he admitted that the cast had at least slept in the Holiday Inn, rather than in a camp.

It later emerged that Spike Jonze had kept himself busy during the filming by making his own mini-documentary on Ice Cube, using a single hand-held camera. This was eventually edited and issued on the DVD version of *Three Kings* as *An Intimate Look Inside The Acting Process With Ice Cube*, a semi-tongue-in-cheek title which reflects the subject matter (Cube does indeed spend some time explaining how he gets into the mind-set of the Chief Elgin character), but is more illuminating for its depiction of the on-set activity.

The publicity done by the actors as the film went to release was light-hearted but sober, with Clooney pointing out perceptively, 'There is a danger...as we go through this [publicity] process, that Cube and

Mark and Spike and I, and David, too, are going to suddenly become experts on the Gulf War... Since we sort of go after the George Bush policy in this a little bit, that's going to become a hotbed. So, suddenly we are going to become these experts on something that we don't know enough about to be the experts on. We know *some*.'

Their knowledge (or lack thereof) of their subject didn't stop many critics from piling praise on the film. The *Chicago Sun-Times'* Roger Ebert said, '*Three Kings* is some kind of weird masterpiece, a screwloose war picture that sends action and humor crashing head-on into each other and spinning off into political anger. It has the freedom and recklessness of Oliver Stone or Robert Altman in their mad-dog days, and a visual style that hungers for impact.' *Slate's* David Edelstein went one better than the Stone/Altman comparison, holding Russell up as a kind of mad genius: 'The movie takes the view of a mordant social scientist who recognizes that consumerism has become the true world religion... *Three Kings* is not the first anti-war movie in which opposing soldiers have recognized themselves in one another before pulling the trigger, but it might be the first to make the point in a way that has nothing to do with liberal humanism.' Wesley Morris at the *San Francisco Examiner* crowed that '*Three Kings*, in all its ragged, sand-swept glory is still a work of strangely bold, distinctly American pop art – proud to be ashamed, ashamed to be proud, unafraid to ignore its commercial bearings 'cause it can laugh all the way to MENSA before it stops at the bank... [It] is a post-colonial, post-war, action-heist-comedy-satire-farce-screwball circus that's like *M*A*S*H* being churned by a sneering, over-amped organ grinder.'

It seemed that Ice Cube could at last boast a bona fide classic film on his CV, to stand alongside *Boyz N The Hood*. But, as usual, he wasn't about to wait around for the plaudits to come to him. His next project was already under way. Although the ripples from *Three Kings* had not yet died down, Cube's next appearance in public came only one month later, when a new film (in which he played a cameo) was released. The movie was a Mack 10 vehicle called *Thicker Than Water*, and it's perhaps just as well that Cube's role was a minor one – the movie was received with lukewarm reviews at best. Talk about peaks and troughs...

Premiered on 31 October 1999, *Thicker Than Water* was a weak attempt at combining the setting of the great ghetto films – *Boyz N The Hood*, *New Jack City* – with the humour of *Friday*. It failed on both counts, although Mack 10 managed to retain some dignity by putting on a relatively competent performance. Other roles were handled by more rappers – Fat Joe as Lonzo, MC Eiht (sometime of Compton's Most Wanted) as Lil' Ant, CJ Mac as Gator and Big Pun as Punny. The plot centred on the rivalry between two Los Angeles gang leaders whose attempts to break into the music business lead them to unite and agree a temporary truce. It soon falls into disarray and, predictably, the guns come out.

The reviews weren't great. Scott Tobias at the *Onion* concluded his review of *Thicker Than Water* with the accurate comment that 'Mostly it's about guns, catfights, unmotivated freeze-frames, and crudely improvised dialogue miked from about a block away. Ice Cube and B-Real show up for an afternoon's worth of scowling and cue-card-reading, respectively, in celebrity cameos well suited to this numbingly obligatory venture.'

But Cube wasn't likely to let these reviews bother him (they weren't even about his own film). He had also contributed to *Thicker* by recording a song for the soundtrack with Westside Connection (a logical move, given fellow WC member Mack 10's role in the movie) called 'Let It Reign'. He told MTV that a new Westside album would appear in May 2000. 'When we all in the studio together,' he said, 'it makes it that much easier, because you got three [people] who been around long enough to know what's going to work and what's not going to work. And it's a lot of fun, a lot of friendly competition with the rhymes, and it's a good thing.'

What has largely been forgotten about the dying months of 1999 is that many people were casting their thoughts forward, not back…to the new millennium, which only a few years later already seems such an antiquated concern. Cube had certainly spent some time thinking about it, telling *Music Monitor* that 'Hopefully after this millennium's over, people will take off all the jackets that they wore during this millennium, all their hang-ups. You know, everybody thinks the world is going to end next year, New Year's Eve. I don't believe that. I believe that once people see that the world is *not* gonna end, it's gonna keep going, I think people will be more like "OK, let's do something about this world." I think right now, people are just riding, trying to ride this out to the end right now, and when the end doesn't come when they think, you know what's left? It's left for them to get busy and try to change things they don't like. Because who wants to go through another millennium like this one?'

A good point. And, as the end of the year approached, Cube flung himself into activity once more. Priority issued a compilation album called *Fox Sports Presents Game Time!* on 28 September, a collection of tunes designed to accompany sports events. Highlights were Snoop Dogg's laconic version of Queen's 'We Will Rock You', Ice Cube's 'In the Zone (Ken Griffey Jr Theme)' and a re-tweaked 'Rock Is Dead' remix of Westside Connection's 'Bow Down'. As a musical project it wasn't particularly important, other than in keeping Cube's name in the limelight while promo duties for 2000 approached. Much more significant were renewed promises that, despite all the difficulties, a revamped NWA would finally appear. Cube had mentioned to MTV that a reunion might come to pass, and on 17 November Dr Dre (whose *Dr Dre 2001* album had restored him to the top of the charts) went on record at the station with the words: 'Me and Cube have been talking for the last two weeks about doing a NWA album, and I'm really into it. He seems motivated. We talked to Ren.'

The greatest revelation for most listeners was the fact that Eazy-E's place would be taken by none other than Snoop Dogg. 'Snoop would be the fourth member of the group. I think it would be a hot project. Myself, Cube, Ren, and Snoop would be incredible,' enthused Dre, not mentioning whether Yella would be involved or not. As for an album title? 'We're gonna call the album *Not These Niggaz Again*,' he said.

Hip-hop fans chuckled in glee at the idea of the multi-millionaires Dre, Cube and Snoop, plus the plucked-from-obscurity Ren, reforming the band and putting out an album with such an apposite title. But their humour turned to shock when it was revealed that in fact a new song had already been recorded by the revised line-up, and that it was set to appear in the new millennium. Who could have predicted it? No one – and, at this point, more than a few dissenting voices were heard, primarily belonging to those fans who believed that Eazy's memory would be tarnished by such a project. These voices remained a constant background for the entire 'new NWA' project...which had only just got off the ground.

Meanwhile, one of the last things Ice Cube did before the millennium ended was to assemble a soundtrack album for the next *Friday* film, which had been titled (yes!) *Next Friday*. A single, 'You Can Do It' – a positive message for the beginning of a new century – was scheduled for release. Observers were mostly pleased to see that he had brought back the huge 'Family Values' bust of himself for the 'You Can Do It' video. As he told MTV Radio, '[It's] basically a performance video, a lot of hot girls in there, the crowd going crazy. I'm on stage rhyming and what's cool about it is that...I got this skull of my head and my shoulders that sits like 17 feet [5.5 metres] tall, so it was cool to bring that out, you know. People would be able to check that out. I took it on the Family Values tour with me and it's cool for people to be able to see it in the video.'

Millennium eve (31 December 1999) came and went. The world didn't stop turning; the much-feared Y2K bug failed to materialise in the world's computer systems; and no messiah, Christian or otherwise, was reported. January 2000 was business as usual, and in Cube terms a high point of the month was the release of 'Chin Check', the first single by the new NWA. The song was as expert as everyone had expected, with all the humour and venom that many had predicted, but it was by no means as raw or as angry as the old NWA, and some listeners felt slightly let down, although Cube's hissed 'Fuck Jerry Heller' line showed that there were plenty of undercurrents still bubbling away. Strangely, Cube himself didn't appear to be wholly supportive of the song, telling a UK *Guardian* journalist in February that 'Chin Check' was 'just an appetiser...'cause everyone knows that the album's gonna be the big record'. Asked why NWA had reformed after so many years, he pondered, 'We were tired of talking about it. For years, every time we'd see each other we'd be like "You know what we should do? You know what we should do? We should do an NWA record." So finally it gets to the point where it's like, "OK, meet me at the studio on Wednesday".'

Of the Jerry Heller reference, Cube claimed: 'That doesn't bother me... History is history, there's no point trying to get away from that. So, yeah, we got baggage, but all we can do now is put together an album that's greater than anybody's expectations. Because when it's done, it's got to be the best record out there.' The band were older now, of course: 'Our lifestyles have slowed down, we got money and families. But the group is like a razor blade, you know what I'm saying? It's bigger than our personal lives. And you gotta keep it sharp. You can't let it get dulled up... It's like sports. The rookies get the attention, and it's the veterans who come through and win the championships when the rookie's at home watching on TV. And I play for the championships.' Rumour even had it that the first NWA video would be directed by none other than Quentin Tarantino, who would have a budget at his disposal of between £525,000 and £700,000 ($750,000 and $1 million). The reunion was clearly causing ripples in high-up circles.

The making of 'Chin Check' had been both smooth and hampered, as Cube told Blackfilm.com: 'The first thing I wanted to make sure of is that the song fit the movie. We talked about a reunion so much over the years, that it was like "Man forget this talking, we can talk about it up at the studio. Let's meet up at the studio". We got up there, Dre started puttin' on some tracks. We found the one that was right for us, we just started going at it... We did that record in a four day period. Because it takes time to vibe and kick it and find out what you wanna do. How you wanna reintroduce NWA to the world. So the first couple of days we were sort of like feeling each other out. Seeing what's been going on for these last 10 years. The second day it was a little looser, and the third day it was almost back to the way it was when we were first making records. On the fourth day we were ready to do more, but by then it was over. We never really got back into the groove that we need to be in to do the record that we need to do. That's why I feel that once we get this paperwork out of the way and we can go somewhere and kick it for two or three months, we can just hang and become NWA again.'

On 12 January 2000, *Next Friday* appeared in American cinemas. 'This time we went for punch,' Ice Cube told MTV. 'We went for the comedy. You know, there was a couple little things but I don't like to beat people over the head with [social commentary], especially with this type of movie. We ain't gonna save the world with this one, but we will bust your gut open.' US audiences were apparently keen to investigate and the film rapidly topped all movie lists after an opening weekend in which 1,100 screens took almost £12 million ($17 million) in receipts – not bad for a movie whose budget was under £7 million ($10 million). The movies it was up against were strong rather than world-class, it's true (*Stuart Little* and *The Green Mile* were among them), but *Next Friday*'s status as New Line Pictures' most successful film after the tedious *Austin Powers* series is not to be sniffed at.

The story of how the film came together is interesting. Chris Tucker, who memorably played Smokey in the first *Friday*, had chosen not to be involved in the sequel, having apparently told Cube that he had found God and didn't want to swear any more. More convincing is the fact that Tucker's career had gone stratospheric (he was now commanding eight-figure fees after appearances in films such as Jackie Chan's *Rush Hour*) and that a come-down to Cube's hood films would have been something of a backwards step. So Cube needed a fast-talking funnyman as a foil to his own, fairly relaxed style (Smokey is said to be 'in rehab' in the movie), and he set up auditions for comedians who wanted an acting break.

Mike Epps, a seven-year veteran of the New York comedy circuit, was the man chosen by Cube and director Steve Carr. 'I feel like the luckiest man in the world,' he told *Cinemayhem*. 'One minute I'm on the road doing stand-up and the next I'm playing opposite a guy I idolize in a sequel to one of my favorite films.' Carr added that 'People have an expectation of how good a sequel should be and generally people think sequels suck...[but] we really felt strongly about using someone new, just as Chris Tucker was introduced as a new talent in the original *Friday*... The hardest and the best thing about directing this movie was picking Mike. He's gonna be a huge star.'

Carr himself was in a similar position to Epps – a man with plenty of experience in the industry (he had previously directed promo clips for Notorious BIG, Public Enemy, the Beastie Boys, Jay-Z and Mary J Blige) who was looking for a break into feature-length work. 'He was just so enthused to do it,' Cube told MTV. 'Much more than that, he's had his hands on a lot of good videos and he was just ready, it seemed. And I'm always into givin' somebody a shot, because somebody gave me a shot, and I'm always into taking chances with new talent. Steve is a new talent, and he was ready to kind of step up to this level, and he did a good job.'

It seems that Ice Cube's development into full-blown movie executive had encompassed most areas of the film-making process. Blackfilm.com asked Cube about the making of *Next Friday*, and learned that the usual test screenings that all studios carry out had had a slightly different focus: 'It's a practice in Hollywood to watch a movie with an audience and then make changes,' said Cube. 'But what we really did was to try to find out what music was working. Or about editing problems that we had. I always look at things like what scenes feel long and should be shorter. I never really go in to see what they laugh at or what they don't laugh at. Because what this audience laughs at, that audience doesn't laugh at. People are different. I just try to put as many laughs in a movie as I can without hittin' you over the head with the idea that this is a comedy. And then from there let it flow. If you don't enjoy the laughs, you enjoy the story.'

Commercially, the movie was an undoubted success. However, the critics were less keen, perhaps due to the plot rather than any other objection – after all, the original *Friday* had the benefit of novelty value, plus the almost elegant concept of events happening to two characters who simply sit on their front porch all day and smoke weed. *Next Friday* tried to be more dynamic on several levels (location, budget, scope) and it seemed that Ice Cube hadn't diversified enough for some, but had remained too static for others – a tricky situation to find oneself in. Cube's concept revolved around the transferral of ghetto values (and events) into a middle-class environment, and his plot engineered this by having his character, Craig, move to a wealthy LA suburb, Rancho Cucamonga, after news comes that *Friday* thug Debo has been released from prison and is seeking revenge. Alarmed, Craig's hapless father takes his son to stay with his lottery-winning uncle Elroy, his voluptuous girlfriend Sugar and his cousin, Day-Day.

This move is the key to the film. As Cube told a press conference, 'We knew we had the makings of a franchise, so we moved into overdrive thinking about how we could keep things fresh but familiar at the same time. The best way to creatively hammer that home was to move the film's setting from the inner city to the suburbs.' This ghetto-comes-to-your-house device was not a new one (remember *The Fresh Prince Of Bel Air?*), but was still an effective stratagem, ensnaring white audiences. It also pointed a sarcastic finger at the black middle class: Cube's depiction of Elroy and Sugar is immediately made humorous by the fact that they indulge in S&M activities – that staple (and stereotypical) foible of the nouveau riche.

Once ensconced in the lap of the bourgeoisie, various subplots develop: Craig falls for a Latino beauty (played by Lisa Rodriguez), enraging her gangsta brothers; it emerges that Elroy and Sugar have spent almost all their money, and Craig elects to help them out of their financial straits by getting hold of some cash; and Day-Day (played with some panache by Epps) is enduring the wrath of his pregnant girlfriend, D'Wana, who is placing demands on him that he is unwilling to meet. All the strands run in parallel, but the overall effect isn't cohesive, unfortunately, making the movie more a series of gags than one with a central thrust. Add to this the rapid, music-video-style direction by Carr, and the film feels too lightweight to take seriously.

All of which could have easily been predicted, of course – the point here, it seems, is to enjoy the foolishness for its simple humour value and not search for any deeper meaning. However, critics (whose job, by definition, is to criticise) have never been very good at this and were mostly pretty snide in their reviews. The humour is everywhere, though, paying homage in many cases to the gross-out wit that film-makers such as the Farrelly Brothers (whose *There's Something About*

Mary had seen Cameron Diaz apply semen to her hair, mistaking it for gel) had made popular in the mid- to late 1990s. Dog turds abound, and characters fall on to them; there's plenty of fart humour, caused by a dodgy burrito; a touch of uneasy incest humour pops up when Sugar greets Craig by running her tongue down his neck; at one point a top lip is stuck in a vacuum cleaner; and there's even a white pothead for amusement value. Cultural references are present, too, with the black sitcom *The Jeffersons* hinted at, a cameo from Michael 'Higher Learning' Rapaport, and the fact that a Latin thug refers to his penis as Mini-Me (the name of the dwarf in *Austin Powers 2*). Craig also smokes dope to the point of hallucination, allowing Carr and Cube plenty of chances to film stupidly trippy sequences.

Despite all the unpretentious humour, the reviewers were fairly brutal. *Box Office* magazine observed that 'This watered-down sequel...has been reduced to multiple skits woven together with a hyped soundtrack... Mike Epps does an adequate job as Ice Cube's sidekick but doesn't come close to filling Tucker's shoes', while the *LA Times* wailed, 'Somebody please remind me that this is supposed to be a golden age for movies... There is plenty of nasty patter and aimless jokes about hard-core sex, soft-core drugs, dog feces and flatulence to keep you occupied while you wait, in vain, for any reason to laugh out loud... If there were any justice, *Next Friday* would be the last *Friday*.'

Others disliked the film's lack of structure, with the *Onion*'s Nathan Rabin stating: 'The first *Friday* didn't exactly boast a screenplay of Shakespearian complexity, but it's a model of structure and ingenuity compared to this directionless mess... [Its] desperate failure to amuse is its most offensive feature.' Still others found it too focused on lowbrow (or even no-brow) humour. The *Austin Chronicle* pointed out that it was 'a story disappointingly similar to the original...populated with sitcom clichés and misogynistic toss-offs, [the film] just can't seem to get enough of the transcendent beauty of getting stoned and the wonder of the human fart.' However, one or two writers managed to swallow their preconceptions and let themselves snigger a little, with the *Toronto Sun*'s Liz Braun observing: 'What's funny in *Next Friday* is mostly politically incorrect material...

[Cube] certainly seems to know what makes people laugh, especially in the adolescent set... [Since] the movie begins with someone falling in dog doo, you may be sure that excrement is a recurring theme. Not without socially redeeming value, *Next Friday* strikes a blow for endangered feces.'

Despite all this, the targets of the film (this being Ice Cube, there have to be some) are clear: middle-class snobs and – more subtly – those who worship at their feet, assuming that the suburbs are safe and peaceful, and therefore a desirable place to be. Interestingly, the barbs that Cube fires at the ghetto in *Friday* (that it's a moronic place, full of violence and pointless obsession) are the same that he directs at the 'burbs five years later – not a point that many reviewers spotted. Not only this, but its success as a near-underground black film in taking over the mainstream was obviously part of Cube's agenda. He told the UK *Guardian* that 'they thought it was just a lightweight black comedy. And I knew that, both from the outside and from inside the studio. They thought, Oh, here's this nice little black movie, we'll give him a few screens and see what it do. And to come out like it did and make $19m [£13m] first weekend, I mean that ain't no fuckin' joke, man. So now the business know all about my nice little black movie.' Asked to comment on the fact that audiences might be surprised at how different the *Friday* films were from classic early 1990s ghetto films such as *Boyz N The Hood*, he shrugged: 'Well, that's the many faces of Ice Cube. I mean, people know me as one way, hardcore, a bad motherfucker, and that's cool. But the fans wanted this and you got to give the fans what they want. Or you're just playing into the hands of the doubters.'

So what went wrong? Astute observers of the gross-out genre (which had probably reached its nadir long before *Next Friday*, with *Dumb & Dumber*, *Kingpin*, *Dogma* and the aforementioned *There's Something About Mary*) might reason that this branch of teen movie, largely perceived to be a white invention, simply did not translate to the black environment. Maybe white critics were still expecting explosions in black films to come from guns rather than rectums. Perhaps they couldn't relax in front of a depiction of the hood enough to enjoy the stupid gags (and the gags really *are* stupid) on their own terms.

Yet audiences flocked to see it, black and white, which means either that the critics were way out of line when they gave the movie a bad review, or simply that Cube was cleverer than they gave him credit for and knew what America's youth wanted to see. And let us not forget the soundtrack: whatever people thought of *Next Friday*, there's no doubt that 'Chin Check' was interesting, musically and historically. A high point of the *Next Friday* soundtrack (which also included work by the Wu-Tang Clan, Eminem and Aaliyah), the song imparted a genuine sense of history at work. Rarely had reunions of any band sparked such interest in mainstream culture (the Beatles for their 1990s *Anthology* series excepted) and *never* in the hip-hop community.

Hardly had the nation's gangsta-rap fans (whether secretly so or proudly advertising the fact) got over the thrill of hearing NWA back in action than Ice Cube unveiled the second part of the *War & Peace* set. *Peace* appeared on 29 February 2000 and caused immediate surprise by being almost as hardcore a record as its predecessor, but with an almost light-hearted atmosphere in parts. Cube was asked to explain the similarities (and differences) between the two records in several interviews, telling MTV: 'Well, there's different subject matter. The single that's out right now…me and Krazyie Bone with "Until We Rich", that's just different for Ice Cube. It's something new. A fresh look, a new kind of flavour.' He was right. The single epitomised the somewhat lighter approach of *Peace* in comparison with *War*, whose 'Ghetto Vet' and 'Fuck Dying' had set a doom-ridden tone from the outset.

A notable cameo on *Peace* came from the comedian Chris Rock, whom Cube asked to lay down some vocal tracks on 'You Ain't Gotta Lie (To Kick It)'. A hilarious skit about boasting and its consequences, Rock's appearance was a returned favour for a stint Ice did on Rock's 1999 comedy album, *Bigger And Blacker*.

Cube told MTV, 'Well, me and Chris go way back. We're good friends. He's always been a fan of mine, and I've always been a fan of his since… his early work. Whenever we see each other it's nothing but a cool vibe, and I saw him at a [New York] Knicks game and I told him, "Yo, I'm down here in the studio. It'll be cool if you could jump on it." I had done something for his album as well. So to get him on the track was just a...bond, because he is the hottest comedian out there right now and funny as hell. I love his sense of reality and that his jokes are based upon reality. I love that about Chris.'

One or two fans drew a sharp intake of breath at the appearance of Sean 'Puff Daddy' Combs on the record – Puff, or P-Diddy as he would shortly begin calling himself, was regarded by some as one of the leading lights of the slushier, commercial end of hip-hop due to his considerable chart success. But Cube was having none of this: 'Puffy not only produces pop music, he produces hardcore music, too. He's a very talented dude, from Warren G to hip-hop... He likes my work, and he wanted to do something for me, so we figured, OK, let's do something that's dope... We came up with a song, called "Gotta Be Insanity"...and it's off the hook. Off the hook.'

The album demonstrates new directions on several levels for Ice Cube. First off, there's the appearance of new collaborators – Combs, Krayzie-Bone, Ms Toi, comedian Chris Rock – although (as usual) Cube himself functioned as the executive producer. Second, the sleevenotes include a full discography and film credits – a new departure for Ice and one that led many to debate whether he was drawing a permanent line under his rap career with *Peace*. Next, no Cube record had included as many inserts (between-song fragments of dialogue) since *The Predator* ('Mental Warfare' and 'Dinner With The CEO' are especially memorable). Finally, a new song with Dre and Ren called 'Hello' opened the record – it's a good song, and one that isn't easily forgotten, but Cube had made an unusual choice by placing it as the opener, with his erstwhile comrades so prominent on the record.

So *Peace* is an oddity. Add up the points above and it's clear that there's an air of strangeness to it that makes it interesting. Not that Cube was answering many questions about his choices. As usual, he was keeping his cards close to his chest about his motives, although he did expand on how he fitted all his activities into his life: 'I guess the best way to explain it is...I come from a situation with basically no opportunities. I mean, if you listen to my early music I'm crying about the conditions and the shit I grew up in. Now, if you offer somebody like me an opportunity, it's almost sacrilegious for me to turn it down.

You know, all the kids wishing they could do it. So, when I get action at something I'm gonna try my best, that's all it is. You know, I'm not just gonna sit there and complain, "Yo, the white man this and the white man that..." So, if I get offered a movie, I better do good in the fuckin' movie. So all I'm doing is taking advantage of action.' And a busy life is a happy one in Cube's world: 'I love kinda overlapping things. I like keeping myself busy, because in this business you can do a lot of sitting around. You can waste your time, and I don't like doing that... This is just normal for me. It's fun.'

'Fun' had also involved setting up a film production company, Cubevision, in partnership with Street Knowledge. 'Cubevision is there to develop the shit that other people are shaky on,' Cube told the UK *Guardian*. 'Raw shit, ideas from the street. When people see the Cubevision logo, they should know it's something good, something worth checking out.' What the 'raw shit' might be is not difficult to define – Ice pointed out that his pre-*Player's Club* scripts were rejected several times: 'I would never rely on the studio system. Because their system is too goddamn fickle. Executives get fired, executives get hired, and you don't even know if your guy is gonna be there when the movie's done... Man, I went through that, and I vowed I'd never do it again. That's why I'm intent on bringing my own shit into the movie house.'

Cube explained the Cubevision set-up to Blackfilm.com: 'When you first get into this the way I did where I had screenplay that New Line wanted, that gives you a little power. Because you have something that the people want, which was the first *Friday*. They let us do it the way we wanted to do it. New Line showed up on the set maybe once while we were shooting the movie. And they didn't say nothing, they just stood back and watched.' He has enjoyed similar non-interference on other projects, too: '*The Player's Club* was the same way. I directed it and showed that I can direct and just took another step into it. And now we're in a position where they know I know what I'm talking about. They know I have a vision and that I know how to go out there and make money, and not spend it all or use all of it. And that's very attractive.'

And it doesn't end there... 'So in the future I want to continue to do more movies. I want to start to bring up the budget more. I want to do more dramatic things. I'm into horror. I'm into comedy. Those are the three things I'm really into. So those are the three things that I'm pursuing. We are looking to acquire screenplays. We're looking to go into television with some of our ideas. More with cable, television is just a little too [constricting]. With cable you can be more raw and real. And that's what we're doing.'

This multifaceted approach was beginning to make Ice Cube a name for himself. None other than Jennifer Lopez, with whom Cube had shared a seat within the coils of an animatronic anaconda, told MTV Radio: 'He's the perfect example of somebody who does [movies and music]. I mean, he's producing movies and directing now. He's an incredible talent. I just think it's silly to pigeonhole anybody into one thing. There are all different types of artists, some people just do one thing and some people do several. You can't do that to somebody who has something to express, I feel like.' She was right – and coming from her the comments mean something. After all, Lopez had developed highly successful film and music careers with an effortlessness that belied the planning that had gone into both.

Meanwhile, Cube was shooting a video for 'Hello', the first single to be released from *Peace*. Once again speaking to MTV, he assessed the song with the words: 'It's just a song about us, kind of letting people know where all this stuff comes from, all the hip-hop that the kids been doing for the last 11 years. It's just a song that's just kind of giving respect where respect is due, and we're kind of giving it to ourselves.' It was also reported that Cube would enter the studio with Dre and Ren to record the long-awaited NWA album, still tentatively titled *Not These Niggaz Again*.

At last it seemed as though the agonising wait might be over, although Snoop – always a wiser man than his years would seem to indicate – counselled caution in *Vibe* magazine: '[If] that record gon' come together, we gon' need to have nothin' to do for two months but be in the studio and create this NWA record. Other than that, shit ain't gonna happen.' Asked when the album might appear, he estimated

'2002, because niggas' schedules is hectic right now'. Cube was still confident, telling MTV that working with the ex-members 'felt good, you know? It felt like, well – for anybody who has moved out of their parents' house, [like] when you go back home and sit in your old room. You feel comfortable. There's just a vibe you get, and that's what we got when we all got back in the studio together. We hadn't worked for 11 years – all of us, together – and to do "Chin Check" for the *Next Friday* soundtrack, and then to do "Hello", this is just the tip of the iceberg.' He concluded with what amounts to a battlecry: 'Once we get in a groove and we start doing the real deal, we're gonna definitely make history again with NWA.'

Even the normally taciturn Dre was relatively loquacious, telling the New Zealand magazine *Selector* that 'We're definitely gonna do it, and hopefully it'll get a release by the end of next year. We're gonna call the album *Not These Niggaz Again*. First of all we have to find out who owns the name NWA, and then we have to make sure there's not a lot of people dipping their hands in the pie. I think we're gonna do a couple of songs live. We won't be starting on the record until the tour is over and we are plannin' on a NWA tour.'

MTV weren't the only people who asked why the focus on an album (rather than a series of singles or a tour) was so strong. Cube explained that 'We've got to put out a full-length record, because there ain't no use to do this unless you put out a whole album. Not just a whole album, but an album that everybody *wants*. I can't wait to start working on it, because I know that it's just gonna be magic. When you get Dr Dre, MC Ren, Snoop Dogg, and Ice Cube in the same room working on the same music, it's got to be magic.' He also praised Snoop for his adaptability – 'We needed that somebody to balance us off. Eazy-E, with his voice, his approach and his lyrics, he balanced me, Ren and Dre. We need that same balance. We thought that we lost a superstar with Eazy-E, and we wanted to bring in another superstar to hopefully, in some way, fill that void. So Snoop Doggy Dogg is the perfect person for that, because ain't nobody down like Snoop.' His next claim might well have upset a few Eazy-E fans, however: 'Snoop can rhyme with the best of them, and to have him on the team makes

NWA as perfect as it was back in 1988, when we came out with *Straight Outta Compton*.'

Of course, Cube has never lost sight of the big picture. Asked where the new NWA album might fit into the grand scheme of things, he answered, 'Well, hip-hop is a beautiful thing, because the music always finds a new home somewhere. You know, the East Coast started out with the music, then the West Coast, we put our own little flavor on it. Then the East Coast put out a new twist on it. Now, the West Coast is puttin' out a different kind of music, and it's a beautiful thing with the South bringing up the middle. It's just cool to see the way it swings this way for a time, and then it swings back to the East Coast for a time, then swings back. Hopefully, I'll still be around when it swings back.'

Note the 'when it swings back' – if you're looking for demonstration that this is a man who knows his place in the scheme of things, you need look no further. Cube is aware that life is cyclical and that it is natural for human fortunes to rise and fall. It's this that has kept him afloat throughout his unique career.

13 Smoked

The year 2000 was turning out to be one of Ice Cube's busiest yet. The double impact of *Three Kings* and *Next Friday* had left many critics asking how one man could produce two movies of such wildly varying quality in such a short space of time, but as usual Cube had moved on, switching his focus from films to the music world once again. The *Next Friday* soundtrack had sold well in all American sectors and respectably enough in many overseas territories, and – as the album's undisputed high point was NWA's 'Chin Check' – its success was encouraging enough for Cube, Dre, Ren and Snoop to proceed with a live show.

The question as to why Yella had not been invited to participate in the reunion was not resolved for some time – in fact he seemed to have vanished into obscurity. Little was known about him except the interview that he gave to *Props* magazine in 1996, not long after the death of his friend Eazy-E. Asked whether a reunion might be possible, he responded: 'I would do it, but nobody has approached me. If I did do it, I'd only do it on a neutral label. Dre won't do it if it's on Ruthless and neither will Cube. I won't do it if it's on Death Row. It's got to be a neutral label with five shares owning the label (Eazy's share too) because I want his kids to get money. Nobody's thinking about Eazy's kids, but I'm always thinking about them. One of his sons, my godson Derek, who was always in his videos, is in my video too. People have been talking about a reunion, but nobody has talked to me about it. If they leave me out, no problem. But if I did it, I'd be doing it for real, not for the money.'

Perhaps the label problem lay at the bottom of his lack of

involvement four years later, when the new line-up was rehearsing for the live show, although the official explanation given by the three ex-NWA members was that they had simply lost touch with Yella. Later, however, reports came that the DJ had in fact been tracked down and was ready to roll when the album sessions commenced.

For now, however, the performance was to be part of the taping of the Farmclub.com show (a joint Web and TV concept) and was ultimately recorded on 11 March at Universal Studios in LA. *Sonicnet* was told by Dre that the forthcoming NWA album – which had not yet been recorded – would 'change the course of hip-hop again', while Cube talked about how comfortable it felt being back in his old band. 'It felt like puttin' on your favorite pair of Nikes or somethin' – comfortable fit, perfect,' he said. 'To look over there and have a megastar like Dre, Snoop and Ren right there with you, you know it's magic. Good things come to those who wait. We've all been patient, and tonight's the night.' He also predicted that recording sessions would commence in June.

The show was a landmark occasion. A celebrity-packed audience including Limp Bizkit frontman Fred Durst and director Quentin Tarantino watched the foursome swing into 'Chin Check', running through it twice for the benefit of the cameras. The revised dynamic of the new band was immediately apparent: this time round, instead of Cube, Ren and Eazy sharing the stage as equals, it was down to Cube and Dre to provide most of the visual impact, pacing aggressively from side to side of the stage while Ren was more static (perhaps intimidated a little in the presence of such hip-hop giants?) and Snoop Dogg provided his usual laid-back, swaying performance, emanating his relaxed cool in a Dogg House Records jacket. They followed the new track with a smooth rendition of 'Straight Outta Compton' and then, in an almost calculatedly democratic move, a performance of Dre's 'Ain't Nuthin' But A "G" Thang' from *The Chronic*. The show also featured songs by Tha Eastsidaz, Nate Dogg and Xzibit, and was broadcast at 11pm on 27 March on the USA Network.

The brief recording was acknowledged as a success. Before the gig, Dre had said, 'We always talked about getting back together, but it's just fate, straight-up. If it's supposed to happen now, it's gonna happen now. There's no magical chemistry or none of that shit.' Ice Cube had reassured one or two journalists, uncertain about Eazy's absence, with these words: 'I think Snoop is the perfect, perfect sub for Eazy. Nobody else could win that slot. There was no other person who ever came to my mind. I'm happy that he was able to come in and get down on our track and make NWA live again.' Snoop himself was confident but respectful about the task ahead of him: 'I've been a fan of NWA since they was selling records out of the trunks of their cars when I was in high school. I was supportive of the cause before, and now that I'm in it, I'm gonna keep it alive.' He sounded almost humble as he added, 'I'm gonna do my best to make sure I don't let anybody down and assist the homeboys in the best way that I can and try to make the best album that I've ever been on... [NWA's] records changed the game; they were the best records that were ever heard.' But, above all, he was excited, saying that he felt like 'a kid who just got his first Atari 2600. This is the illest group ever to come out the West Coast. They founded what is known as gangsta rap.'

The rappers were uniformly pleased with the show, with Dre telling *USA Today* that 'It went really well considering that we didn't get a chance to rehearse or anything', and Ren adding, 'It was like being in 1989.' Cube explained the lead-up to the event, as he had been obliged to do so many times already, with these words: 'We were sick of talking about it and saying what we should do. I said the only way we can do all of this stuff we're talking about is to just go do it.' *Farmclub* co-founder Jimmy Iovine (who also happened to be the co-chairman of Interscope Records) also had a moment to speak, comparing NWA to the Beatles and the Rolling Stones: 'They opened things up in terms of not only what artists could say, but how they could say it. I'm not talking about the words they used, but the whole intensity that they brought to what they did.' Cube was more specific, stating that 'We held a window [open] and let the world see things through our eyes.' Dre was blunter still, claiming, 'We said what a lot of people wanted to say for a long time but never had the balls to say on record... I don't think America was afraid of us, not really. We sold a whole lot of records. I think a lot of it was just the way people talked about us in the media.'

Ice Cube was able to take the wide view, as usual. 'When you think about it, we've followed the pattern of American celebrities – at least young ones, anyway. You start out being loved by the kids and hated by the parents, but pretty soon the parents come around. We have so many people out there who grew up on our music. Now there's a whole new generation taking over things, and their minds are more open than the generation before them.'

It's an interesting point. Are the teenagers of the 21st century really more liberated than those of 1987? In some ways, perhaps, yes. Look at the rise of the Internet, for instance, and the spread of universal communications through the now-common mobile phone, which every 14-year-old seems to own. One of the effects of this rise in access to cheap communications technology has to be the increased availability of information. And what is the effect of this? Simply that children and teenagers know more than they did a generation ago, for better or worse, which means either that they're less shockable or just more interested in 'extreme' media in the face of so much ordinary, bland information. It's a point worth thinking about, because it's outspoken artists such as Ice Cube who are talking to the kids – perhaps *your* kids. Understand what they are saying.

Ice also talked about Eazy at the show – inevitable, given the drive that the late rapper gave his band. He thought Eazy would be happy to see the reunion: 'That's what he was trying to get done for the longest time. But just about the time I had made up with him, he was mad at Dre. Before we could get serious about it, Eazy died.' Apart from making sure that no one who was not directly involved with NWA tried to rip off the new line-up – as Ren expressed it, 'coming out of the woodwork and getting their pockets lined' – the reformation had been smooth and almost relaxed, with the members even acknowledging that ego problems had hindered them before. 'When Cube called and set it up, we all went to the studio and were just chilling,' Ren says. 'Nobody was talking about old beefs. Even if it was in the back of your mind, it was over with, and there's nothing you could do about it but just move on... Snoop is West Coast. He represents that to the fullest. He's like somebody coming from college onto a pro team – he has all the stats, and he broke all the records.'

In April 2000 it was reported that Cube had signed a deal with HBO to develop and produce a TV series about the hip-hop music industry called *Be Careful What You Wish For*, in which he might play a small recurring role. When asked how he managed his time with all the projects he worked on, he told MTV, 'I'm always using my time, and, you know, people wouldn't think that... with all that I'm doing, that I can make it home [at] 6:30 every night if I want to, because I use my time well. That's the key. When I'm not doin' nothing, I kick back. Shoot a little hoop, play with my kids, hang out with my boys, and just have fun, man. Try to enjoy life.'

Despite Cube's commitments, the road now seemed clear for an NWA album and tour. Dre said of 'Chin Check' that it would be re-recorded with a new track (an old version had been used): 'I wasn't totally happy with that record because it sounds rushed. We're going to get in there and shock the world...' Always the cautious one, he also pointed out that the new band had not yet determined who owned the rights to the name NWA and that a distribution deal was also still to be finalised. But Ice Cube was more confident about that issue: 'I'm not even thinking about that, because that is just going to be a distraction, and our thing is to make a good record. Once you do that, it's amazing how things work out. Besides, we all have enough money right now to do it without a record company if we have to... People were asking me about this record...all the way back in 1996, so we've got to do it. I would stop making movies for us to tour.'

Momentum was gathering: the new NWA had laid down its gauntlet successfully. Word came that a super-tour was being prepared: not the eagerly awaited NWA outings, but a different set-up, which would bring most of the new line-up together on one bill before the revised band focused on its own activities. As the excitement grew, Ice Cube found himself back in the limelight to a certain extent – and on 3 June was asked to hand out a trophy at the MTV Movie Awards at Sony Pictures Studios in California, along with a stellar list of presenters including Janet Jackson, Mel Gibson, Samuel L Jackson, Sarah Michelle Gellar and Freddie Prinze Jr. The show went out on 8 June on MTV, hosted by *Sex And The City* actress Sarah Jessica Parker. It's interesting to note that Cube was being asked by a music corporation to appear at an event celebrating the film industry – proof that, for him at least, the two worlds had become one. Coincidentally, he had just been on the other side of the podium when, along with LL Cool J, Christina Aguilera and the Backstreet Boys, he was given a Blockbuster Award. In Cube's case the award was given in the Favorite Action Team category, which he shared with George Clooney and Mark Wahlberg for *Three Kings* – a film that had clearly made a mighty impact among the video-rental company's members, and presumably had made some serious cash for its shareholders, too.

As the summer began, the news broke that the hip-hop supertour that everyone had been talking about for some time was finally to happen. To make its agenda clear right from the off, its organisers had named it the 'Up In Smoke' tour – and it was destined to feature one of the most inspired hip-hop bills ever assembled.

The tour, which began on 15 June 2000, was unprecedented on many levels. Although hip-hop tours had existed before – the Def Jam roster had famously hit the road in the 1980s to legendary effect – this time around the cream of rap's current crop would be hitting huge arenas, armed with a production budget unlike any other that had been previously witnessed in the field of hip-hop. The line-up was simply the finest live hip-hop ensemble that had ever been seen on one stage – Ice Cube would open the shows, with Eminem following him, and then a triumphant double act (in the shape of Dr Dre and Snoop Dogg) would headline.

Cube's position as the lowest artist on the bill was appropriate despite his stardom. Eminem was, quite simply, the hottest hip-hop phenomenon to emerge since Public Enemy. Other artists had possessed more credibility, were more talented or more musically pioneering, but a combination of his whiteness, plus a massively controversial profile due to his tumultuous family life and the furore caused by the homophobia and misanthropy in his raps (which he defended as non-literal, although many critics didn't believe him), had ensured that his rise to the top was faster than anyone before him. Also, the Dre/Snoop dream team was one that had been unsurpassed in hip-hop for some years, meaning that the line-up (Cube as the dependable veteran, Eminem as the young upstart on his way up, and the kings of it all on top) was a masterpiece of marketing strategy.

Not that Ice Cube was expected to find it hard to hold his own on this tour. If anything, it was Eminem on which the expectations of the press and public were focused. Could the young white boy make it on the same bill as the original gangsta rappers from the streets of Compton? He fielded the question, which came in many forms, with a confidence that belied his age: 'I don't try to compete, man. I just do what I do. I go out and [do] whatever it is I been doin'.... I don't remember the last show to the next.' In fact, his slot was the most entertaining part of this uniquely entertaining show: he even exploited his position on the tour to aim some disrespectful jibes at a rap-rock band called the Insane Clown Posse, who had publicly commented on him in less than positive tones.

The 40-date tour was a marathon of organisation. Initially only intended to encompass 25 shows, due to phenomenal public demand Dre added another three weeks on to the tour, which meant that the show would commence in California and swing through Oregon, Indianapolis, Ohio, Pennsylvania, Minnesota, Illinois, New York, Massachusetts, Connecticut, Maryland, North Carolina, Georgia and Florida before the extra dates (which would continue without Cube, as he had announced that he would be leaving to start filming yet another movie). The remaining 15 shows would be performed in Louisiana, Texas, Arizona, Nevada and Colorado before the tour finally came to a halt on 20 August.

And what a show it was! Ice Cube's opening set may have been the shortest (he only performed four or five songs per night), but it was perhaps the most dramatic. Observers would have been forgiven for assuming that the years of acting had perhaps lent him a sense of melodrama – his entrance was presaged by a passage from Carl Orff's famous *Carmina Burana*, the stadium was bathed in white light, and he emerged, dressed in white, from a cage that dropped from the roof. His set started with 'Hello', a stamping opening statement which kept audiences' attentions focused on his current work, before dropping into 'You Can Do It' (which, along with 'Chin Check', had helped the *Next Friday* soundtrack to sell so well) and then 'The Nigga You Love To Hate', taken from *Amerikkka's Most Wanted*. On most nights he ended the show with the *Player's Club* tune 'We Be Clubbin'' before exiting to a storm of applause. This old-/new-school approach was welcomed by the crowds, who were delighted at the inclusion of material from both ends of his career, but it was a populist set all right, without much of a sense of the insurrectionist Cube of old. Perhaps, given the confines of the tour, there was little he could do other than deliver a crowd-pleasing set with few surprises.

Eminem's set was precise and to the point, with most of the controversy the fans expected delivered in the form of insults to the Insane Clown 'Pussies', whom he brought on stage in the form of two blow-up sex dolls wearing clown masks. He underlined his point by placing one of the dolls' mouths on his crotch. The message was crude but clear. His set was based on 'Kill U', 'Dead Wrong', 'Under Influence', 'Marshall Mathers', 'Criminal' and the audience-arousing 'The Real Slim Shady', which left the crowd baying for more with its infectious, no-brainer chorus. His potential was clear – and at this stage he was yet to release his biggest hit to date, 'Stan', or to perform with Elton John – both moves that made him much, *much* bigger in the public eye than he was at the time of the 'Up In Smoke' tour. If it were to be repeated at the time of writing, there is no doubt that Eminem would be the headliner.

Dre and Snoop chose to introduce themselves with a brief film, in which the two rappers are seen chilling before a show – in fact, the 'Up In Smoke' show itself. They have a few hours to kill, so they visit a hotel where a bevy of purring, semi-naked beauties await them. It's immediately clear that we're in hip-hop fantasy land, and there's plenty of hood humour going on – 'I needed my hair doing,' says Snoop by way of introduction, 'and Dre wanted his dick sucked.' The camera then focuses in on Snoop's enormous Afro, and the pair are welcomed into an executive suite by a bunch of impatient groupies.

Much bathtub-based nooky ensues (although the director keeps it soft-core for the kiddies) and Snoop lights up a fat joint while his hair is being plaited. Dre calls him and they arrange to go out to score some 'chronic' (why a duo who could afford such luxurious down-time couldn't send a lackey out to pick up some weed is not explained, but this is fantasy, let us not forget...). The two enter a convenience store, where an employee is about to deal them some dope – but robbers burst in and the two rappers hit the floor. Dre runs out of bullets and is stalked by a gloating gunman – but is saved by Snoop, who shoots his attacker through a shelf of food.

Like the best gangsta-rap films, there's a sickening touch of violence at the end of this rather cartoonish clip, when Snoop and Dre are debating whether or not to deliver the coup de grâce to the wounded robber. Snoop leans over to the camera and asks the viewers (that is, the 'Up In Smoke' audience) if they should kill him or not. Receiving a bellowed 'Yes', both men dispatch the unfortunate hoodlum and exit stage left. They then appear on stage, wearing the same clothes they'd worn in the film, and launch straight into the first song, the legendary '(Who Am I?) What's My Name?' It's an incendiary start to a vibrant set, which features 'Ain't Nuthin' But A "G" Thang', 'Bitch Please', 'What's The Difference', 'Forgot About Dre' (the last two feature Eminem), 'Fuck You', 'Let Me Ride' and 'Still D.R.E.'

Taken as a whole, it's a powerful show – it's little wonder that audiences flocked to see it, nor that the video and DVD of the tour (which included plenty of backstage footage, primarily of Eminem fooling around with his posse) sold well. Teenagers loved it for its obvious dope references and parent-scaring vibes, while the press admitted that nothing this impressive had come out of the hip-hop arena in years.

But this wasn't just a tour. The 'Up In Smoke' concept was something quite new in popular culture, and a far bigger milestone than a simple commercial venture. What the tour did was nothing less than legitimise both gangsta-rap and dope-culture values in the minds of many thousands of people, both those who physically witnessed it and those who heard it pass. No, the tour didn't make society a more 'hip-hop' place. However, it did focus a sharp spotlight on changes that had been happening throughout white American culture for some years – ever since the emergence of Ice Cube and Dr Dre, with their seminal *Predator* and *Chronic* albums eight years previously, in fact.

When Dre was asked by the *NME* if the 'Up In Smoke' tour had seen any of the artists get on-the-road cabin fever, he responded, 'Nah, nah, nah! I mean, um, of course there was a few arguments here and there. You know, minor internal arguments within our family. And I got into it with a couple of our production people a few times when, um, some of the pyro-blasts didn't go off, leaving us standing up there looking fucking stupid. It was crazy, but other than that it was perfect. Mission accomplished, we didn't have any problems as far as violence goes.'

More proof of the tour's enormous success is to be seen in the presence of a white artist – not headlining, but beneath more successful black performers. How often does this happen? Very rarely indeed, and the nation found it entirely acceptable. Furthermore, this was no P-Diddy or Will Smith hip-hop tour; this was a gangsta tour, in musical and visual terms. This, and nowhere else, was where gangsta rap entered the mainstream, saw that it was good, extended its hand…and took America's money. After this, there was no point in pretending that hip-hop culture was an underground phenomenon, and least of all its violent subdivision, gangsta rap. This is the turning point the rappers had forecast throughout the 1990s. This was where one era ended and another began. This, and it had been a long time coming, was the point where all bets were off. And the new era it signalled is just beginning.

As an ironic epitaph (and yet more evidence that the cultural tides had turned), both Cube and Dre found themselves invited to *Source* magazine's Hip-Hop Music Awards 2000, scheduled to take place on 22 August in Pasadena. Both men must have laughed when they saw that they were to be given Lifetime Achievement awards: after all, these were the men whom the FBI had warned after 'Fuck Tha Police', and who had once threatened to kill each other in rhyme. The wheel had turned, all right. Amazingly for an artist whose selling power had been in doubt after he departed Death Row and built a new label, Dre also picked up awards for Album of the Year (*Dr Dre 2001*), Single of the Year ('Still DRE') and Solo Artist of the Year.

Cube had to settle for a nomination for Live Performer of the Year along with Method Man, Redman, DMX, Hot Boys and Puff Daddy, but he appeared to be unfazed. If anything, he was somewhat overawed by his trophy: 'When they told me I was receiving the Lifetime Achievement Award, I said damn, I'm only 31,' Cube said as he stood onstage next to Dre. 'But when I look back at the work Dre and I have done in the last 15 years, it *is* a lifetime of work.' A lifetime only partly passed, however, and certainly in NWA terms, whose second phase was about to begin. Fans had now seen the new line-up on stage (both on *Farmclub* and – individually, at least – on the 'Up In Smoke' tour), and had heard their recorded work, with 'Chin Check' still a club staple six months after its release.

Then the shock came. In December 2000, Dre announced that the NWA project had been put on hold indefinitely. Many observers were surprised, others were disappointed – but others curled their lips in sarcasm, claiming that this development hardly came as a surprise. Had the rappers fallen out? Had they disagreed over money *again*? Apparently not. The reason given by Dre, and later corroborated by Ice Cube, was that each artist had finally run out of time. Cube was acting in another movie; Dre was working hard as a record label chief; Snoop had a record and label to develop.

Dre told MTV that a couple of sessions had been recorded. 'We got a couple things down, nothing that I'm happy with, so they don't mean anything – the status of NWA right now remains in limbo, because everybody that's supposed to be a part of this record has their own careers, and they're out doing their things... Ice Cube is working on a big special-effects movie, Snoop Dogg has a record coming out and is gonna promote that, and I'm working with my new artists, trying to do my thing.' The death knell for the new NWA came when he said, pointedly, 'I have no idea when that record's gonna happen, or *if* it's gonna happen.'

Ice Cube confirmed this when he told a fan that Dre simply did not have the time and that, as the chosen producer, his availability was paramount: '[Dre is] producing the album, and unless he says, "Yo, I'm ready, I got music for you," then it's no project. It's just a mess that nobody is ready to dive into, because everybody wants to get paid. It's gonna cost a fortune for the record. So it might not ever happen.'

So the wheel had almost come full circle. Not completely, but almost, and its final revolution had been prevented by a simple lack of time. However, perhaps some hip-hop-aware deity is guiding the course of events here and maybe the time is not right for NWA's return. Perhaps the time will *never* be right. After all, the righteously angry young men of the 1980s are hip-hop's senior statesmen now that tomorrow has arrived, and maybe their anger was best expended back then, when times were different.

NWA seems to be on hold, but that may be a good thing. Like a weird kind of urban King Arthur, whose Excalibur is an AK-47 rather than a sword, perhaps we need them to stay dormant until the time is right and they are needed again. That day may still be distant, or it may be just around the corner.

14 A Piece Of The Pie

NWA might have been dormant but Ice Cube was very much still in action, facing the future much as he always had – with a mixture of confidence, realism and raw attitude. An artist who received the Ice Cube guest-appearance touch at this time was Ms Toi, whose debut album, *That Girl* (she had been labelled 'That Girl' since her cameo with Cube and Mack 10 on 'You Can Do It' from the *Next Friday* soundtrack), featured his rapping skills on 'My Dogs & My Locs'. The record also featured MC Ren on 'Bangin''.

However, much of Cube's attention in the early months of 2001 was focused on a new film, which he had chosen to appear in largely because of the reputation of the director – legendary John Carpenter, whose name had been made with *Dark Star*, *Halloween*, *Escape From New York*, *Christine* and *They Live*. In the wake of *Three Kings*, many critics hoped that Cube would react well again to the presence of a strong director and produce a knockout performance.

Ghosts Of Mars duly appeared on over 2,000 screens on 24 August 2001. Put simply, it was a B-movie, based on a schlocky concept and throwing as many horror and action sequences into the mixture as would fit. Initially Cube had been intended to star alongside Hole frontwoman Courtney Love, who had made her name as an actor in *The People Vs Larry Flynt* – but Love injured her ankle during pre-production and it was not to be.

Events in the film take place 200 years into the future. Cube plays a violent criminal called James 'Desolation' Williams, who is in the process of being transferred to a prison in an outpost city called Chryse on the planet Mars. Geoformers have given Mars a breathable atmosphere, and at first sight the team tasked with escorting him – led by intergalactic cop Melanie Ballard, played with aplomb by Natasha Henstridge, who had played an alien in *Species* and its sequel – doesn't seem to have too hard a job on its hands, as long as they keep all weapons out of Cube's reach.

But (of course) there's a hitch. In a similar turn of events to *Alien*, a nearby mining party has triggered an ancient Martian device that summons aggressive ghosts of the now-extinct Martians, which possess most of the mine workers. Ballard, Williams and the team must work together to defeat the not-particularly-creepy, Marilyn Manson-alike zombies in order to survive. Quite simply, it's a blood bath, with some characters dying and some making it out alive – which is a surprise best left unrevealed. Filmed in White Mesa, San Ysidro, New Mexico, the desert location managed to provide a suitably otherworldly look to the scenes.

It emerged that Cube had played more of a role than that of mere actor. The production company, Screen Gems – a new division of Sony – had urged Carpenter to choose him for the role, although the director had initially wanted Cube's co-star Jason Statham (best known for his role as Turkish in *Lock, Stock And Two Smoking Barrels* and *Snatch*) for the role of Desolation Williams. The choice of Cube proved to be fortuitous, however, as Carpenter revealed to Blackfilm.com that 'When he came in and we started talking about the character, he had some great ideas. He's a very interesting and smart man. Very focused on what he's doing. I'm very happy to have him.'

Furthermore, Cube had had a creative input. 'We do nightly rewrites during the first week of rehearsals to adjust for…the input the actors bring to the table. Making a film is constant adjusting. It's Darwinian. You drop what doesn't work, and something better develops out of the process… I told Cube this new idea I had been kicking around for the ending, and the next day he came in and he'd written the whole thing and it was just great. So we incorporated that.'

Henstridge told Zap2it.com that working with Cube was 'cool, it was really cool. The first couple of days that I met him and realized that I had to have a very sort of head-to-head... [The] relationship we have in the film is very strong and even. The first couple of days I met him I was like, "He scares the hell out of me. How am I going to do this?" So I started to joke with him a little bit because he's very intimidating, but really, he's just a sweet guy, he truly is. He just comes across as intimidating when you first meet him. We ended up joking around and having a great time.'

Carpenter was equally complimentary, revealing that Cube had changed the way the director composed music. 'Ice Cube was the one who set me on to ProTools. ProTools is basically a computer system where you can load in your basic tracks and begin to manipulate them in kind of interesting ways. So, I started experimenting with it, and it's fascinating. It's a whole new process.'

The pleasure was mutual, according to Cube. 'John and I talked a lot about Desolation, and he took a lot of my ideas. He appreciated the fact that I came to the table with ideas about character, interaction. He was with it! Hell, the man gets his name above the titles of his movies and to have him welcome my suggestions and changes was more than I could ask for.' But Cube was learning all the time, not just practising his screenwriting: 'I'm learning a lot from him, always looking over his shoulder, asking questions. He's been doing this as long as I've been alive and still he always takes the time to give me the benefit of his knowledge.'

The film's concept was a gripping one, however, with or without Cube's intervention. Carpenter mused that 'Basic human nature will follow us to wherever we decide to live. There will be cops and outlaws, demons and saints, good and bad. And in some instances, the line between good and evil might be blurred.' This appealed to Cube: 'Here's this highly intensive character who is a high-security risk to move. Then you have this situation where the town has been taken over by ghosts, and we have to band together to get out of there. They need his help, and he needs theirs. That's the cool twist to it.'

The role wasn't too stressful, it seemed: 'I feel like a big kid, playing with a lot of big toys. *Anaconda* was much more physically demanding. This is actually one of the easiest movies I've worked on because John is actor-friendly. He doesn't demand a lot from his actors. When he hires you for a part, he hires you for your expertise and what you do. It's really about what your character is thinking and would want to do.'

Like many of the characters Cube had played before – think Doughboy, Savon and even *Friday*'s Craig – Williams was a multilayered role. 'Desolation is an outlaw born on Mars, but he dreams of Earth,' said Cube. 'He has all these films and videos about Earth, so he's really a product of its entertainment, news and media. He becomes an outlaw because he's dissatisfied. He does everything he can to do wrong, and he ends up locked up.' And Carpenter knew that Cube's presence was a definite bonus: 'Ours is a very different kind of Mars movie,' he said. 'First of all, we don't have the budget they had on those films. Secondly, it's a more futuristic Mars, so there's actually breathable air on the planet. This is not a spacesuit movie. Besides, in terms of Mars movies, which other one do you know that has Ice Cube starring in it? I rest my case.'

Statham, who played a fast-talking young gun called Jericho, seemed to be more than a little starstruck by Ice Cube, gushing, 'It was great working with him. He is so cool. The thing is, he is not trying to be cool, he just is. Some people try to be cool and they so are not. He is just cool. The personality he has is great and it was cool to work with him.'

So far, so good? Unfortunately not, for both critics and audiences largely shunned the movie, castigating the veteran Carpenter for a film they regarded as both beneath him and poorly executed. The UK *Guardian* called it a 'cheaply made farrago', while the *LA Times* said that 'Carpenter is skilled at allegory but doesn't make much of the fact that Mars is under female rule' and that 'the film does have the sense of scale of some of Carpenter's previous futuristic adventures, but it unfortunately has few other pluses'. Jeffrey M Anderson at the *San Francisco Examiner* was more charitable, overcoming any intellectual snobbishness and proclaiming it 'a real, honest-to-goodness B-movie'. He also stated that 'Carpenter is acutely aware of his position as a B-movie maker and has always stuck to it' and that the director 'stands his ground, even in the face of a new-fangled industry that doesn't really know what to do with him'.

Most of the negative vibes seemed aimed squarely at Carpenter rather than his actors or camera crew. Michael Atkinson at the *Village Voice* hailed him as 'the last of a dying breed: a cheesy, puberty-suspended mad scientist making the best of arrested development, modest ambitions, moviemaking impatience, and a headful of Ace-paperback ideas endearing for their mustiness', but that *Ghosts* was 'written, directed, and edited with the offhand shoddiness of a day worker thinking about his evening beer'. Meanwhile, Bob Graham at the *San Francisco Chronicle* dubbed the film 'a tired and dispiriting affair that takes forever to get going'. There was some faint praise for Cube, though: 'Ice Cube is a distinctive personality, pudgy and authoritative at the same time, but he needs something to work with.' In the end Graham concluded that 'The best thing this movie has going for it is the end-of-the-world bunker look of the colony and its heavy-duty train-to-nowhere.'

Perhaps some of these statements were unfair – after all, a B-movie should be treated as such. One or two of the critics sniggered at the film's admittedly implausible ending, but then unlikely plot twists are traditionally part of the fun of this genre of film, rather than something to be mocked…as long as the viewer accepts that the movie shouldn't be taken seriously. However, this is a trick that takes time to perfect, and for the moment it seems that *Ghosts Of Mars* will have to go down as another inessential movie in Cube's growing list of projects.

A mere 18 days after the release of *Ghosts*, Cube – like everyone else – was shocked profoundly by the attacks on 11 September on the World Trade Center in New York. Like many observers he was horrified, but, as he revealed in a Webchat hosted by *Blender* in early 2002, he had had a feeling that something of this nature might occur some day. When asked, 'You never pulled any punches when it came to criticizing the US government. Were you surprised by the attacks on September 11?', he responded, 'I was surprised. But I kinda knew something was coming someday. More things probably will come. I don't think anybody is above criticism, especially the government.'

The whole of hip-hop culture was seen to pull together after the attacks: Dr Dre, for example, donated £700,000 ($1 million) to the disaster relief fund. Subsequent events took place, as they did in every other arena, in a gloomy atmosphere; in fact, the shock waves were still reverberating when Ice Cube's press office announced that he would be releasing a greatest-hits package in December. This was not an unexpected move. After all, Cube now had several full-length albums to his name and a huge number of side-projects and collaborations to hand. Furthermore, after ten years as a solo artist, the time was commercially right to reach out to a new generation of listeners, who might not wish to find their way into Cube's work through earlier albums such as *Death Certificate* and *The Predator* (which remain fresh, but lack the late 1990s self-awareness of his more recent albums) or contemporary releases such as the *War* and *Peace* discs (which don't have the classic old-school edge). A best-of was certainly the answer, and fans began to debate which songs should and should not appear on it.

Titled *Ice Cube's Greatest Hits*, the 17-track album (as many songs as would fit on a single CD) duly appeared on 4 December 2001. Cube presaged its appearance with a few interviews, telling writers that quality had won out over commerciality in most cases – 'It's a mixture of things. Songs that were big on the radio and chart-wise, like "It Was A Good Day", but also songs like "A Gangsta's Fairytale" from my earlier years on *Amerikkka's Most Wanted*. A video was never made, the song never charted, but clearly one of my greatest hits. "Jackin' For Beats" is on there. "Pushin' Weight", "We Be Clubbin'", "Check Yo' Self", a whole lot of them.'

Many fans had voiced concern that Cube might be quitting the music business with this collection, but he merely pointed out that 'This might be my last record for a while, 'til I get rejuvenated. Right now I do records more for fun. The hustle and bustle of the business is boring, it's wack, it's depressing. I refuse to play the record game at this point in my career... The business part is always the part that's wack. You gotta do it, but it's always a drag.' More surprising was his casual admittance that acting might be a more preferable way forward:

'I been doing records so long, movies is the natural progression for me. I can show my creativity on the big screen. Not only audio, but visual.' A bombshell, perhaps? Maybe, but not an unexpected one. Some observers might well interpret this statement as a full-blown acknowledgment that Cube's preferred career path did not lie in the world of music – but it's more likely that, after ten years as a media everyman, he has decided to sit back, take a breath and think carefully about where exactly it is he wishes to go. And, after so much multi-platform experience, the world truly is open to him. Why should he confine himself to one particular medium?

Always mindful of the marketability of a product and the hard-earned cash of his fanbase needing to be exchanged for genuine value for money, Ice Cube had recorded two new songs for the collection. The first, 'Late Night Hour', was recorded with the help of the producers du jour, the Neptunes – a vocal contribution had initially been scheduled to come from Limp Bizkit singer Fred Durst, but his packed timetable prevented him from getting to the studio on time, and the collaboration failed to take place. Time was short, but results were good, as Cube told *Sonicnet* – 'It's coming out kinda tight... The record companies kinda hooked [the Neptunes] up. When they heard they was going to work with me, they put some stuff together in Virginia and flew it out here. As a rapper, when you get some producers like the Neptunes to have something tailor-made for you, that's kinda what you look for.' The song also contained a shout-out to the old school with a line paraphrased from 'Straight Outta Compton' – 'Straight outta Compton, crazy motherfucker named Ice Cube, and I'm rollin' with the motherfucking Neptunes'.

'We went and got the Neptunes but we kind of went in and did an underground hardcore track,' he told NME.com. 'I got with them and I let them produce the record totally. I just told them, "What you want to hear from Ice Cube?" and they put it down.' He also explained the situation with the other members of NWA: 'We could do a record, but we couldn't do a *great* record without time to kind of marinate, feel each other, figure out which way we want to go. So for the best interests of the name and what we built with NWA, we owe it to that not to do anything, and just to wait. I wouldn't say we were best friends, but we're definitely on good terms. Ren comes out and shoots hoop at my house all the time. Dre, Snoop, we just got off this "Up In Smoke" tour, we had a chance to kick it with each other for the first time in like ten years. I think we mended a lot of wounds, on that tour. It was all love.'

The album's second new song was '$100 Bill Y'All', a hard-hitting track produced by Rockwilder, with its title a play on the name of Limp Bizkit's first album, *Three Dollar Bill$ Y'All*. Together, the two new tracks made the record more of a draw for the average fan than a simple selection of singles. As best-ofs go, this one was compiled with more sensitivity than most. The hotly debated track-listing turned out to be a multifaceted one: the album begins with 'Pushin' Weight' and is followed up by 'Check Yo' Self', 'We Be Clubbin'' and '$100 Bill Y'All', which form an introduction to where Ice Cube is at in the 21st century. (Perhaps easing the listener into the Cube experience, before the barrage of old-school beats comes in, was part of Ice's agenda?) Then it's into more aggressive territory with 'Once Upon A Time In The Projects' – perhaps the best post-NWA statement Cube had ever made about the environment he came from – and 'Bow Down', which was the high point of the Westside Connection album of the same name.

Two very different collaborations follow. The first is as new as they come: 'Hello' (which featured Dre and Ren) was the new-/old-band comeback single which kickstarted the *Peace* album, while the second was more laid-back – 'You Can Do It', including the talents of Mack 10 and Ms Toi. A party flavour comes in with 'You Know How We Do It', before the classic mid-period Cube of 'Bop Gun (One Nation)', where George Clinton's vocals remain sublime, and 'It Was A Good Day'. There's a mixture of old and new with 'What Can I Do?', 'My Summer Vacation' and 'Steady Mobbin'', before the killer classic sounds of 'Jackin' For Beats' and the awesome 'The Nigga Ya Love To Hate'. The set is rounded off with 'Late Night Hour', which bids the listener farewell for the moment – until Cube is, as he puts it, 'rejuvenated'.

Not that Cube had withdrawn entirely from the music world. In early 2002 he made a cameo appearance in a P-Diddy video, 'Bad Boy

For Life', which depicted the ructions caused in a middle-class neighbourhood when the rapper and his associates move in. Basically it's a scenario in which the rich white folks are intimidated by the even richer black guy, who moves in and disrupts their suburban tranquil with his party lifestyle – although there's little social commentary here, as the two sides get on quite amicably. 'You've got this perfect middle-American town,' said P-Diddy. 'They keep their doors open and everybody gets along with everybody. There ain't no parties thrown. Everybody goes to bed at 9 o'clock. Then P-Diddy and the Bad Boy family move in. You see how the cultures mix and we're all able to get along.' Cube played his trademark frowning role along with brief appearances by Shaquille O'Neal, Mike Tyson, Snoop Dogg, Xzibit, ex-Jane's Addiction/Red Hot Chili Peppers guitarist Dave Navarro, Travis Barker of Blink 182 and actor Ben Stiller.

As far as I am concerned, Ice Cube can appear in videos with whoever he likes and still maintain his artistic credibility, but it should be noted that there are those in the hip-hop community who regarded this last step (a buddy role in a P-Diddy promo clip) as the end of a road that had led Cube from hardcore underground excellence to a bland mainstream stance. After all, P-Diddy is the man who pioneered the 'ghetto fabulous' image (which translates as wearing a lot of gold over an old T-shirt, it seems), scored platinum sales with some rather tepid tunes, and dated a bevy of celebrities including Jennifer Lopez – hardly the voice of the streets that Cube had once so ably represented. The truth will depend entirely on how important the observer believes the underground to be – if, indeed, one remains.

On 8 March, Cube's filmic profile – which had inevitably taken a hit from *Ghosts Of Mars* – was lifted a good few notches by *All About The Benjamins*, an unashamedly good-time movie which saw him reunited with *Next Friday*'s Mike Epps. 'With Epps, the first project we worked on together, he was new to it,' Cube told the press during a satellite press conference from LA. 'He didn't know what to expect from the whole experience. He's done a few movies in between, [so] he's just more comfortable with acting [now]. The chemistry seems to flow. We're...in such a flow that it's kind of like some of them old-school teams of comedy pairs you used to see. We plan on doing three more movies together.'

The decision to stick to an odd-couple theme was a wise one on Cube's part, it turned out, with most critics applauding the interplay between Cube's sourpuss character (a bounty hunter named Bucum Jackson – that's 'Bucum' as in 'book 'em') and the hyperactive Epps, whose portrayal of a con artist named Reggie Wright was compared with the most memorable work of Eddie Murphy, Martin Lawrence and Chris Tucker. Epps explained where his comedic background came from in an interview with Blackfilm.com: 'My family is funny. Everybody in my family is funny. I'm just the one who went out and made it happen. In school I was a straight fool. One time I took some crazy glue... This girl was asleep, I took it and I glued her hands together... I went to juvenile center for four months for that. She woke up and her hands were glued. I guess I wasn't interested in what the public schools had to offer. They weren't teaching me what I was going to be doing. I was a comedic actor as a kid and didn't know it. But I was practising it.'

Set in Miami – permitting the director, video-clip maker Kevin Bray, to make the most of the glamorous beach-life locations (this was his debut as a full-length film-maker, like F Gary Gray and Steve Carr before him) – the plot focused on the relationship between the two men. Originally mutual enemies (Epps is a persistent bail-breaker, whom Cube has arrested twice before), the two must unite in order to retrieve a lost lottery ticket that has won Epps £42 million ($60 million), make Cube enough money to launch his own detective agency (the 'Benjamins' are $100 notes [worth £70], which bear the face of Benjamin Franklin), and save both their necks from the threats of a vengeful criminal gang. It's a complex plot – perhaps unnecessarily so at times – but Bray's rapid-fire editing keeps the viewer engrossed, and plenty of interspersed violence and comedy maintains a certain dark aura around the proceedings.

The film recouped two-thirds of its budget with its opening weekend take of £7 million ($10 million), and most reviews were positive both about the central characters and the basic premise of the film. As one of the producers, Cube must have been delighted with the critical response, not least because it augured well for the reception of the third *Friday* film, which he had announced would be called *Friday After Next* and would appear in the autumn of 2002.

The *LA Times* was cautiously impressed, observing that 'its dark-edged crime-caper plot is so formulaic it seems almost ritualized', but 'Ice Cube and Mike Epps enact their standard odd-couple tango with...ease and brio' and 'Cube shows greater confidence and flexibility as a leading man. His comic timing, though not as precise as it could be, is adjusting nicely to the demands of the mainstream genre.'

The *San Francisco Chronicle* couldn't quite decide whether *All About The Benjmains* was a good or a bad movie, oscillating between 'sit people down in front of [this film] and they won't necessarily want to go away. At least they won't run away screaming' and 'I can't totally trash a movie that I halfway enjoyed. The plot holds interest, and the lurid Miami atmosphere has its allure [and] the outrageousness of the humor...makes Ice Cube an original voice.'

Perhaps a phrase written by the *Village Voice*'s Nick Rutigliano summed up the film best – and summarised the acting styles of Cube and Epps succinctly, too: 'Director Kevin Bray lets the multimillionaire boyz be boys, allowing motormouth Epps to piss in any flower bed while preventing Cube, who often resembles a disconcerted but undeterred rottweiler, from seeming a dumb bunny.' And Margaret A McGurk of the *Cincinnati Enquirer* made an astute comparison when she said that '*All About The Benjamins* is a twisted crime caper that lifts its best moves from *Lock, Stock And Two Smoking Barrels* and *Midnight Run* and plunks them into a retread of *Friday*', although she also warned that 'Balancing comedy and violence is a tough trick, which *The Benjamins* does not entirely master.' However, she concluded with, 'Still, the movie has its charms, in the buddy-flick interplay between Bucum and Reggie... *Benjamins* shows progress both in the ghetto-action genre and in Cube's evolution into an actor and moviemaker who's in it for the long haul.'

The 'long haul' is right. Cube had begun to show signs of serious experience as an actor – he had carried several movies already, if not by the director's intentions then certainly according to critical reaction – and has the makings of a lifetime actor of obvious talent. Mike Epps pointed out that Cube had taught him a lot. 'Cube is an expert. He's a good coach. As a player, you just have to listen to him. After doing this many films with him, I know what he wants. I know what his comedy consists of.' But Ice had never been too harsh a taskmaster, it appeared, allowing Epps to improvise when he wanted to. 'I went off the script a little bit,' Epps said. 'It's hard staying on the script. Ice Cube allows us to ad lib. He'll let me get mine in, tell me to say an extra motherfucker. He always gives me extra leeway.' The lessons learned by Cube in *Friday*, in which Chris Tucker's improvisation skills convinced director F Gary Gray to use many of his spontaneous scenes, was evidently a side that Cube valued in his co-actors, and chose to develop – just as he himself was eager to make a creative input into his other film roles, as he had done in *Ghosts Of Mars*.

This brings us to the time of writing. *All About The Benjamins* is his most recent work, apart from an excellent appearance on an album by the British DJ and producer Paul Oakenfold, *Bunkka*, which was released in May 2002. Refreshingly, the song – 'Get 'Em Up' – is one of the high points of the record, with Cube rapping with a venom not heard since the days of Westside Connection. Oakenfold told UK Radio One that the album would feature a host of guest artists including Nelly Furtado, Billy Corgan and the Neptunes, describing it as 'based around guitars and breaks, it's kind of a step on from dance'. A second Cube/Oakenfold collaboration entitled 'Right Here Right Now' was also scheduled to appear on the soundtrack to the Wesley Snipes vampire movie, *Blade 2*.

Cube being Cube, several projects are lined up and ready to go, including several movies on top of *Friday After Next*. An £8.5 million ($12 million) movie called *The Barbershop* is wrapped and scheduled for release on 12 July, co-starring rapper Eve and centring on a day (not necessarily a Friday, before you ask) in Cube's barbershop on the south side of Chicago. On the choice of newcomer Eve as his co-star, Cube told MTV that giving new talent (as he did for Epps and Tucker) was a job he felt bound to do: 'Somebody gave me a shot. Somebody looked at me *not* in an audition, and that somebody is John Singleton. He saw me being myself and he knew I was right for *Boyz N The Hood*. I took a page from that.'

'[The film] takes place in Chicago, a neighborhood barbershop, winter time,' Cube told the *NME*, 'and my character inherits a barbershop from his father, but I don't really want to run it because my mind is somewhere else. In the course of the movie I find out really what the barbershop means to the neighborhood. It's a place for men to talk. It's like figuring out what the priorities are, but it's also funny.'

Around this time a blast from the past was also felt in the shape of The DOC. He had spent the years since he left NWA recovering from a crushed larynx (suffered in a car crash) and building a name in the rap world as a co-writer for Dr Dre. A DOC album, *Deuce*, was scheduled for release on his own Silverback label in spring 2002 and featured contributions from Dre, Cube, Ren and Nate Dogg.

As for the long-awaited *Friday After Next* – which Cube fans will be hoping is as good as *Friday*, or at least better than *Next Friday* – the movie is booked to open on 27 November. Cube and Epps revealed to MTV recently that it is a Christmas ghetto movie. 'I don't think we exposed America to what a black Christmas can really be... We're just exposing how Christmas can really happen in the hood. We're back in the hood, Craig and Day-Day live together. Mr Jones and Uncle Elroy own the barbecue spot, and we work as ghetto security at the little strip mall.' And what can Craig be up to this time? 'He's taking his authority too far,' said Epps of Cube's character. 'He's walking around the mall wearing house shoes. A security guard with house shoes? One thing about working with Ice Cube, you ain't never gonna lose your core audience. You can go in the ghetto somewhere and see a *Next Friday* poster in a crack house.'

Many fans had hoped that Chris Tucker would return for the third *Friday*. Ice Cube explained his continued absence in a Webchat with these words: 'He told me he doesn't use profanity anymore. He found God, and he doesn't cuss anymore.' Fair enough, you might think? After all, Cube is a religious man himself... But no; it appeared that the real reason was money. 'He's going on the radio saying he didn't get paid right the first time. But everybody got scale the first time, including me. I just happened to produce and write the shit. It ain't my fault that gets me a little more. But he still hasn't come to me face to face and told me that. He makes $20 million [£14 million] a movie now, because of that little ol' movie called *Friday*. How fucking mad can he be?' You have to admit, Cube has a point.

To date Tucker's only public explanation for his actions was when he told Well-Rounded.com that a *Friday* sequel wouldn't be his preferred acting option. 'I hope [Cube] ain't doin' it, 'cause I ain't doin' it. I don't want to mess it up. 'Cause I mean, why mess somethin' up? That's like doin' *The Mack* twice. But, you know, that's up to him. They'll just have to find another Smokey. But write that good, you know, that's my dog.' And there the matter must rest.

Other movie projects which have been tentatively publicised, but have no film release date as yet, include: *Big Ticket*, a comedy in which Cube stars opposite none other than Johnny Knoxville, the prime mover behind MTV's insane *Jackass* series; and *Stray Dawgz*, a werewolf drama set in the San Francisco Bay area in which Cube discovers that his ancestors were werewolf hunters and is called into action himself. Most interesting of all – on paper, at least – is *Pimp*, the biopic of Robert 'Iceberg Slim' Beck, a much-feared Harlem underworld figure from the 1940s whose 1969 autobiography *Pimp: The Story Of My Life* would be the basis of the script. Could *Pimp* be Cube's *Citizen Kane*? Or his *Plan 9 From Outer Space* (which was crowned 'The Worst Film Ever Made' at New York's Worst Film Festival in 1980)? By the time you read this book, the answer might already be known.

MTV asked Cube if more films were on the way, but he responded that 'We've got a couple things in the works, but I'm a real superstitious person. I feel if you talk about what you've got going on, especially in Hollywood, then it never comes true. But we have some things percolating with my new company, Cubevision. You know, just tryin' to drop bombs in all aspects of entertainment.' Asked if *Next Friday* had been the film that made him commit himself to the film world in recent years, he demurred, 'Nah. Way before the success of

Next Friday I knew I wanted to make my mark in the film business like I did in the music business. I want to be a pioneer for any young kids out there that come from the same background that I came from. You can do anything you want to in this world if you apply your mind, your determination, and a little sweat. You can make it happen.'

Finally, the last rumour circulating the press offices and Internet chatrooms is Ice Cube's endlessly going-to-happen collaboration with Nine Inch Nails (NIN), the alternative industrial-rock band fronted by the charismatic Trent Reznor. An interview with Reznor appearing in *Raygun* magazine claimed that Dr Dre might also be involved. 'Dre's a fucking genius. [Producer] Rick Rubin and I met him in the Valley like two weeks ago... [He's] expressed interest in working with me in some capacity, and Ice Cube, I think, is the best rapper I've ever heard.' However, the concept was to be more grandiose than a simple rock-meets-rap 'Fuck Dying' scenario. '[Our] whole thing [is] not to make it a remix situation, where it's like a white boy remixed by so and so, or me singing on a Dre track, or Ice Cube singing on a NIN track. The idea is to have it become the impetus to make some new kind of music. When I talked to Dre it was like, "Let's change music".'

NIN and Cube have had a working relationship since the mid-1990s, when Westside Connection had sampled the rock band's 'Hurt' for their 'The Gangsta, The Killa And The Dope Dealer' on *Bow Down*. Cube said at the time, 'I like [Reznor] because he just do what he want to do... He puts music together that's so original, and so above what everybody else is doing, and so like creative. You can just tell he's always thinking about how he's gonna put his music together... We just knew that that was gonna be an underground hit.' He also told *Addicted To Noise* that 'I want to work with him. I dig what he do; he dig what I do... I think he's off the hook. The way he does the sound, the mood, the music. The way his videos are put together – they're, like, the eeriest videos ever. The whole concept is off the hook.'

Note that Ice Cube seems to admire Reznor – one of rock's most introspective characters – for two main reasons: the depth and scope of his vision (like Cube, he assembles collages of sound from a plethora of sources) and, perhaps more important, the certainty of his direction.

To Cube, a ghetto-raised-boy-turned-global-phenomenon, this is an attractive characteristic, simply because he recognises himself in it. It's this confidence (which David O Russell had called 'shameless', remember, during the filming of the mighty *Three Kings*) that has made him the man he is. And the example of this confidence, more than anything else he might say or do, is the lesson many listeners will take away from the Ice Cube experience – a lesson only the rarest of men can teach.

15 Prophecy

So there it is – the story of Ice Cube. I'm sure you'll agree that it's a remarkable one. After all, how many other artists can claim such an influence across so many media platforms? How many others can claim to have weathered so much controversy, and emerge victorious with a loyal, intact fanbase? And how many artists (indeed, any public figures) can offer the world that observes them a genuine core of authenticity like that of Ice Cube? This is a man who (let us not forget) came from the modern equivalent of Dante's ninth circle of hell – an urban wasteland which claims many of its children for its own and which most of us will never see for ourselves. There's no posturing or fakery here, for life depends on authenticity too much.

The fact that Cube has risen as far as he has says much about his resilience and talent, of course, but it also says a great deal about the society that carried him to these heights. In 2002, he can boast no fewer than four platinum-selling releases: the *Amerikkka's Most Wanted*, *Death Certificate* and *The Predator* albums, plus the *Kill At Will* EP. Cube partly agrees with the public's endorsement of these records, telling the *Bay Guardian*'s Billy Jam that his favourite of his own albums are '*Amerikkka's Most Wanted* and *Death Certificate*. The records that I don't like are *The Predator* and *Lethal Injection* because with those two I was taking the whole rap game for granted. But now I'm rededicated and refocused.'

Music Monitor asked Cube why he thought hip-hop had spread into so many areas of society. 'I just think that shows you the power in the music. One thing about raps, they got a whole lot of words. They got way more words than any song could have. And people are just starting to get turned on by that, on all levels. Where I think you always had the cool white kids bumpin' the music, now you got lawyers, you got professional corporate people bumpin' rap music, buying rap music, getting involved in what we're involved in. I think it just prepares us to get better, it prepares us for better rap music, for it to go to the next level. Because if we don't take it to the next level, that same enthusiasm that we're getting now, is gonna start downsliding.'

He was then asked if his success was taking him away from his mass audience. 'I don't feel out of touch with my audience, because I'm not living the Hollywood lifestyle,' he said. 'I still hang around the people I hung around before I had anything. So that keeps me grounded. And right now you got a crowd out there that loves hip-hop from 4 to 40, so ain't no way in the world you're gonna be in touch with *everybody*, but most people know what I'm about, at least Ice Cube fans. And that's all I'm gonna concern myself with nowadays, because I've been in this game too long to try and get more people to like me. Either you're down with what I'm down with, or you're not – and if you're not, I'm cool with that too.'

As well as the obvious commercial impact of his work, critical plaudits for the best of his records have been similarly unstinting, with *Amerikkka's* and *Death Certificate*, as well as NWA's *Straight Outta Compton*, entering *Source* magazine's Top 100 Hip-Hop Albums list at the end of the 20th century. What can he possibly have left to achieve?

The answer seems to lie in his activities of late. Like any good business strategist, Cube is in the process of diversifying his approach and spreading himself into other fields. It isn't hard to imagine him, for example, stretching his entrepreneurial activities into Internet commerce, software development, sports, leisure activities and straight-ahead retail as well as moving deeper into music and film. At the time of writing, industry watchdogs are producing report after report revealing the growing tendency for music fans to download and distribute their music from the Web. Therefore, it involves no great leap of faith to picture Cube playing a central role in making this process faster, more efficient or simply more profitable.

He explained this move towards diversification to MTV with these words: 'The rap game plays out after a while. I've been in it for 15 years. The same doing videos, going up to the radio station, "Buy my record." Fifteen years of that, you want to show how creative you are on different levels. We don't want all the pie. We just want a little piece of it.'

But he's a stubborn character, with integrity. This means he will not allow his move into other areas to compromise the quality of his music (which remains central to his career ambition). 'It's cool being a screenplay writer, an actor and a director, but my first love is music,' he told Launch.com. 'No matter where I go, I'll always come back to that.' *Music Monitor* asked him specifically if he could avoid the trap of issuing unoriginal work. He pondered his answer before carefully replying, 'That's something that all artists get caught up in at one time or another, including myself. But if you really look at the situation and understand what's going on, hopefully you'll pull yourself out of that, and say "Man, I need to take pride in what I do, I need to put good songs together before I release them".' In other words, is he saying he would rather not release records at all than release a substandard record? 'That's what I do. I could make a whole lot of money just releasing, releasing, releasing, releasing, but I'd rather try and do something that's gonna stand the test of time, something that people are really gonna love and people are gonna really get into.'

These are no mere slogans. Cube appears to have a solid career plan worked out. For example, he told the UK *Guardian* that his way into a new directing project would hinge on getting more acting roles under his belt (the verdict on his first, *The Player's Club*, seems to be that it was solid rather than scintillating): '[I plan on] getting my name a little bigger through acting, so next time I direct, it'll come out a little stronger.' And his inside knowledge of the way the music business works can only help make the way even smoother in that direction: as he told *Addicted To Noise*, '[Hip-hop is] a straight business. It was something new at first but now it's just part of music. It's just what rock'n'roll is. There are certain ways you work a rock'n'roll record, and there are certain ways you work a rap record. It's all standard.

There ain't nothing new to it, there's no flash or pizazz. It's just part of the music system.'

Parenthood has also broadened his horizons. 'The best thing about fatherhood is that you can look at all the mistakes you made and lay down a blueprint for your kids,' he told *Canoe*. 'When you're by yourself you bottle up everything you learn, but when you have kids you can give 'em the game... What I love most about being a father is that I can teach 'em all about life and watch 'em sidestep some of the shit. I wish my father would've told me some of the things I tell my kids.'

And still we know so little about Ice Cube's private life – an achievement on his part. He has let occasional morsels of information slip – journalist Farrah Weinstein got a lot of personal information out of Cube in one interview, asking him about his taste in fashion and other usually unexplored avenues. For example, he revealed that his clothing style is 'Simple. Not over the top and not under the bridge. I'm not a person that's too busy or too flamboyant. I go buy a coat and it lays straight down, three-quarter, and not too many puffs or wrinkles. I buy a lot of tennis shoes, jeans and thousands of T-shirts.' We know that his only accessories are a diamond earring in his left ear and 'a diamond Rolex that I don't wear that much. It's too gaudy. I wear a simple watch that my wife bought me. And a silver chain.' Cube also admitted that he couldn't live without his TV: 'I love watching sports. But I can't get into the TV programs. I can get into movies, but they have to be real good.'

Interestingly, he hands a lot of responsibility to his wife Kim when it comes to style. 'My wife is very stylish. She knows everything, what's in style, what's not in style. So she usually hooks me up. She'll come home with stuff and say, this might be good for you to wear on that show. She styles with love... Sometimes she'll clean my face for me with these cleansers. She's always coming home with new products to try out. I'm a guy – a *guy* guy. And she's like, well, how you look represents me.'

His pragmatic mind-set has also helped Cube deal with the pressures of fame – an abstract set of issues which appear to vary from famous person to famous person. For him, as a man who clawed his way out of the ghetto, the material trappings of fame would have been an obvious instant gratification. Remember how NWA, ghetto boys all, laughed at Cube for refusing to sign Jerry Heller's contract which promised £53,000 ($75,000)? They are not to be blamed, given the environment that had spawned them. But a man of Cube's intellect and political awareness would never remain satisfied with the baubles of wealth for long. 'You start out wanting the fame, the money, the glamor, but then when you get it, you start wanting other things,' he said. 'I mean for some guys, they chasin' the ghetto style, the bling-bling style, but then what?... You know, you spend all yo' time comin' up, tryin' to get people to notice you and stand out, but then once you do, you spend all your time tryin' to be normal.'

The rise and fall of popularity is always a thorny issue. But in Cube's case it is one he shrugs off with the words, 'Well, you can't care about that stuff. It's like, first the public loves you, then they get sick of you, then you spring back up again. You're always fallin' on and off the radar.' He is similarly succinct in his approach to life's more practical issues. A fan in Fort Worth asked him if he ('Mr Fuck The Police', as he put it) would call the cops if his house was broken into. Cube replied, 'Hell, yeah. I'm paying them motherfuckers enough,' and he was only half joking. 'They work for me, too,' he added. 'They ain't just there to fuck me up and abuse me. Put they ass to work. Come get 'em. Be in the bushes, hop the fence, all that shit. You do it. You get paid to do it. If you have to get into a shootout, do it. Better you than me.' The Police Department, it seems, have a long way to go before they will be welcome in Cube's world – 'Police are a lot friendlier to me now, now that I'm Ice Cube,' he once said. 'But just think if I was the average everyday brother driving down the street. How would they be to me?'

As his future plans seem almost limitless in scope, it's not surprising that Cube is – conversely – not in the business of regrets. But an operator such as he, to whom efficiency and time management are important, the few misjudgments that he has made across his career manage to retain a little sting. One of the most obvious ways he has grown across the years is in the slow reduction of his venom towards social groups, be they demarcated by race, gender or religion. Therefore his answer to a fan's question, 'The songs you did ten years ago that talked shit about Koreans, Jews and homosexuals – "Cave Bitch", "Black Korea", "No Vaseline" – do those songs represent who you are now?', was both honest and reflective. 'I would be crazy to say no, those songs have nothing to do with who I am,' he mused. 'But ten years later, my understanding of the world is totally different. That's how I felt then. My views have changed slightly. Some things I'm still stuck on. But I'm not the same person.'

Would the hip-hop community of today find such sentiments attractive, now that the ashes of the LA riots have been cool for a decade and the focus on police brutality less sharp? Perhaps not. 'Would I record them songs now? I don't think so. For a couple of good reasons. They don't make real good hip-hop songs; in some ways, they're too heavy.' This is an interesting point: the vengeful Cube of the early 1990s would hardly have shunned any subject as being too 'heavy'. Experience has led to subtlety, it seems. 'I'm just a wiser record-maker now. And I still got a lot of shit to say that is going to fuck up people's heads like that did. I'm not into repeating what I said. You want what I said in '94, go back. It's still available.' As he said on *The Predator*, 'Said it? Yep. Regret it? Nope', and as he later explained even more specifically, 'I've said things, and there's no reason to [restate] them or no reason to go over old ground... I'm always into going into new records, new things.'

When it came to movies, however, the concept of regret is more fully formed, with Cube displaying a trace of disappointment about those films that met with little appreciation. '*Ghosts Of Mars* didn't turn out good. I didn't like *The Glass Shield* or *Dangerous Ground*.' But, as always, he tempers his complaint with a philosophical aside, and in this case a solid industry epithet: 'That's part of the business: script's good, idea's good, location's good, director's good – movie sucks.'

Perhaps the most revealing angle is to examine Cube's self-awareness – that hard-to-find, impossible-to-buy quality which shapes, aligns and empowers us all – and ask how he regards his own development from enraged hood youth to sober elder statesman (and a 30-something elder statesman to boot). He recently revealed to *Icecubeworld* that 'We all grow up...hopefully. When you're young, a lot of crazy things go through your mind and come out your mouth. Who's to say that when I'm rapping, I'm not talking about a circumstance that a homie of mine went through? Everything I write about doesn't necessarily happen to me, even though I have been harassed by the police for no reason. And I have to look out for me, because I have a family to take care of, so those experiences you hear may be true.'

Journalist Jack Chance asked Cube how having money and fame had affected him. He said, 'I'm pretty cool. My fame has not really crippled me in any way, without me doing it to myself. I always try to be approachable. That's what makes me being famous different than other people who have 100 bodyguards and a big entourage. I feel I can get out of my car and walk anywhere. You have a couple of people saying, "Whassup?" and recognizing you, but for the most part, people look at Ice Cube, and I'm always myself.' He recognises that, like most people, his moods fluctuate. 'Put it this way: Ice Cube can have a conversation with anybody in the world. And Ice Cube can also laugh with anybody in the world. Some mornings, I wake up mad at the world. Some mornings, I wake up happy to be alive. But I'm always myself. I never put on fronts or acts for people.'

Being genuine is clearly a quality that is important to Ice Cube. No faking, no following trends, no false allegiances and no swerving from the path of righteousness might as well be the whole of his law – but he's big enough to accept that his place in the scheme of things is not at the top (not yet, anyway). 'The new booties, the youngsters, they don't like to give it up to where they got their skills from. That's cool. I've been doing this 17 years. I don't expect nobody in this game to tip their hat to me. We competing out here.' And perhaps this is just the way it should be – remember, Cube joined the rap game when it was in its infancy. 'Hip-hop is all about being cocky, having attitude. It's a lot of arrogance and egos involved. It's like the NFL – nobody's going to give you an inch. Don't ask for it. And don't give none.'

He went on: 'I think everybody knows that Cube comes from the heart and that I'm not going to sell a muthafucka out, and I'm not going to sell myself out. When the devils come with their shit, I don't shake and quiver... I tell everyone the real deal, and they respect that in me. I bring light to them in that way, and they say Cube is a person who has taught me something through the music. I kind of give them a service that school doesn't provide, 'cause school doesn't want to be straight-up and real with the kids.'

This brings us neatly to the role of teacher, which many a prominent black figure (Malcolm X, Quincy Jones, Ice-T) has come to occupy after years of struggle. 'I haven't changed my program. And I'm not gonna change my program,' insists Cube – but, while sticking to his chosen path, he finds the time to impart what he has learned to the generation that follows him. Just as he had stuck closely to director John Carpenter to learn his trade, and passed the torch in turn to young newcomers such as Chris Tucker and Mike Epps, he handed out instructions about screenplay writing to a young hopeful with these words: 'If you can't tell a good story to a friend, I mean just a good story about something that you witnessed, then that's the first thing you work on. Two: you need to know what movies you like and what made you like 'em. That helps you not write boring stuff. Last: find a book on screenplays so you can understand the format. I learned from reading screenplays. But the real thing to do is get a book.'

Addicted To Noise perceptively asked him how he saw his role in the early years of the new century. The status of teacher, social commentator and entertainer had already fallen to him, so how might he fit into the world in other ways? Cube – ever the moving target – wouldn't give a straight answer. 'I don't know. I don't really look at it that heavy. I'm just devoted to my fans – that's all you can do once you've been in it as long as I've been in it. I can't play the politics of rap, get all involved and all that because, in a way, we united, and we competed, too. I can't really get caught up in that. Maybe when I was new into the game, just trying to make my mark – but my mark has already been made. I have just as many fans as I have enemies, you know what I mean? That's what it's going to be like once you reach a certain level.'

'My job is to not get sidetracked by all these issues, and to just make good music, 'cause good music is the only thing that's gonna ensure my spot into this rap game – as long as people want to hear what Ice Cube gotta say,' he continued. 'So I can't really worry about that. I gotta worry about studio, records, production, making it bigger and better – you know, giving people what they want to hear. And they can deal with all those politics.'

But people want to know what leaders think of the politics that surround them, so he was asked if he felt he had been credited appropriately for his impact on rap. 'You really never get your credit', he answered, 'until you either fall off or die – that's when you really, truly get your credit. And I'm not really even looking for credit, I'm just looking for fans who keep buying my records and keep supporting me.' He pointed out that the hip-hop scene was only healthy for those who 'can rap good. If you can put together good records, this is a good time for rap. But if you think you gonna just be famous because of this, or you gotta gimmick, and that – no. Right now it's about putting together good songs. Gimmicks and stuff like that are no good.'

A *Maxim* interview from February 2002 revealed Cube to be both humorous and contented, looking at both the past and the future with a realistic eye. Asked what would have happened if he had stuck with architectural draughtsmanship all those years before, he answered that 'I think I would've pursued drafting for a while, seen how far it took me. I know what the hell I *didn't* want to do; I didn't want to do hard fuckin' labor, 'cause I'm not into that. I got into drafting because I was the kind of kid who, if I liked Magic Johnson, I would draw pictures of Magic Johnson. But I think that job would've been too boring for me. I'm not a nine-to-five kind of cat.'

He also admitted that 'Ice Cube' is not his only nickname. 'My brother, to this day, still calls me Juice because of the way I played football on our street. I was fast, could catch and run, and since my real name is O'Shea Jackson, my initials are O.J. But I don't know how much I like it. Everybody's got a strange nickname in the ghetto. Everybody. I know a dude named Barefoot Pookie who goes barefoot all the time. He might have a suit on, but he's still barefoot. I mean, he's not a rapper, but after you've heard so many weird names, what's wack?' And, most tellingly, he confirmed that film, rather than music, would be his immediate focus. 'I've kind of shied away from the rap world a little bit to do movies, because I kind of feel like I've outgrown it. I've been rapping since I was 16, and I'm 32 now – that's 16 years of learning. I'll do another album someday, but it might not be for two years.'

The issue of NWA still remains, of course, and is not one to be lightly dismissed, even by its main progenitor. Cube admitted that 'It still trips me that from when *Straight Outta Compton* dropped in '89 to almost ten years later, that gangsta rap is still the most interesting, exciting, and the most money-making form of rap there is.' However, his career appears to him to be a continuous thread rather than a series of alliances: 'I still sell the same amount of records. I still get a big reception,' he told journalist Jeff Chang. 'In hip-hop, people always want new artists, but when I really get down, *nobody* puts a record together better than me. So I'll always be here. Long as I stay consistent and keep my heart in it, I'm a be here.'

How has Ice Cube changed hip-hop? The answer is 'profoundly', and 'on more than one level'. As a solo artist he helped introduce the idea of mining the archives of soul and R&B for his sounds, with his sharp production a direct inspiration from the hardcore beats of the Bomb Squad. The lyrical dexterity he introduced to his music was a spur to many – remember what he said about the healthy competitiveness of hip-hop? – and the anger that infused his work gave life to a whole host of followers in his wake. But, more than this, Cube was one of a vanguard of performers, along with Dre, Eazy, Chuck D, Ice-T, Tone Loc, 2 Live Crew and even lightweights such as MC Hammer and (later) Puff Daddy, who changed the face of hip-hop in a period of a few years, most notably in the early to mid-1990s, after the contribution of early pioneers such as Kool Herc, Grandmaster Flash, Afrika Bambaataa and the whole Sugar Hill coterie had faded. His contribution to this angry, articulate, often crude platoon of performers was a crucial one.

Not that this impact fell solely on music... On revisiting that angst-ridden time in 1990, 1991 and 1992, it's clear that American (and therefore Western, reluctantly or otherwise) society was being churned up by the wrath of the music coming from Cube and his brethren. Look at the rise of black film, or the spread of black culture – TV, radio, comedy, drama – into the white mainstream. The growth of the cult of personality around black icons in politics, sports, entertainment and all other areas of public life – these were all led by the black pioneers of the 1990s. Cube is an honourable member of that esteemed group of seminal figures, and his presence in so many areas is equalled in hip-hop culture perhaps only by Queen Latifah, whose books, chat show, movie career and chart impact make her a kind of female equivalent to Cube.

As he has grown, so have the hard-line parameters of Cube's personal beliefs both crystallised and receded. For example, he is no longer such a passionate advocator of the Nation of Islam, it seems. He told the UK *Guardian* in 2000 that 'I never was in the Nation of Islam... I mean, what I call myself is a natural Muslim, 'cause it's just me and God. You know, going to the mosque, the ritual and the tradition, it's just not in me to do. So I don't do it.'

But those of his fans who fear that a slackening of Cube's famous anger is on the cards can be reassured. His determination has not faded, and it is the aspect of his character that will ultimately carry him through. Asked if he had new arenas of endeavour to explore, he stated that 'I want to master everything I'm into so I'm just gonna work harder at what I do. And I'm gonna try and do it all till I start to getting fan mail saying "Cube, give it up, please, please, please".' This may seem unlikely – but the smartest of the hip-hoppers take nothing for granted and expect even the most unlikely scenarios. Ice-T, so close in his thought processes to Cube, once pertinently observed that 'When I come on tour I watch every band, every night, every day... I don't leave till the last one, you know [because] one day my records might stop selling, and I might need to learn how to set up equipment.'

The best questions are those which reveal more than they set out to reveal, and one of the ways to ask them is to make a person think in the long term – beyond careers, beyond life, and into death. Ask someone what their epitaph would be and you learn a lot about them and their priorities, so when *ROC* asked Ice Cube how he wanted to be remembered, his answer was both piercing and passionate. 'I want people to remember that Ice Cube always told the truth,' he said. 'I want to go down like Marvin Gaye or Bob Marley. You can still pick up their records to hear the deal. I want muthafuckas to do that with me. I want to be an icon. I just want to be remembered as somebody who never *shook*.'

Contrast this apocalyptic statement with the Ice Cube who set out his stall on *Straight Outta Compton*, promising death and violence at every turn, and you might be forgiven for thinking that his agenda hadn't changed so radically after all. But you'd be missing the broader point. Where he threatened vengeance with an assault rifle in the 1980s, the Cube of today works his way into the listener's psyche with a far more powerful weapon – the force of his personality, that of a man who fully comprehends both the world he moves in and his place in it. And the possession of this knowledge is no small advantage.

Before closing, let's take one last look back at the bad boys, those niggas with attitude, offending the world in general back in April 1989. Taking a moment – perhaps involuntarily, and certainly unintentionally – to rise above the guns'n'bitches'n'hoes diatribe, Cube revealed a hidden side to this most violent of bands. 'We wanted some people to get offended. We wanted people to say "Yeah, that's cool". We wanted some people to laugh. We like mystery. We like controversy... As long as what we say is true and what we say is real, then we don't feel bad if somebody looks at it differently.'

Professor Mary Ellison takes the view that 'Cube tries things out like a mask – it doesn't mean that it's who he is. He's playing at it. After all, he's playing at being the mack, and has worked through all the idioms associated with being the mack.' This is a revealing comment, and could even lead us to view Cube in a whole new light. Is he who he seems to be? Is he some kind of hip-hop trickster (in the classical sense of the word)? Perhaps, after all these years, it's time to realise that he has been leading his audience along all the time, with a breathtaking degree of skill, and is now exactly where he wants to be, exactly *because* of this skill.

Taking this thought a step further, perhaps those teenage boys – the NWAs, the Tupacs, the Biggies – were less antisocial than we imagined.

Perhaps they were no more or less kind and humane than the rest of the population. Perhaps – take a breath – they were just like us? Maybe. But Ice Cube remains a prophet, and prophets don't appear unless there is a good reason for it. Think of the great orators of history, of what they said, what they did, and what happened to them. In every case they had a message to deliver, and on delivering it they found that its effect was in every way greater and stronger than they could have imagined. Look around you. In how many ways is the society you live in ready (if not overdue) for some changes?

People like Ice Cube are messengers. They often appear to have many messages, but in fact the essence of their stance is simple, and goes something like this.

Get ready. A storm is coming.

Discography

SOLO ALBUMS

Amerikkka's Most Wanted (1990)
Death Certificate (1991)
The Predator (1992)
Lethal Injection (1993)
Bootlegs & B-Sides (1994)
Featuring...Ice Cube (1997)
War & Peace: Volume 1 (The War Disc) (1998)
War & Peace: Volume 2 (The Peace Disc) (2000)

NOTABLE GUEST AND SOUNDTRACK APPEARANCES

'Burn Hollywood Burn' with Big Daddy Kane and Public Enemy (Public Enemy, *Fear of A Black Planet*, 1990)
'How To Survive In South Central' (*Boyz N The Hood* soundtrack, 1991)
'Played Like A Piano' with King Tee (King Tee, *At Your Own Risk*, 1993)
'Westside Slaughterhouse' with Mack 10 (Mack 10, *Mack 10*, 1994)
'Big Thangs' with Too Short and Ant Banks (Ant Banks, *Big Thangs*, 1997)
'The World Is Mine' (*Dangerous Ground* soundtrack, 1997)
'Only In California' with Snoop Dogg and Mack 10 (Mack 10, *Based On A True Story*, 1997)
'Ghetto Vet' (*I Got The Hook Up* soundtrack, 1998)
'Cheddar' with Mack 10 and WC (WC, *The Shadiest One*, 1998)
'We Be Clubbin'' (*The Player's Club* soundtrack, 1998)
'Get 'Em Up' with Paul Oakenfold (Paul Oakenfold, *Bunkka*, 2002)

Filmography

ACTOR

Boyz N The Hood (1991)
Trespass (1992)
CB4 (1993)
Rap, Race & Equality (1993)
The Glass Shield (1994)
Higher Learning (1995)
Friday (1995)
Dangerous Ground (1997)
Anaconda (1997)
The Player's Club (1998)
I Got The Hook Up (1998)
Three Kings (1999)
Thicker Than Water (1999)
Next Friday (2000)
Ghosts Of Mars (2001)
All About The Benjamins (2002)
Friday After Next (2002)
Barbershop (2002)

PRODUCER/EXECUTIVE PRODUCER

Friday (1995)
Dangerous Ground (1997)
The Player's Club (1998)
Next Friday (2000)

All About The Benjamins (2002)
Friday After Next (2002)

WRITER

Friday (1995)
The Player's Club (1998)
Next Friday (2000)
All About The Benjamins (2002)
Friday After Next (2002)

DIRECTOR

The Player's Club (1998)

Online Resources

http://www.icecubemusic.com
http://www.icecube.cjb.net/
Ice Cube sites

http://www.africanpubs.com
Useful archive of prominent black figures

http://www.blackfilm.com
Comprehensive black film archive

http://hiphopca.com
Guide to hip-hop in Canada

http://www.rapworld.com
The title says it all

http://www.strictlyrap.co.uk
Lyrics, biographies and general hip-hop info

http://www.daveyd.com
Excellent, comprehensive hip-hop guide

http://www.losangelesalmanac.com
Everything you could ever need to know about LA

http://www.crimsonbird.com/history/rodneyking.htm
A compelling version of the events leading up to the 1992 LA riots

http://www.eazy-e.com
The best Eazy-E guide

http://www.nwaworld.com
NWA live on in cyberspace

http://www.priorityrecords.com
http://www.ruthlessonline.net
http://www.heavyweightrecords.com
Cube-related record company sites

http://www.mtv.com
http://www.rollingstone.com
http://www.sonicnet.com
Wide-ranging archive sites on Cube and many other artists

http://www.google.com
http://www.webferret.com
http://www.altavista.com
Search engines

Index

Note that stage names are listed as read (for example, *Ice Cube* and *Snoop Dogg*, not *Cube, Ice* and *Dogg, Snoop*) but conventional names are listed with the surname first.

2 Live Crew 42, 273 (see also *Campbell, Luther*)
2Pac (see *Shakur, Tupac*)
11 September 2001 252–3
311 212

A&M Records 208
Adler, Bill 63
Afrika Bambaataa 21, 27, 273
Aftermath Entertainment 172
Aguilera, Christina 241
Ahlerich, Milt 52
Ali, Muhammad 81
All About The Benjamins (film) 256–9
Amerikkka's Most Wanted (album) 73, 74–5, 104, 264, 265
Anaconda (film) 182–6
Arabian Prince 31, 36, 44
architecture 39–40, 45, 272
Arnold, Benedict 90
Arvizu, Reggie 'Fieldy' 195, 196, 197

B-Real (Cypress Hill) 124, 145–6, 169–170, 171

Backstreet Boys 241
Banks, Tyra 142, 143
Barbershop, The (film) 259–60
Barnes, Dee 77–8
basketball 12, 130–1
Be Careful What You Wish For (TV series) 240
Beastie Boys 226
Bennett-Speed, Carolyn 116
Bernard, James 96, 97–8
bicoastal rivalry 72, 124, 144, 158–9, 163, 165, 167–8
origins 62, 63
Big Daddy Kane 72, 166
Big Pun 221
black culture, and mainstream 274
Blade 2 (film) 259
Bloods (see *gangs, Bloods and Crips*)
Boatman, Michael 160
Bomb Squad 71, 72–3, 273
Bone Thugs-N-Harmony 148
Bootlegs & B-Sides (album) 141

Bow Down (album) 167, 171–3
Boyz N The Hood (film) 83, 85–8, 109
Bradley, Omar 151–2
Bradley, Tom 100, 107
Bray, Kevin 257, 258
Brazil 182–3
breakdancing 26
Broadus, Calvin (see *Snoop Dogg*)
Brown, James 20, 22
Brownstone 193
Buchanan, Pat 109–10
Bush, George 95, 107, 110, 220
bussing 18–19
Busta Rhymes 22

Calhoun, Monica 189
Campbell, Luther 65
Cannon, Lou 103
Carpenter, John 248, 249, 250, 251–2, 271
Carr, Steve 225–6, 227
Carraby, Antoine (see *DJ Yella*)
CB4 (film) 137
Cermai, Mike, and NWA early releases 37–8

Chance, Jack 178, 179, 270
Charbonnet, Pat 69, 71, 75, 190
charity 120-1
Chic 20
Chilly Chill 78, 92
Christopher Commission 103-4, 108
Chuck D (Public Enemy) 22, 27, 55, 64, 72-3, 99, 273
  and Cube's recordings 74, 78, 187
  on integrity 71
  on racism 129
CIA (rap outfit) 22, 26-7, 30
Ciby 2000 160
Clinton, George 135, 138, 177, 187
Clooney, George 213, 214, 215, 219-20, 241
Combs, Sean (see Puff Daddy/P Diddy)
Common Sense 176-7
Compton, Los Angeles 13, 16
Compton's Most Wanted 16-17
Coolio 157
Cortez, Jayne 21
Crenshaw, Los Angeles 11, 12, 23
Crips (see gangs, Bloods and Crips)
Cross, Brian 44-5, 75, 147
Cubevision 232-3, 261
Cumberbatch, Guy 91
Cypress Hill 111, 169

Da Lench Mob 73, 92, 139-40 (see also J-Dee)
Dangerous Ground (film) 178-82, 269
Dark, Gregory 212
Davis, Jonathan (Korn) 195, 197, 202
Davis, Nathan 202-3

Death Certificate (album) 92-3, 96-7, 98, 99-100, 109, 264, 265
Death Row 121-2, 159
Del (Ice Cube's cousin) 79
DJ Muggs (Cypress Hill) 18, 118, 119, 170
DJ Pooh 155
DJ Yella 41, 54, 65, 125, 150, 152-3
  and NWA 36-7, 44, 45, 121, 236
  and WCWC 24, 30, 31
DOC, The 31, 36, 38-9, 67, 77, 260
Dole, Bob 95, 96
Don Jaguar 119
Drayton, William (see Flav, Flavor)
Dre, Dr 28-31, 32, 130, 132, 172, 253
  contribution to hip-hop 273
  and Dee Barnes 77-8
  and Eazy-E 149
  and Gary Gray 157
  and Hip-Hop Music Awards 245-6
  influence 66-7
  and Nine Inch Nails 262
  and NWA 44, 45
  100 Miles And Running 76-7
  beginnings 34
  early live appearances 38
  early releases 36
  Efil4Zaggin 90, 92
  reunion 211-12, 222
  reunion album 234
  reunion ends 246, 247
  reunion show 237-9
  split 121-2
  Straight Outta Compton 47, 54, 65
  Up In Smoke tour 241, 242, 243-4, 245
  and Peace 231
  rap style 199, 209

relationship with Cube 25, 26, 27, 210-11
relationship with Eazy-E 124-5
The Chronic 122, 123
  and The DOC 260
  and WCWC 24
Durst, Fred 197, 200, 202, 237, 254 (see also Limp Bizkit)

Eastsidaz, Tha 237
Eazy-E 27-31, 32, 130
  and charity 120
  contribution to hip-hop 273
  and Death Certificate 94-5, 98-9
  and Dee Barnes 78
  and Dr Dre 124-5
  and finances 69, 76
  illness 148, 149
  invitation from Republicans 95-6
  last message 150-1
  and MC Ren 125
  on motivation 54
  and NWA 44-5
  early days 33, 34, 35
  early releases 37
  Eazy-Duz-It 40-1
  Efil4Zaggin 90, 91
  reunion 222-3
  reunion show 239
  split 121
  and Snoop Dogg 234-5
  and The DOC 67
  ups and downs 146
  and Yella 236
Eminem 47, 172, 230, 241-2, 243, 244
Epic Mazor (Crazytown) 19, 99
Epps, Mike 271
  All About The Benjamins 256, 257, 258, 259
  Friday After Next 260
  Next Friday 225-6, 227, 228

Epps, Omar 142, 143
Evans, Faith 163, 174
Eve 259

Family Values '98 195–201
Fard, Wallace D 80–1
Farmclub 237, 238
Farrakhan, Louis 80, 81,
    82, 119, 145
Farrell, Perry 111, 112,
    120
Fat Joe 221
FBI 52, 136
Featuring...Ice Cube
    (album) 187–8
Firm, The 198
Fishburne, Laurence 85,
    86, 142, 143
Fitzpatrick, Frank 193
Flav, Flavor 55, 72, 74
football 12
Fox Sports Presents Game
    Time! (album) 222
Fresh Prince 54
Friday After Next (film)
    258, 259, 260
Friday (film) 154–6
'Fuck Tha Police' (NWA
    song) 50–3, 104
Funkadelic 20

G-Funk 59, 122, 123
gangs, Bloods and Crips
    11–12, 14–16, 19, 106,
    109
Gates, Darryl (LAPD chief)
    32, 106, 108, 151
Gaye, Marvin 275
gays, Cube's attitude
    towards 269
Gellar, Sarah Michelle 241
Ghosts Of Mars (film)
    248–52, 269
Gibson, Mel 241
Glass Shield, The (film)
    160–1, 269
Gooding, Cuba 85, 86,
    128
Grand Wizard Theodore
    21

Grandmaster Flash 21,
    27, 141, 273
Gray, F Gary 154, 156–8,
    259

Hancock, Herbie 21
Hayes, Charlie 218
HBO (rap outfit) 29
Heavy D 38, 55
Heavyweight Records
    208, 213
Heller, Jerry 39, 92
    and Death Certificate
    94, 95, 97
    on Eazy-E 151
    and NWA
    early releases 37–8
    finances 69, 268
    reunion 223, 224
    split 121
    Straight Outta
    Compton 45
    tour 67
Henstridge, Natasha
    249–50
Herc, Kool 21–2, 27, 273
Heston, Charlton 110–11
Higher Learning (film)
    141–2, 143, 144
Hill, Walter 126–7
hip-hop, origins 20
Hip-Hop Music Awards
    245–6
hooks, bell 59–61
Hurley, Elizabeth 178
Huston, John 126

Ice Cube
    approachability 270
    assassination threat
    136–7
    and bicoastal rivalry
    167–8, 169–71
    on bodyguards and
    recent deaths 175–6
    and Dr Dre 172–3,
    210–11
    early life 11–13, 17–31
    and Eazy-E 148, 152
    effect on hip-hop 273

epitaph 274–5
films
    future as director 266
    past 269
    prospects 261
    roles contrasted 181
    and finances 69–70, 76
    further education 39–41
    future 265–76
    hiatus in album
    production 253–4
    and Hip-Hop Music
    Awards 245–6
    on influence 65–6
    lecture at LA high
    school 140–1
    millennial concerns
    221–2
    motivation 60
    and Nation of Islam 80,
    82, 83
    and parenthood 267
    rap style 209
    retrospective interview
    53
    on women 58, 59
    (see also NWA [Niggaz
    With Attitude], albums,
    films and tours under
    individual names)
Ice Cube's Greatest Hits
    (album) 253
Ice-T 27, 47, 129, 207–8,
    274
    assassination threat
    136–7
    on bicoastal rivalry 63–4
    Body Count 110, 111
    on bodyguards 55–6
    contribution to hip-hop
    273
    early days 22
    fanbase 50
    and Louis Farrakhan 81
    and Featuring...Ice Cube
    187
    on finances 76
    on gangs 15
    influence 62–3
    on integrity 71

Lollapalooza tour 111
on MTV 131
and *New Jack City* 84–5, 89
on rap's influence 129
The Ice Opinion (book) 138
and *Trespass* 126, 127
on women 58–9
Incubus 203
Insane Clown Posse 242, 243
InSite (see *Kid Chill*)
Intimate Look Inside The Acting Process With Ice Cube 219
Iovine, Jimmy 172, 238
Island Records (UK) 97

J-Dee 92, 140, 170 (see also *Da Lench Mob*)
Jackson, Clyde (Ice Cube's brother) 12, 13, 17, 272
Jackson, Daryl (Ice Cube's son) 138
Jackson, Doris (Ice Cube's mother) 11, 17, 22, 39
Jackson, Hosea (Ice Cube's father) 11, 12, 22, 39
Jackson, Janet 142, 241
Jackson, Kim (Ice Cube's wife) 59, 92, 111, 112, 267
Jackson, O'Shea (see *Ice Cube*)
Jackson, O'Shea (Ice Cube's son) 111, 112
Jackson, Samuel L 241
Jamaica 20, 21–2
James, Rick 20
JD (Da Lench Mob) (see *J-Dee*)
Jews, Ice Cube's attitude towards 269
John, Elton 243
Johnson, 'Magic' 153
Jones, Quincy 33, 64–5, 66
Jones, Teren Delvon 79
Jonze, Spike 214, 215, 219

K-Dee 26, 135
Kam 92, 140, 170
Kid Chill 15–16, 26
Kid Disaster (see *K-Dee*)
Kiddo (Ice Cube's childhood friend) 23
Kill At Will (EP) 78–9, 264
King, Rodney 100, 102, 104–5, 109, 146
Knight, Marion 'Suge' 121–2, 124, 159, 164, 172
Koreans 104, 269
Korn 195, 196, 199, 202, 203, 205, 213, 214
Krayzie-Bone 231
KRS-One 49, 55, 64, 163
Ku Klux Klan 97

LAPD (Los Angeles Police Department) 15, 50–2, 152, 160, 268
and 1992 riots 103–4, 105–8
and Rodney King 100
Lee, Spike 84, 89
Lethal Injection (album) 132–6, 264
Lezan, Mik (see *Arabian Prince*)
Lightning Rod 21
Limp Bizkit 195, 196, 200, 202
LisaRaye 188, 191
LL Cool J 22, 241
Llosa, Luis 182, 183, 186
Lollapalooza tour 111–12, 196
Lopez, Jennifer 182, 183, 233, 256
Los Angeles 13, 14–16, 23, 101–13, 117 (see also *Compton*; *Crenshaw*; *South Central*; *Watts*)
Love, Courtney 248

Mac, Bernie 155, 189
McCartney, Paul 78

Mack 10 167, 171, 193, 213
and *Thicker Than Water* 220, 221
McLaren, Malcolm 21
Macola 30, 42
marijuana, and Snoop Dogg 123
Marley, Bob 275
Marrow, Tracey (see *Ice-T*)
Mathers, Marshall (see *Eminem*)
MC Eiht (Compton's Most Wanted) 16–17, 221
MC Hammer 273
MC Ren 54, 95, 125, 151, 231, 260
and NWA 43, 44
Efil4Zaggin 91
reunion 211, 237, 238, 239–40
split 121
tour 68
media, and Los Angeles riots 104–5
Michel'le 24, 28, 94
Mighty Mighty Bosstones 212
Miller, Craig (see *Kam*)
Miller, Donald 42
Million Man March 145
Miramax 160
Ms Toi 231, 248
MTV 22, 49, 131, 240
MTV Movie Awards 240–1
Muhammad, Elijah 80, 83, 120
Muhammad, Khalid 94, 134
music, importance to Ice Cube 266

N-hood (see *Crenshaw*, *Los Angeles*)
Nate Dogg 237, 260
Nation of Islam 73–4, 145, 174, 274
and *Death Certificate* 92, 93

influence 80–2
as reconcilers 177
and *The Predator*
116–17
National Guard 105, 106
Neptunes 254, 259
New Jack City (film) 84,
89
New Line Pictures 193,
225, 232
New York 72, 108
Next Friday (film) 223,
225–30
nigga, contrasted with
nigger 32–3
Niggaz With Attitude (see
*NWA [Niggaz With
Attitude]*)
nigger, contrasted with
nigga 32–3
Nine Inch Nails 262
Notorious BIG 148, 159,
163, 226
NWA (Niggaz With
Attitude) 32–46
100 Miles and Running
76–7
1987 tour 38
and bicoastal rivalry
63–4
and *Death Certificate* 94
and Dee Barnes 77–8
departure of Cube 70–1
early releases 35–6
Efil4Zaggin 90–2
and finances 69–70
formation 31
and Los Angeles riots
109
NWA And The Posse
42–3
prospects 273
question of reunion
210–12, 222
reformation 222–4, 236
relationships 254–5
reunion album 233, 240
reunion show 237–9
second tour 67–8
split 121

Straight Outta Compton
45–6, 47–62, 65–6, 265
influence 64
video 49
Up In Smoke tour
241–5

Oakenfold, Paul 259
O'Connor, Sinéad 91
O'Neal, Shaquille 256
Orff, Carl 242–3
Orgy 195, 196, 200

P Diddy (see *Puff Daddy/
P Diddy*)
Parker, Sarah Jessica 241
Parliament 20
Patterson, Lorenzo
(see *MC Ren*)
Pearl Jam 111, 123
Phoenix Institute of
Technology 40
Player's Club, The (film)
188–94, 232
Polygram Records (UK) 91
Porno For Pyros 111, 112
Predator 2 (film) 117, 118
Predator, The (album)
113, 114–20, 264
Prince 66
Prinze, Freddy 241
Priority 37–8, 69, 92, 121
Public Enemy 55, 71, 103,
130, 226
influence 22, 47, 49
Puff Daddy/P Diddy 148,
159, 173, 186, 231,
246, 255–6, 273

Quayle, Dan 101–2, 110,
195
Queen Latifah 274

R&B 115, 273
racial origins, finance
contrasted with music
64
racism, rappers on 129
Rage Against The
Machine 99, 111–12

Rammstein 195, 196, 200
Randy (Ice Cube's
childhood friend) 18
rap, origins 20–1
Rap, Race & Equality
(film) 137–8
Rapaport, Michael 142,
228
Reznor, Trent 262
Ridenour, Charles
(see *Chuck D*)
Robertson, Geoffrey 91
Robinson, Ross 195
Rock, Chris 137, 230–1
Rodriguez, Lisa 227
Roodt, Darrell 178
Roxkwilder 255
Rubin, Rick 262
Run-DMC 22, 26, 44
Russell, David O 214–19,
263
Ruthless Records 28–9,
31, 152–3

Saber, Danny 213
Sadler, William 127
St Ides (brewing company)
99, 203
Salt-N-Pepa 38
Schooly D 62, 63, 64
Scott-Heron, Gil 21
Screen Gems 249
Seattle, and Los Angeles
riots 108
Seldon, Bruce 164
September 11, 2001 252–3
Shakur, Tupac 123, 172,
174
All Eyez On Me 163,
164
and bicoastal rivalry
144–5, 159
death 164–5
final pronouncement
165–6
on mortality 56
Poetic Justice 142
rap style 209
Shorty 92, 140 (see also
Da Lench Mob)

Simpson, OJ 11, 162–3
Singleton, John 41, 103, 158
Boyz N The Hood 83, 85–9
Cube's debt to 260
Higher Learning (film) 141–4
Sir Jinx
and Cube 71, 133
and *Death Certificate* 92, 94
early days 23–4, 26, 30
and *Kill At Will* 78
and Yo-Yo 79
Smalls, Biggie (see also *Notorious BIG*) 164, 165, 168, 173–4
Smith, Will (see *Fresh Prince*)
Snipes, Wesley 84
Snoop Dogg 66–7, 147, 167, 172, 256
and bicoastal rivalry 173
and Dr Dre 122, 123
and Eazy-E 152, 234–5
and NWA
reunion 222
reunion album 233–4
reunion ends 246
reunion show 237, 238, 240
Up In Smoke tour 241, 242, 243–4
rap style 209
and Shakur 164, 165
and violence 57
soul 273
Soundgarden 111, 123
South Africa 179
South Central, Los Angeles 11–31
sport 12
Statham, Jason 249, 251
Stereo Crew 26

Stern, Howard 32, 151
Stoltz, Eric 182, 183
Stop The Violence rap coalition 55
Street Knowledge Productions 76, 208, 213, 232
Sugarhill Gang 20, 21, 115
Swanson, Kristy 142

T-Bone 92, 140 (see also *Da Lench Mob*)
Tarantino, Quentin 224, 237
Tha Eastsidaz 237
Thicker Than Water (film) 220–1
Three Kings (film) 213–20, 241
Trespass (film) 125–8
Tucker, Chris 154, 156, 157, 225, 259, 260–1, 271
Tyson, Mike 164, 256

Up In Smoke tour 241–5

Van Peebles, Mario 84
Voight, Jon 182, 183, 184–5

Wahlberg, Mark 213, 214, 215, 219, 241
Walker, Randy 'Stretch' 159, 163
Wallace, Christopher (see *Notorious BIG*)
War and *Peace* (albums) 204–8, 230
Warren G 66
Watkins, Gloria (see *hooks, bell*)
Watts, Los Angeles 11, 13–14
Webster, William 108
Weinstein, Farrah 267

West Coast/East Coast rivalry (see *bicoastal rivalry*)
Westside Connection (WC) 167, 171, 200, 221, 262
Wheatob, Tony (see *Sir Jinx*)
Whitaker, Yolanda (see *Yo-Yo*)
Williams, Lonzo 24, 28, 30
Winfrey, Oprah 43, 61
Witherspoon, John 157
women
and *Amerikkka's Most Wanted* 74
Cube and bell hooks on 60, 61
portrayed by NWA 35, 36, 41–2
Straight Outta Compton 49, 57–9
as song subject 134–5
Wonder, Stevie 66, 78, 114
Woods, Tomika 148, 149
words, importance to rap 264–5
World Class Wreckin' Cru (WCWC) 24, 25, 28, 30, 31, 45
Wright, Charles 61, 115
Wright, Eric (see *Eazy-E*)
Wu-Tang Clan 124, 147, 166, 186, 230

X, Malcolm 81, 83, 117, 119
Xzibit 237, 256

Yella (see *DJ Yella*)
Yo! MTV Raps 67
Yo-Yo 74, 79, 92, 125, 139
Young, Andre (see *Dre, Dr*)

Lightning Source UK Ltd.
Milton Keynes UK
UKOW06f1854230915

259169UK00021B/682/P